The Egyptian Oracle Project

Bloomsbury Egyptology
Series Editor: Nicholas Reeves

Ancient Egyptian Technology and Innovation, Ian Shaw
Burial Customs in Ancient Egypt, Wolfram Grajetzki
Court Officials of the Egyptian Middle Kingdom, Wolfram Grajetzki
Hidden Hands, Stephen Quirke
The Middle Kingdom of Ancient Egypt, Wolfram Grajetzki
Performance and Drama in Ancient Egypt, Robyn Gillam

The Egyptian Oracle Project

Ancient Ceremony in Augmented Reality

Edited by Robyn Gillam and Jeffrey Jacobson

Chapters contributed by
Josephine Anstey and David Pape, Ph.D.,
University of Buffalo, New York, U.S.A.
Erik Champion, Ph.D., Curtin University, Perth, Australia
Lisa Aimee Sturz, MFA, Red Herring Puppets,
Asheville, North Carolina, U.S.A.
Mary-Ann Pouls Wegner, Ph.D., University of Toronto, Canada

Bloomsbury Academic
An imprint of Bloomsbury Publishing Plc

BLOOMSBURY
LONDON • OXFORD • NEW YORK • NEW DELHI • SYDNEY

Bloomsbury Academic
An imprint of Bloomsbury Publishing Plc

50 Bedford Square 1385 Broadway
London New York
WC1B 3DP NY 10018
UK USA

www.bloomsbury.com

BLOOMSBURY and the Diana logo are trademarks of Bloomsbury Publishing Plc

First published 2015
Paperback edition first published 2017

© Robyn Gillam, Jeffrey Jacobson and Contributors, 2015

Robyn Gillam and Jeffrey Jacobson have asserted their rights under the Copyright, Designs and Patents Act, 1988, to be identified as Editors of this work.

All rights reserved. No part of this publication may be reproduced or transmitted in any form or by any means, electronic or mechanical, including photocopying, recording, or any information storage or retrieval system, without prior permission in writing from the publishers.

No responsibility for loss caused to any individual or organization acting on or refraining from action as a result of the material in this publication can be accepted by Bloomsbury or the authors.

British Library Cataloguing-in-Publication Data
A catalogue record for this book is available from the British Library.

ISBN: HB: 978-1-47423-415-3
PB: 978-1-7809-3216-3
ePDF: 978-1-47424-925-6
ePub: 978-1-47424-926-3

Library of Congress Cataloging-in-Publication Data
The Egyptian Oracle Project : ancient ceremony in augmented reality /
edited by Robyn Gillam and Jeffrey Jacobson ; chapters contributed by Josephine Anstey and David Pape, Ph.D., University of Buffalo, New York, U.S.A., Erik Champion, Ph.D., Curtin University, Perth, Australia, Lisa Aimee Sturz, M.A., Red Herring Puppets, Asheville, North Carolina, U.S.A.
pages cm
Includes bibliographical references and index.
ISBN 978-1-4742-3415-3 (hardback) – ISBN 978-1-4742-4925-6 (ePDF)–
ISBN 978-1-78093-216-3 (ePub) 1. Oracles, Egyptian–Computer simulation.
2. Temples–Egypt–Computer simulation. 3. Rites and ceremonies–Egypt–History–30 B.C.-640 A.D. 4. Egypt–Religion. I. Gillam, Robyn Adams, 1952- editor. II. Jacobson, Jeffrey, 1961- editor.
BF1770.E3E39 2015
299'.3138–dc23
2015010973

Series: Bloomsbury Egyptology

Typeset by Fakenham Prepress Solutions, Fakenham, Norfolk NR21 8NN

Contents

Illustrations	vi
Acknowledgments	ix
Background to the Project and this Book	xiii
Introduction *Robyn Gillam and Jeffrey Jacobson*	1

Part 1   The Egyptian Oracle

1	Historical Foundations *Robyn Gillam*	17
2	Cross-Cultural Analysis *Robyn Gillam*	57
3	The Virtual Temple of Horus and Its Egyptian Prototypes *Robyn Gillam*	79

Part 2   The Performance

4	Technical Description *Jeffrey Jacobson*	109
5	Mixed Reality Theater and the Egyptian Oracle Project *Josephine Anstey and David Pape*	131
6	Educational Purpose and Results *Jeffrey Jacobson*	153

Part 3   The Technology

7	Puppetry and Virtual Theater *Lisa Sturz*	167
8	Introduction to Virtual Heritage *Erik Champion*	185
9	The Virtual Temple: Construction and Use *Jeffrey Jacobson*	197

Conclusion *Robyn Gillam and Jeffrey Jacobson*	211
Appendix A: A Funeral Procession in Modern Rural Egypt *Mary-Ann Pouls Wegner*	217
Appendix B: After-Show Questionnaire	221
Bibliography	223
Index	247

Illustrations

FIGURES

0.1 The priest interrogates two audience members playing the parts of neighbors in a dispute. He will appeal to the spirit of Horus in the sacred boat for judgment.   2

1.1 Map of Egypt.   18

1.2 Plan of the temple precinct of Amun-Re at Karnak in the 21st Dynasty (1070–946 BCE).   21

1.3 Southern end of the processional way in front of the temple of Luxor.   22

1.4 Temple of Amun-Re, Karnak, entrance to the hypostyle hall from the courtyard of the Second Pylon, giving onto the riverbank entrance of the temple in antiquity.   23

1.5 Temple of Amun-Re, Karnak, courtyard of the Tenth Pylon, facing south.   24

1.6 Modern perspective drawing of the barque of Amun.   29

1.7 Temple of Amun-Re, Karnak. Twentieth Dynasty commemorative of Nesamun in the courtyard of the Tenth Pylon.   36

1.8 Vignette of the Saite Oracle papyrus, Brooklyn Museum, showing the four prophets of Amun (center) interceding with the god in his shrine (left) for the questioner (on the right).   40

3.1 Plan of the temple precinct, Medinet Habu.   86

3.2 Temple of Medinet Habu. First courtyard, looking through the second courtyard to the sanctuary at the back of the temple.   87

3.3 Temple of Medinet Habu. Second courtyard, showing the southern colonnade with reliefs of the Festival of Sokar.   89

3.4 Temple of Horus at Edfu. Sanctuary of the temple, showing the monolithic stone shrine that held the god's image that was the

	subject of the daily cult. The processional barque in front of the shrine is a modern replica.	93
3.5	Plan of the temple of Horus at Edfu.	94
3.6	Temple at Edfu. Courtyard facing façade of the main temple, showing the screen wall separating the courtyard from the festival hall. The Pure Walkway is located between the back and side of the main temple and the surrounding wall.	95
3.7	Temple at Edfu. The façade of the pylon, showing emplacements for the flagstaffs, as well as scenes of the king dispatching his enemies before Horus.	104
4.1a	The sacred barque of the god Horus.	110
4.1b	The barque of Khonsu as depicted in the temple at Medinet Habu.	111
4.2	The high priest, Petiese.	112
4.3	Musicians. Relief from the tomb of Djed-nefer, 4th century BCE, Heliopolis.	113
4.4	Physical arrangement of the equipment and participants.	115
4.5	Virtual temple layout.	118
4.6	Priest puppet (in the festival hall) and live actress communicate across the "fourth wall" of the virtual stage.	120
4.7	Layout of the mixed reality space in the sixth scene.	122
4.8	The god does not approve!	124
4.9	The spirit of Horus moves the sacred boat to choose a woman (center) for a great honor. This is the moment when many realize the priest is a puppet and not a program.	126
5.1	The *Woyzeck* side of *WoyUbu*, with the performers in front of large projections.	135
5.2	"Woyzeck" observes a projection of the green-screened *Ubu Roi* performers	138
5.3	The *Ubu Roi* side of *WoyUbu*, with the audience watching performers in front of the green screen.	139

7.1	"Lewis Latimer" and "Thomas Edison" and their incandescent bulb.	169
7.2	Blue-screen setup for "Uncle Argyle."	172
7.3	Lisa Sturz (in blue) controlling the puppet "Archie," with Wendy Morton (left) assisting.	173
7.4	(a) "Teenage Mutant Ninja Turtle" built by All Effects; (b) Puppeteers (from left to right) Jim Martin, Noah MacNeal, Gord Roberson and Rick Lyon.	178
7.5	Digital input device (DID) used to control a large dinosaur puppet in *Jurassic Park*.	179
7.6	Digital input device (DID) used to control a digital puppet, *Scooby Doo*.	180
9.1	The front of the virtual temple.	197
9.2	The artwork finished, textured and applied to the inner sanctuary gate of the virtual temple.	203

TABLE

6.1	Interview responses, Museum of Science, Boston (N=4).	163

Acknowledgments

Many people have contributed to this book and the project described in it. To begin, we would like to thank Nicholas Reeves, editor of the Bloomsbury Egyptology series, and the staff at Bloomsbury for their support of a work that is both innovative and unusual among the books so far published in this series. Valuable contributions from our chapter authors Erik Champion, Josephine Anstey, David Pape and Lisa Sturz have given the book much more depth and breadth than we could have provided on our own. Thanks to Mario Salinas for his graphic design help with the temple maps. Thanks also to our primary editor, Gillian Watts, who edited the entire book and wrote the index, and to our contributing editor, Richard Graefe.

Contributions to the Egyptian Oracle Project and its foundation, the virtual Egyptian temple, are listed below. However, we wish to especially emphasize Friedrich Kirchner's central contribution to the project: he wrote the code and developed much of the animation and interaction design for the puppeteer. Our puppeteer, Brad Shur, provided the heart and a voice for the god and his priest. Working together, Friedrich and Brad made the ancient drama come to life. Special thanks also go to David Hopkins, who did the 3-D artwork for both the temple and the priest, and to Kerry Handron, who contributed her insights into educational theater for children.

We would like to thank Robyn Gillam's students at York University, Toronto, who enacted oracular ceremonies in 2010 and 2014. We have also been extremely fortunate to have the steadfast support of Christopher Innes, Canada Research Chair in Drama and Performance at York, who made it possible to film the student performances in blue screen and place them in the virtual temple of Horus, providing invaluable research and development for the project. Amanda Wagner of the Information Commons at the University of Toronto magically repaired, merged and generally cleaned up a number of problematic digital images.

The U.S. National Endowment for the Humanities made this project possible with a $49,913 grant to PublicVR (HD-5120910). PublicVR, Pittsburgh, PA, was the lead institution for the project, providing administrative support, additional funding and significant in-kind support.

Puppet Showplace Theater, Brookline, MA, provided the performance venue and crucial staffing for the dress rehearsal on 19 April and the performance on 20 May 2010.

The Carnegie Museum of Natural History, Pittsburgh, provided an excellent venue, educational context, audiences and evaluation. William Diamond Middle School, Lexington, MA, both provided a venue and gathered data for the September 19, 2011 performance, as well as assisting with development of a testing protocol. Boston Cyberarts (AXIOM) provided a venue for the performances on May 1, 2011 and February 16, 2012, which was generously hosted by Anstey and Pape. The Boston Children's Museum simulcast the 1 May performance in its exhibit space. The Grid Institute, Boston, provided a performance opportunity and an excellent audience for the May 13, 2011 performance at its immersive education conference. Boston College provided the performance space. The University of Buffalo, New York, provided space for our mid-project dress rehearsal on February 12, 2011. The Boston Museum of Science sponsored a one-time performance at the museum and sent us the results of their evaluation.

Jeffrey Jacobson (project and technical management) was responsible for evaluation design and analysis, configuration management, interim and final reports, and distribution websites. Robyn Gillam (Egyptologist) provided source materials, identified constraints and provided an educated viewpoint during our creative process. Friedrich Kirchner did the programming; his extensive background in film and previous experience with digital puppetry was crucial and very welcome. Brad Shur (puppeteering) performed in all the shows and provided invaluable advice and insight on the dramaturgical needs of the performance. Kerry Handron, leader of the narrative team, developed and managed all the performances at the Carnegie Museum of Natural History, gathered the data there and was the live actress for all those shows. David Hopkins did the artwork and animation; the remarkably beautiful virtual temple was also his work from a different project.

Brenda Huggins was the live actress in all our shows and assisted Brad with final adjustments to the script. Jon Hawkins created the current non-dialogue sounds and music for the Egyptian Oracle performance. Asa Gray created the original music for the performance and the ambient sounds for the temple. Ajayan Nambiar engineered the traveling kit for performances, which features a surround-sound system. He created effects for the music and ambient sounds of the temple to give a greater sense of depth and realism. Natthaphol Likhitthaworn improved the animations and software performance; his ability to do both artwork and programming was valuable. Michael List was the puppeteer for the Carnegie Museum of Natural History shows.

Ken Hargrove, Heather Bloss and Ted Grindrod were independent evaluators for the performances. Siddhesh Pandit developed the networking code that allows the puppeteer to control the show via the internet or a LAN; he also provided technical assistance at several performances. Brianna Plaud made the costume worn by the actress in the Boston area performances.

Lowry Burgess gave valuable advice on the psychological and aesthetic impact of the show and assisted with securing Institutional Review Board support for our evaluation efforts. Christopher Innes, D.Phil., assisted in efforts to gain additional funding and facilitated the live performance at York University, Toronto. John Baek, Ph.D., gave valuable advice on the evaluation protocols. Michael Nitsche, Ph.D., provided valuable advice on the software and on the production in general. Semi Ryu, Ph.D., offered valuable advice on the dramatic structure of the production and possibilities for further improvement.

The Virtual Egyptian Temple

The temple comes in five major versions: the original 1994 project (version 1.0) which used WorldToolkit; a web-enabled translation of version 1.0 (VRML); the current public distribution (UT2004); a completely rebuilt version (Unity3D); and the second complete rebuild (also in Unity3D). PublicVR provided most of the development funding, technical support, public distribution, research design for educational testing, and evaluation and management for versions 2.0 and later. The Carnegie Museum of Natural History (CMNH) provided a public venue for version 3.0 (2005–11), development of tours and educational materials for the public, and venue for testing; it also provided funding for version 4.0 as a sub-award under NSF award 0916098. The Art Institute of Pittsburgh and Art Institute of New England contributed objects and artwork by students, via coursework and internships, part of a collaborative curriculum developed in concert with the CMNH and PublicVR.

Jeffrey Jacobson (PublicVR) was project director, sponsor, human-factors designer and lead educational researcher, handled overall media design and maintained the communication software (forum) and managed contributions. Robyn Gillam (York University) provided historical content and source materials for version 5.0, some of the artifacts for version 3.0 and later, and interpretation and design of the temple artwork. Kerry Handron (CMNH) was in charge of exhibit and presentation development, testing, and supervision of staff, resources and schedule. Lowry Burgess (Carnegie Mellon University) was the senior advisor for all versions and producer of version 1.0.

Other contributors to various versions of the temple included Michael Darnell, PublicVR (model, textures and lighting, v. 3.0); Vashti Germaine, Carnegie Mellon University (ambient music, v. 1.0 to 4.0); Billy Gonsalves, Art Institute of Pittsburgh (AIP) (geometry and textures, v. 4.0); Asa Grey, Berklee School of Music (ambient music, v. 5.0); David Heimann PublicVR (sound programming, v. 5.0); Lynn Holden, PublicVR/Carnegie Mellon University (historical content and source materials, v. 4.0 and earlier; many of the artifacts in v. 3.0 and later; media design); David Hopkins, PublicVR/AIP (all artwork, modeling and lighting, v. 5.0; modeling and artwork, v. 4.0); Yelena Kamenetskaya, AIP (geometry and textures, v. 4.0); Singer Ko, AIP (geometry, lighting and textures, v. 4.0); Reginald Laurenceau, AIP (lighting, v. 4.0); Brian Relay, AIP (camerawork for fly-through video, v. 4.0); and Casey Schenery, AIP (lighting, v. 4.0).

Under the direction of Jeffrey Jacobson, students at the Art Institute of Pittsburgh produced artifacts for the virtual temple as class assignments. Ricardo Washington (2009–10) and Jeffrey Zehner (2006–07) coached the student volunteers. Historical content and review were provided by Lynn Holden or Robyn Gillam. Students whose work appears in the virtual temple are Janelle Desborough, Geoffry Bowker, David Bakos, Octavo Garcia-Rivera, Sean Van Gorde, Jason Wilson Linen, William Everett, Damico, Gabe Strickland, Cyrus Conner, Michael Jones, Bram de Beer, Cody McLachlan, Monica Mulneix, Anthony McKeever, Amber Johnson and Colleen Nachtrieb.

Last but not least, we thank our friends and families, without whose love and support neither the Egyptian Oracle Project nor this book would have seen the light of day.

We would like to thank Prof. Ron Sheese and the Department of Faculty Relations at York University for recommending and providing funding that made possible the completion of this book in the Summer of 2014.

Background to the Project and this Book

This book consists of a series of essays or studies that document the educational project, the Egyptian Oracle, which is its main subject. Since a number of collaborators from different fields have worked on it, we feel it may helpful to the reader to explain the layout of this book and the methods used in it in order to better understand the project it describes.

Because the Egyptian Oracle Project is an interactive educational performance in mixed virtual and live reality, some of the media that document it, including a short video and additional illustrations, have been made available online on the publisher's website. It is strongly recommended that the reader make use of these additional resources in order to gain a fuller understanding of what the project consists of. It is also important that the book be read all the way through, as it follows a clearly articulated path: from a preliminary discussion of media and educational theater, through an overview of the historical material used to develop the content of the performance, a description of the performance and its educational outcomes, and a series of essays locating the technology used therein in the wider context of developing educational and artistic applications of virtual reality. It concludes with an overview of the project and its implications for both educational outreach and research applications.

Rationale for the reconstruction of the Egyptian Oracle

The historical section of the book comprises chapters describing reconstruction of the oracle ceremony, its cultural context, its prototypes from ancient Egypt and some cross-cultural analogs. It is useful here to explain the rationale behind this particular reconstruction, indicating where in these chapters more information can be found. Chapter 1 presents an imaginative reconstruction of the ancient oracular ceremony and the sources on which it was based. The reconstruction is for the most part based on commemorative documentations of oracular ceremonies held by the social elite in the temple of Amun-Re during the Third Intermediate Period, c. 1100–800 BCE (pp. 17–20; 38–44). The reason for doing this is that, although the ceremony was performed across most social classes over a long time period, these sources provide the clearest indication of its performative sequence and spatial enactment (pp. 39–41; 42–4). Chapter 2 provides a brief cross-cultural analysis of similar practices in neighboring ancient cultures, as well as modern analogs in Egypt (see also Appendix A), western Africa and the diaspora in the Americas. Such material not only gives the reader something with which to compare the ceremony but also provides additional information about its social, cultural and affective content. This information is indispensable to effective realization of the performance at the heart of the Egyptian Oracle Project.

The virtual temple of Horus, in which the Oracle Project performance took place, predates Gillam and Jacobson's collaboration. As explained in Chapter 9 (p. 198), it was conceived not as a reproduction of an actual building but as an exemplar, meant to demonstrate the main characteristics of a structural type for educational purposes and spatial research. It combines structure and details from the well-preserved cult temple of Horus at Edfu (third to first centuries BCE) and the mortuary temple of Ramesses III at Medinet Habu (mid-twelfth century BCE). Since the combination of two different types of temple into one could be seen as problematic, Chapter 3 provides some background on the origin and development of the Egyptian temple (pp. 82–7), as well as more detailed descriptions of the layout and purpose of the Medinet Habu and Edfu temples (pp. 86–91). Many of these explanations are directed toward the relationship of oracle and processional religion with the temple and the larger community.

Chapter 9 gives a detailed description of the history, construction and uses of the virtual temple, including its historical sources (also discussed in the historical section) and technical specifications. The original virtual temple underwent substantial modifications after Gillam became a consultant to the project, including the use of more Late Period material in the wall decorations. It was hoped that some of the peripheral buildings associated with temples (described in the historical section of this book) could be added, along with additional wall decoration, but the necessary funding was not available. At present these aspects of the virtual temple are unfortunately incomplete.

Although much of the evidence for the existence of the processional oracle, and all the material relating to the nature of the performance, predates the mid-first millennium BCE, it was decided to locate the time of the performance in the fourth century BCE (Chapter 4, p. 109). The reasons for doing this were based on pedagogy and interdisciplinarity. In our work with students in universities and museums, we teach about different time periods and cultures to a multicultural audience. The fourth century BCE, at the beginning of the Ptolemaic period, allows for discussion of cultural change and interaction in a way that enables participants in the performance to reflect on their own contexts. The Ptolemaic period also brings Egypt into relation with Graeco-Roman culture, a subject area that school-age students and members of the public are most likely to be familiar with.

As described in Chapter 4, the performance brought together the overall designer of the project, the educational programmer, the Egyptological consultant and computer programmers with the puppeteer, actor and audience. The script was a result of negotiations among all those participants, and the elite protagonists of the original imagined oracle ceremony were replaced by more "ordinary" people such as those documented at the New Kingdom village of Deir el-Medina. As such they fitted better into the inclusive mandate of museum education, as articulated by the educational programmer (pp. 114, 121–6). Likewise, the script presented a simplified version of the ceremony, suitable for a school-age or randomly selected adult audience. The virtual puppets, the head priest and the bearers of the god's shrine were articulated by the programmers and presented by the puppeteer as dignified but highly stylized, to avoid the "uncanny valley" effect (see pp. 112, 146, 192).

The Egyptian Oracle Project in the context of virtual heritage

In Chapter 5 a discussion of mixed reality theater locates the Egyptian Oracle within this rapidly developing medium, and Chapter 6 discusses audience reactions and learning outcomes as documented in post-performance questionnaires. The third section of the book examines the technology used in the performance in the wider context of virtual heritage. Chapter 7 explores virtual puppeteering; it combines technical descriptions of the practice with autoethnographies by Lisa Sturz and Brad Shur, showing how it relates to embodied subjectivity as well as technical know-how. (Autoethnography is also used by Mary-Ann Pouls Wegner to locate her observation of a modern Egyptian funeral in Appendix A.) In Chapter 8, Erik Champion examines the Egyptian Oracle within the wider project of virtual heritage that has the aim of reconstructing what does not physically survive from the past. He suggests that its particular contribution lies in introducing greater interactivity though employment of the techniques and strategies of computer gaming in an educational context.

Finally, the Conclusion provides an overview of the book as well as some suggestions for further applications of the basic software and the types of activities suggested for it in both educational and research contexts.

Introduction

Robyn Gillam and Jeffrey Jacobson

The Egyptian Oracle performance described in this book was a first attempt, produced on a relatively small budget (less than $80,000) and made possible by considerable donated time and resources, especially the pre-existing virtual temple of Horus (Chapter 9). It was intended to be a prototype, a proof-of-principle demonstration that captures the essential character of the original oracle ceremony.

This book consists of a collection of essays contained within a framing discussion by the coordinators of the Egyptian Oracle Project, Jeffrey Jacobson and Robyn Gillam. The concept and technical design of the project is the work of Jacobson, while Gillam contributed the content, as well as some pedagogical and performance-based research and development arising from work by her students. However, the execution of this project would not have been possible without the contribution of a number of expert practitioners, including software designers, program writers, analog and digital puppeteers, theoreticians and practitioners of educational technology, actors, and experts in dramaturgy and the history of theater. Their explorations of this project are framed as part of a larger discussion of the uses and possibilities of web-based educational technology combined with live on-site educational performances.

Form

The Egyptian Oracle Project is a cooperative multidisciplinary undertaking that involves a mixed reality performance using digital projection. The projection comprises a virtual reality environment and a digital puppet, or avatar, operated by an offstage puppeteer. The setting and the puppet are introduced by a live performer who represents an element of the projected environment. The live performer also interprets and facilitates the interactions of a live audience with the puppet and its environment. As this performance is part of an educational activity, it is preceded and followed by a briefing and debriefing session.

The performance itself is a live reenactment of a public ceremony from ancient Egypt's Late Period. A life-sized projection of a virtual Egyptian temple extends the physical theater into virtual space. The central actor is a virtual priest controlled by a professional puppeteer located offstage. The main supporting actors are a real person, in costume, and a (virtual) sacred boat bearing the spirit of the god Horus. Audience members participate by playing citizens of the ancient populace, giving them an immersive learning experience.

The processional oracle, which is documented in the Third Intermediate and Graeco-Roman periods of Egypt's history, figured directly in the life of the community. The performance and its virtual temple setting conform to a high level of historical accuracy, suitable for any museum setting (see Chapter 1). Members of the audience, as in the ancient past, come before the god with questions to be answered and problems to be solved. The priest poses questions to the god and interprets the movements of the sacred boat as divine revelation, which has the force of law.

The processional oracle was an essential feature of Egyptian public life during this period. More broadly, religious ceremony was central to ancient Egyptian culture, and the performance is built to convey that idea to the public, to inspire empathy for other cultures and to advance our understanding of immersive

Figure 0.1 The priest interrogates two audience members playing the parts of neighbors in a dispute. He will appeal to the spirit of Horus in the sacred boat for judgment.

media. The National Endowment for the Humanities funded this work in 2010–11 (Digital Humanities Startup Grant HD-5120910) and the resulting production has toured in Boston and Pittsburgh. See Chapter 6 for more information on the immediate educational uses of the show, and Chapter 7 for a broader discussion of educational puppetry.

To really understand the performance, we urge the reader to view the full-length (approximately twenty-five minutes) recorded version of this performance at the project's website, http://publicvr.org/egypt/oracle/longvid.html. Bear in mind, however, that the performance is intended for the people participating in it, and the repetitive nature of its structure may seem tedious to the outside observer. Also, this version is intended as a prototype for a larger production that we hope to construct in the future. For more discussion on those future plans, see the Conclusion.

PublicVR is a 501(c)3 non-profit corporation dedicated to free software and research in virtual reality for education and human factors. The software that generates the puppet and the digital environment was developed with Unity3D (2013), a generally available and easily downloaded software used for online gaming. The entire program is available as a wiki on the project website; it may be freely downloaded and adapted for form and content by any educator who wishes to use it. The code, artwork and script are open source and are available at http://publicvr.org/html/pro_oracle.html. The background environment can be created in any built space (or a portable dome) using an LED projector and a laptop computer.

Historical content

The Egyptian Oracle represents a public religious event that was commonly enacted in Egypt between 1500 BCE and the early Christian period (fourth to sixth centuries CE). In this event, which was generally part of a public procession that marked a religious festival, an image or symbol of a god, carried by men who were priests or important community members, showed volition or a preference in response to a question or request by moving unexpectedly. Although such events were sometimes completely spontaneous, they were often coordinated by a high-ranking priest or community member, with the questions, whether written or oral, agreed on beforehand. The movements of the god's image, which was often hidden inside an elaborate portable shrine, were also generally predictable and interpretable. These events, witnessed by the community as a whole, often took place in the vicinity of a temple, in a setting that superimposed greater cosmic significance onto life in the everyday world. The oracle was used to decide all kinds of social and religious issues, from local disputes and personal matters to major political questions. During its very long existence, the ritual evolved and its emphasis, use and setting changed over time. Although other forms of oracular consultation were used in Egypt, the so-called processional oracle is the best known and best documented. It is the processional oracle that provides the basis for this project's mixed-media performance (see Chapter 4).

Originally developed to show the possibilities of modeling and reconstructing ancient structures and sites in virtual reality, the temple evolved into an educational gaming space designed to teach K-12 students basic ideas about ancient Egyptian culture. The virtual temple of Horus was installed in the Earth Theater, a planetarium-like display space at the Carnegie Museum of Natural History (CMNH) in Pittsburgh. Objects from the museum's substantial Egyptian collection were modeled for virtual inclusion in the temple to strengthen its relevance to the overall educational experience of the museum (see Chapter 9). It was decided to add the Egyptian Oracle to CMNH's educational programming as a more authentic and involving introduction to Egyptian culture than the priestly guide avatar originally used. In mid-2010, Jeffrey Jacobson's educational software company, PublicVR, obtained a starter grant from the U.S. government-funded National Endowment for the Humanities, which allowed a complex and diverse cast of actor/participants to be assembled.

Disciplines and personnel

As noted above, the Egyptian Oracle Project brought together specialists from many different fields, including a software designer, a computer programmer, an Egyptologist, a museum education programmer, analog and digital puppeteers, an actor, builders of VR environments and a digital composer. This group involved not only different individuals and personalities but, more important, a number of very different discursive fields. Mixed virtual and live performance—itself a new and emerging field—brings together different areas of action and expertise that are not without their contradictions. It also raises important issues of education and its role in understanding the past that have been, and remain, controversial (see pp. 12–14 and Chapter 6).

The diverse disciplines and approaches deployed in this project may be summarized as follows:

- the construction of virtual reality and gaming software, along with its theory and practice;
- the art of acting and puppetry, with its history, training, theory and practice;
- the practice of teaching, its history, training and theory, especially in relation to applied or educational theater;
- the discipline of Egyptology, with its history, training and theory; and
- archaeological theory, especially spatial analysis and post-processual understandings of phenomenology and embodied subjectivity.

The stated aim of the Egyptian Oracle is to provide students engaged in the activity with an instructive documented experience that seeks to resemble as closely as possible an oracular consultation with an Egyptian god. However, it must be conceded that the various actors and contributors may unintentionally distort and undermine this stated aim, simply by virtue of what they do and who they are.

Egyptology is an academic field whose intellectual genealogy stems from classical and Oriental studies. It is based on a close philological study of ancient texts and material culture as revealed through museum objects and archaeological practice. Although the archaeological side of the discipline makes extensive use of scientific techniques and quantitative analysis, its philological art-historical and historical side uses approaches and heuristic frameworks more commonly found in the social sciences and humanities (Shaw 2004: 20–5). Its area of study—the history and culture of ancient Egypt—is spread over three to four thousand years and is plagued by gaps in evidence and uneven distribution of information (Gardiner 1961: 52–61). Although it may be theoretically preferable to present materials unified by time and place, it is not always practicable, so a diachronic approach, using evidence from one period to fill gaps in another, is often used. Although care is always taken to make these substitutions in an informed and logical way, such an approach can never present a truly "authentic" picture of a time and a place. This was the approach used in the Egyptian Oracle Project. The period we chose for our performance, the fourth century BCE, is not the most well documented for the oracle, but it better shows evidence of cross-cultural contact, especially with the Greek world (Lloyd 2000: 385–96; Myśliwiec 2000: 158–78). Multiculturalism is of particular interest to the creators of the project, as it mirrors the world in which we and the students who take part in the activity live. The educational aims of the project are just as important as its content; in fact, they should work together seamlessly.

It was the educational programmer Kerry Handron who, provided with materials by Egyptologist Robyn Gillam, led the writing of the scenario on which the performance activity is based. Her work was later checked by Dr. Gillam, but it was felt that only an educational planner had the expertise to create a script that would fulfill the pedagogical aims of the project in a way that was interactive and engaging for the students. Handron's work on this project is informed by the theory and practice of applied or educational theater, an important element in pedagogy at all levels of education since the middle of the twentieth century (Jackson 2007). However, before addressing this field in more detail, we must examine more closely the relationship of theater and acting to the project.

Theater and the space of performance

Acting and the theater in Western culture trace their origins back to the classical world, as preserved in texts, sites and representations. The writings of the philosopher Aristotle on drama have been an important influence on theater theory (Pavis 1998: 53–4, 131, 387–8; Schechner 1988: 1–6, 9, 16–21). Living traditions of practice can be traced back as far as the late Middle Ages and Renaissance. Although practically every human society we know of creates some form of dramatic performance (Schechner 1988: 153–84, 207–49), acting theory and practice in our culture remain firmly rooted in Western traditions, although there has recently been much interest in other traditions and in the staging and interpretation of ethnographic material (Pavis 1998: x, 83–5, 131; Watson 2002).

Western drama operates with a series of conventions that underlie the basic assumptions shared by the playwright/director, actors and audience, encompassing the staging, acting, text and site of performance (Pavis 1998: 78–80, 113–14). The basis of all these assumptions is that theater shows human communication by means of humans communicating (Pavis 1998: 71). Beginning with Aristotle, drama has been defined as a routine based on an agonistic structure that acts out a conflict-based storyline and provides the audience that watches and reflects on it with a sense of release or closure (Aristotle 1996: 4.3, 5–6). The actors convey this story by "showing" (*deixis*) rather than "telling" (Aristotle 1996: 4; Pavis 1998: 91–2). The actors are understood to be separate from the characters they portray; they are sometimes described as "bringing them to life," as are puppeteers (Engler and Fijan 1973; Pavis 1998: 47). The costumes and bodily deportment of the actors (Pavis 1998: 34), as well as their speech and facial expressions, are understood to portray the character through a process of abstraction and readability (Pavis 1998: 80–1). Just as the actor is understood to be a person in disguise, so the entire event is understood by the audience to be an illusion. While the viewers accept the illusion aesthetically, they respect the fact that it is unreal, by virtue of the convention of "distance" between the actors and themselves. It is distance that allows the actors to create and maintain their illusory world that is contemplated, interpreted and reflected on by the audience (Pavis 1998: 108–10, 146, 217). This fantasy is informed by the common social and cultural knowledge of the playwright, the actors and the audience (Pavis 1998: 75), and it is also underpinned by decorum, or compliance with common moral and social conventions (Pavis 1998: 90–1).

However, since the late to mid-nineteenth century and the onset of full modernity, rapid social change has challenged Western theater from both without and within to examine these basic assumptions and to look at and reflect upon other performance traditions. This period saw the emergence of "New Drama," as exemplified by the works of playwrights such as Henrik Ibsen and George Bernard Shaw. They challenged their bourgeois audiences not only to think about but to act on social problems and issues, presented in settings that referenced everyday life rather than abstract reality (Jackson 2007: 49–60). While such an approach to theatrical text or scripts continued to be an important thread in activist or educational theater down to the present, significant formal innovations of the past hundred years are more important for this study.

Although often close to "New Drama" in terms of social activism, twentieth-century innovators emphasized the formal aspect of theater, often deconstructing its mimetic, dramatic character (Pavis 1998: 71–2, 84–5, 109, 133). Inspired by traditional Chinese theater, Bertolt Brecht emphasized the artificiality of the stage and its devices; he has his characters tell rather than show, in order to push his audiences toward discussion and revolutionary action rather than reflection (Brecht 1964: 91–8, 101–3, 179, 205, 277). Antonin Artaud insisted that actors create characters that were more symbolic and ritualistic than mimetic and that the theatrical event be returned to the ritual experience from which it was thought to have originated (Artaud 1958: 63–73). Unlike Brecht, Artaud sought to completely abolish the distance between the audience and the actors, in a sublime immolation that signified the death of theater and the privileging of authentic, non-rational experience (Artaud 1958: 84–8, 89–100, 113–16). While Brecht and Artaud obviously represent two extremes of modern theatrical theory and practice, their individual influences can be felt both in the development of educational theater and more widely, throughout the cultural postmodernity of the late twentieth and early twenty-first centuries.

Educational theater

Educational theater originated in the mid-twentieth century, in the 1930s and 1940s, encompassing both public education and agitprop events (Jackson 2007: 66–126). It was first used in connection with the school curriculum in Britain and was conceptually related to child-centered educational models based on constructive play. Theater in the schools developed alongside conventional theater performances for children, but it drew on the aims and techniques of modernist and experimental theater (Hornbrook 1989: 7–9; Jackson 2007: 60–5). Of special importance to its evolution was the work and writings of Augusto Boal (1931–2009), a Brazilian director and theorist who developed the "theater of the oppressed" as a tool for educational and political activism (Jackson 2007: 135–6). Eliminating the distance between actors and audience is a fundamental part of Boal's practice of "invisible theater," in which the audience—initially unaware that they are part of a play—become "spect-actors," or active participants, and hence, from an educational perspective, active learners (Boal 1979: 119–26, 142–50). The practice also makes use of a neutral party or facilitator who coordinates the proceedings and leads discussions—a model well suited to pedagogical purposes (Boal 1979: 182–6). Although theater in the schools originally made use of professional actors in performances and workshops (Jackson 2007: 130–6), theater-based techniques such as role-playing and workshopping have long been a part of classroom activities and have become an important part of assignment and curriculum design for active learning (Courtney 1980; Heathcote and Bolton 1995).

Virtual spaces, virtual learning

Computer-assisted technologies were originally developed in the mid-twentieth century as an aid to large-scale scientific mathematical calculations. They have since expanded to control virtually all mechanically based operations and industrial and communication technologies, as well as the management and storage of every kind of digital and analog information. The development of microchip technology has made computer-assisted technology less expensive and, over time, generally available to most of the world's population. The wholesale digitizing of most print and image sources, now largely available on the internet, and almost universal access to word processing have greatly changed education at all levels. Not only are students able to access information and communicate about it through computers and PDAs, but they also spend increasing amounts of time in online virtual environments, often playing games.

Computer games and other virtual environments such as *Second Life* incorporate many elements from contemporary theatrical and art practice. They involve scenery, actors and audience participation. Like installations and multimedia, they use electronic media to create effects related to space, visual perception and lighting. And they tell stories, often of a very traditional Aristotelian agonistic character. Also, like Boalian educational theater, they create "spect-actors" who can learn from their experiences and advance through a kind of curriculum (although their only reward is winning a game). In their portrayal of overwhelming violent events in which the gamer participates, online games may also reference Artaud's "theater of cruelty," with its privileging of affect over rationality. However, even when a computer game involves the death of a player, it happens only in the unreal online virtual environment. The body operating the console remains intact.

From archaeological theory to educational practice

Archaeological theory and practice deal with actual locations and the traces of past inhabitants and their material culture. Archaeologists have studied the quantifiable aspects and cultural character of these materials but have recently become more interested in their implications for the reconstruction of embodied subjectivity. Spatial analysis looks at the mathematical and architectonic relationships of spaces in built structures and suggests possible social meanings for them (Hillier and Hanson 1984; Seibert 2006). Post-processual archaeology, a movement in archaeological theory and practice that engages with social and gender relations in an ecological framework (Thomas 2000: 1–6, 8–10), has led to the exploration of how bodily existence was experienced in past societies (Hamilakis 2001), especially through the negotiation of both natural and built spaces (Lane 1996; Richards 1993).

This line of enquiry is informed by the approaches of phenomenology, a branch of philosophy developed by Heidegger (1962) and Merleau-Ponty (2002) and based on an examination of immediate experience that investigates the nature of embodied consciousness. Information gathered from the physical remains of subjects from the past, as well as any indications of the cultural significance to them of the landscape and their settlements, is part of this picture (David and Thomas 2008: 245–333). Practitioners will sometimes try to experience the space or landscape themselves in order to arrive at a perception analogical to those of past subjects (Ingold 2000; Tilley 1994). As described below, Egyptian formal temples are a particularly rich source for this sort of cultural information. Their extensive inscribed surfaces not only describe the religious significance and uses of different parts of the building (Fairman 1954), but they also commemorate individuals who staffed or visited them, as well as sacred events such as enactments of the processional oracle (Spencer 2010: 268–72).

A Multidisciplinary project: Possibilities and limitations

The Egyptian Oracle Project fulfills several of the desiderata of current educational practice. It is interactive and immersive and makes theater central to its pedagogical method, as dictated by drama-centered curricula. Although the priestess-presenter is part of the scenario, she does fulfill some of the functions of Boal's facilitator. As in the Theatre in the Schools program, both the presenter and the puppeteer are theater professionals and the scenario, based on academically verified materials, has been created by a museum educator well versed in interactive pedagogical techniques. The virtual reality setting is also suitably theatrical. Computer-generated settings have often been compared to theater (Laurel 1993) and have proved particularly effective for staging everything from teaching simulations to the dramatic scenarios of popular video games, providing an effective spatial substitute for physical social interaction, as on sites like *Second Life*. The fact that the environment is projected onto a wall or screen rather than being experienced in a more immersive environment provides the Brechtian distancing effect so important for reflection and interrogation—the best environment for active learning.

However, it must be admitted that an activity such as the Egyptian Oracle cannot truly reproduce the kind of event that it represents. First, it cannot recreate a world that existed 2,400 years ago or the cultures and activities experienced by its people. The physical and geographical environment of an

Egyptian temple and its surroundings of this period bears no resemblance to the climate-controlled spaces of museums and other educational institutions where the Egyptian Oracle performance has been staged. The puppeteer and the actor can represent the actions of the priests and, in accordance with modern acting theory and techniques, explore what we know of such people in order to "bring them to life." What they cannot do is produce actual persons who were involved in such events or in any way inhabit their states of body and mind, although the setting does allow for some spatial indicators. The audience participants—the "spect-actors"—are even less connected to the event represented, an event about which they are to be informed by its professional participants. Although they are given enough information to take part in the scenario, they cannot attempt to act "in character" or to represent the persons indicated, even to the extent of the puppeteer playing the priest.

Even more problematic is the central fact of this presentation: the presumed presence of the god whose spirit moves the image in the shrine. While we have elected to present the event as a cultural phenomenon without trying to explain it in a "rational" way, this perspective fails to take into account that present-day opinions about the existence or character of spiritual beings are much less homogeneous and far more contested than in the ancient society therein depicted. The choice to represent such an event was always a risky one; while it underlines the difference of the past, it also by its very means of representation calls into question the reliability—as it were, the "truthfulness"—of what is being shown. Since the actors and the virtual reality environment cannot themselves produce a spiritual event or presence, it must be simulated by other means. In this case it is the puppeteer behind the curtain who inhabits not only the chief priest but also the god in the shrine with its bearers. This recalls innumerable accounts of religious hoaxes (Frankfurter 1998: 150–1, 164) as well the generally negative concept of God as a puppeteer, depriving the human actor of any semblance of free will (Pavis 1998: 292–3). Thus, from the point of view of either a faith-based or an atheist perspective, a performance such as this can summon up extremely negative connotations: one that recalls the "false gods" of the Judaeo-Christian tradition (Geller 2004: 2028–9; Young 2000: 644–50) or, on the other hand, the suggestion that all religions are a combination of confidence trick and wishful thinking, born of intellectual laziness and emotional immaturity (Dawkins 2006).

Of course such viewpoints are a product of a particular time, place and cultural legacy, like the activity being depicted, but they unfortunately point to a longstanding tendency to link such ideas to theatrical presentation as an inherently duplicitous medium, incapable of transparency or honesty, its participants disguised and deceitful (Boal 1979: 113–14). Such ideas, going all the way back to Saint Augustine's objection to theater (in his time still a religious celebration in honor of Dionysus) as an idolatrous and untruthful representation of imaginary personages (Augustine 1991: 35–6 [III.2]), bring us to the disputed value of historical reenactment, to which educational and mixed reality theater has been connected.

Reenactment and its discontents

Although historical reenactment—in the sense of the re-presentation or acting out of events such as battles and pageants by persons equipped with appropriate props and costumes—can be traced back to eighteenth-century Europe (During 2010), it has achieved particular prominence in the present because of the growth of historical reenactment societies, their widespread popularization through the media and, especially, the proliferation of historical "reality" TV shows. These presentations, which tend to focus on life-ways and material culture rather than historical events, typically choose members of the general public to act out roles in a scenario that often focuses on class differentiation and the physical hardships of past lives ("nasty, brutish and short"). In a theatrical sense, their drama derives from the inability of the participants to adapt to their circumstances (the "rules of the game") or from their developing relationships with one another. These programs clearly owe a great deal to the game-based genre of reality TV shows where participants triumph over adverse environments and each other, with their interpersonal conflicts providing the entertainment (Agnew 2007; Schwarz 2010).

To be fair, not all reenactment is like that. It runs the whole gamut from role-play gaming, in which the participants engage in fancy-dress play, to serious attempts by amateur historians to reconstruct significant details of events such as battles in the American Civil War or life on the home front in Second World War Britain (de Groot 2011: 288–9; Lynskey 2013; McCalman and Pickering 2010: 5–6). Reenactors have interacted with and influenced live museum interpretation as their activities have become more visible and accepted in the culture at large (Magnessen and Justice-Malloy 2011: 1–5). On a less academic level, they now often appear in popular history documentaries and act as extras in movie costume dramas (Hall 1994). Popular non-academic ideas about history, and especially reenactment and its corresponding mass-mediated equivalents, provide an alternative to academic discourse that can play a role in community dialogue and political negotiation. Reenactment has played an important role in the negotiation of political and social disputes and has forged significant links with the practice of performance artists as a way of enacting longstanding events and conflicts with a view to their resolution (de Groot 2011: 588–9, 590–4; Schneider 2011).

As noted above, the practice of reenactment tends to focus on more recent historical periods; it often relates to knowledge or experiences of the reenactors' relatives or ancestors, as well as the recovery of past folkways and technologies. More remote periods tend to be the preserve of more fanciful game-playing— like the Middle Ages for the Society for Creative Anachronism (McCalman and Pickering 2010: 6)—although groups such as Roman Army enactors are often extremely meticulous in their activities (Roman Military Research Society 2013). Generally speaking, however, the two main spurs to reenactment are a desire to find out more about daily life and material culture and, most important, a wish to experience it in an emotional and bodily fashion. Detailed knowledge and physical immersion in the past presuppose a high level of documentation, and an affective connection most often hinges on a temporally close, often family-based connection (de Groot 2011: 588–91; Kitamura 2010; Magnessen and Justice-Malloy 2011: 1–5). Neither of these conditions is generally possible for more remote time periods, so reenactment of earlier epochs is generally carried out by the for-profit entertainment industry. Experimental archaeology has been incorporated into mass media history presentations, as have phenomenological, spatial and ethnographic approaches (Cline et al. 2008).

There has been much discussion about the value of reenactment and popularization generally among both archaeologists and historians. Many archaeologists, and those in the related field of anthropology, see considerable value in reenactment as a strategy for recovery of community histories and cultures and acknowledge the cultural validity of its experiential character (Cline et al. 2008: 176–8; de Groot 2011: 390–1). However, they often express disappointment about the selective and distorting use made of their expertise by the popular media (Cline et al. 2008: 172–4). A considerable number of historians, on the other hand, have strongly expressed disapproval of all forms of reenactment, which they define very broadly as a misleading, even fraudulent representation of the past that often serves merely to massage the feelings of the participants and the audience. They have noted the insurmountable epistemological and ontological problems presented by any attempt to enact past events (mentioned above), as well as the tendency of many enactors to confuse their own activity with the original event.

Some historical commentators see all forms of performance as reenactment; they are particularly suspicious of educational performances, labeling them as examples of defective pedagogy that absolve students of the need to aspire to any higher-level academic activity. Such critics see learner-centered teaching as a sign of the decline of educational standards, not their expansion (Agnew 2007: 303–9; McCalman and Pickering 2010: 2–4, 8–11).

Unfortunately these scholars show a lack of historical awareness of their own time and place. While the changing culture and demographics of schools and universities have presented challenges in classrooms and many take refuge in the simulacrum of the virtual world, an informed basic understanding of historical and cultural change, perhaps leading later to meticulous engaged scholarship, can still be imparted to students and other members of the community, but in different ways (Cline et al. 2008: 178–9; Pearce 2003). The Egyptian Oracle performance is one attempt to develop a twenty-first-century pedagogy, using both very ancient and very modern materials.

Part One

The Egyptian Oracle

1

Historical Foundations

Robyn Gillam

The heyday of the oracle: Historical and cultural context

At the turn of the first millennium BCE, Egypt was no longer a great political power in the ancient East. It was economically bankrupt and politically divided between the Nile Valley and the Nile Delta, on the Mediterranean. Loss of its empire in Canaan and Nubia, along with a shift in climate patterns, had brought famine and disease. This left the people of the lower Nile Valley vulnerable to social unrest and conflict, as well as attacks from the desert dwellers living alongside them, who had suffered even more from adverse weather patterns (Kitchen 1996: 243–71; Myśliwiec 2000: 16–22; Redford 2000; Yurco 1999).

At the end of the twelfth century, Egypt had been ruled by a group of kings named after Ramesses II, the Great. However, apart from Ramesses III, who saved Egypt from foreign invasion at the beginning of this period (but was later murdered by members of his court) (Van Dijk 2000: 304–6), they were a fractious and undistinguished lot. The reigns of the later Ramessides were increasingly distinguished by administrative incompetence and political infighting (Černý 1965: §I; Kitchen 1996: 245–6). While the last of these kings, Ramesses XI, was on the throne, a war broke out between the governor of Nubia, which lay to the south of Egypt, and the high priest of Amun, the city god of Thebes, the southern royal residence city. This led to the disappearance of the two antagonists and Egyptian rulership over Nubia, and of the pharaoh himself. When calm was restored, years were no longer numbered according to the reign of the king; the new era was called the "Renaissance." Egypt (see Figure 1.1) was divided into two states, one comprising the Delta and the lower Nile Valley to the Faiyum, which was ruled over by kings who seem to have been related to the former ruler. The other, consisting of the southern part of Egypt

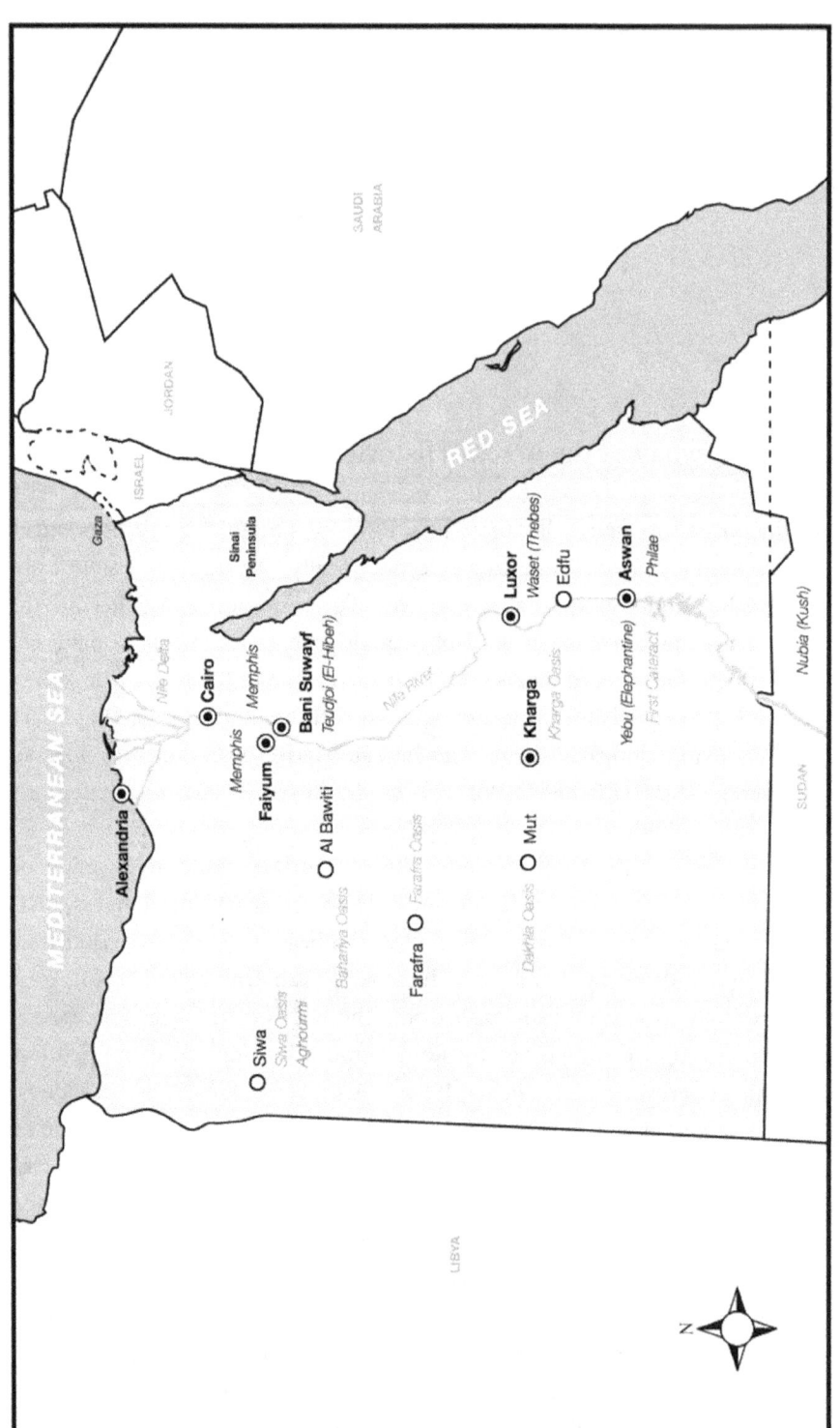

Figure 1.1 Map of Egypt.

up to its border at present-day Aswan, was simply the estate of the god Amun (see Figure 1.1) and was administered by his high priest (Černý 1965: §IV, §V; Kitchen 1996: 248–54; Niwinski 1992).

The god Amun, whose name means "the hidden one," had come to be associated with the city of Thebes more than a thousand years before this time, when the local rulers of the city gained control over the whole of Egypt after another period of political fragmentation and civil war (Callender 2000: 153–5, 158–62; Otto 1972: 237–8). More than half a millennium later, another Theban warrior clan drove foreign invaders from Egypt and gained a great empire, extending to the Levant in the north and Nubia in the south. Much of the spoils of war and the tributes of foreign nations flowed into Amun's temple, which became larger and more magnificent with each passing reign (Redford 2013: 9–10). The kings from northern Egypt who succeeded these rulers in the thirteenth century continued to expand the house of the god and its related structures (Myśliwiec 1996: 14–27; Van Dijk 2000: 273–4). And not only did Amun's house become more magnificent than that of any other god (Grimal 1992: 298–306), his land, personnel and disposable wealth stood unrivaled by anyone, finally surpassing even that of the king.

By the twelfth century, documentary evidence from the reign of Ramesses III and his successors suggests that the temples owned much of the arable land and population of Egypt. Control of both the estate of Amun and the power over taxation of royal land had been consolidated in the hands of the family of the First Prophet (high priest) of Amun, the earthly controller of the god's estate (Černý 1965: §II). While earlier kings had controlled the estate of Amun by making their own appointments to positions within it, the rulers of this period lacked that ability. The domain of the god quickly came to overshadow the Egyptian government, which, faced with this and other pressures, withered away. When the over-mighty First Prophet Amenemope disappeared in the civil war described above, his place was quickly taken by another, a military man of obscure background named Herihor.

Herihor married the daughter of his predecessor, initiated the "Renaissance" era and proclaimed himself king as well as First Prophet. While the Prophet's royal claims did not extend beyond the temple walls, he and his son Piankh carved out a realm for themselves with cooperation from the rulers of northern Egypt who had replaced Ramesses XI (Kitchen 1996: 248–54). The border between the two realms was marked by a strongly fortified outpost at el-Hibeh in the northern Nile Valley just south of the Faiyum, later known as Teudjoi, or "their walls" (Kitchen 1996: 256–71, 272–7, 283–6).

Less than twenty years after the end of the Renaissance era and the death of Ramesses XI, Piankh's son, the First Prophet Pinudjem I, proclaimed himself king, followed by four of his descendants. Given that the power and authority of the family derived from the role of their head as First Prophet (in Egyptian, *hem netcher tepy*, or "first servant of the god") (Kruchten 1989: 182–4), only the god himself—Amun-Re, the king of the gods—could mediate difficult legal and political situations in those trying times. Although the procedure was not unknown in earlier periods, as time went on it seemed that the god's advice was being sought on almost every occasion (Černý 1962: §V). At the turn of the first millennium, this advice was being dispensed in a magnificent and very public ceremony.

The setting of the performance: The domain of Amun-Re

By 1000 BCE, the *per* ("domain" or "estate," literally "house") of Amun (Figure 1.2) centered on "the most esteemed of places," that is, the temple proper around the main sanctuary inside the Fourth Pylon (Barguet 1962: 1n2). It was already one of the largest sacred installations on earth, although it had not yet reached its full extent. A thousand years earlier, the nucleus of the temple, around the sanctuary of Amun in the middle of the ancient city of Thebes, had been erected by the kings of the early 12th Dynasty (Ullmann 2007). Beginning in the earlier 18th Dynasty, the kings who created Egypt's overseas empire expanded this structure, creating an extensive sanctuary area as well as a series of halls, courts and gateways extending in a westerly direction (Hirmer, Lange and Otto 1968: 488–90; Lauffray 1979: 49–65). At the front of the temple (the Fourth Pylon) they also began a series of gateways and courtyards leading to the south (Seventh and Eighth Pylons) (Aufrère, Golvin and Goyon 1991: 96–9).

The north–south axis of the temple extended south toward the temple of Mut ("mother"), the wife of Amun, and then joined a processional way (Figure 1.3) leading to the southern or Opet temple of Amun, just over two kilometers to the south (Barguet 1962: 243–4; Hirmer, Lange and Otto 1968: 494; Lauffray 1979: 134–53). This was the site of a major festival celebrated during the annual Nile flood, when the god and his wife would travel along the processional way to the southern temple to celebrate their marriage. Returning by river to the northern complex, Amun's magnificent river boat, crafted of cedar from Lebanon, would then dock at the western façade of his temple (Murnane 1980a).

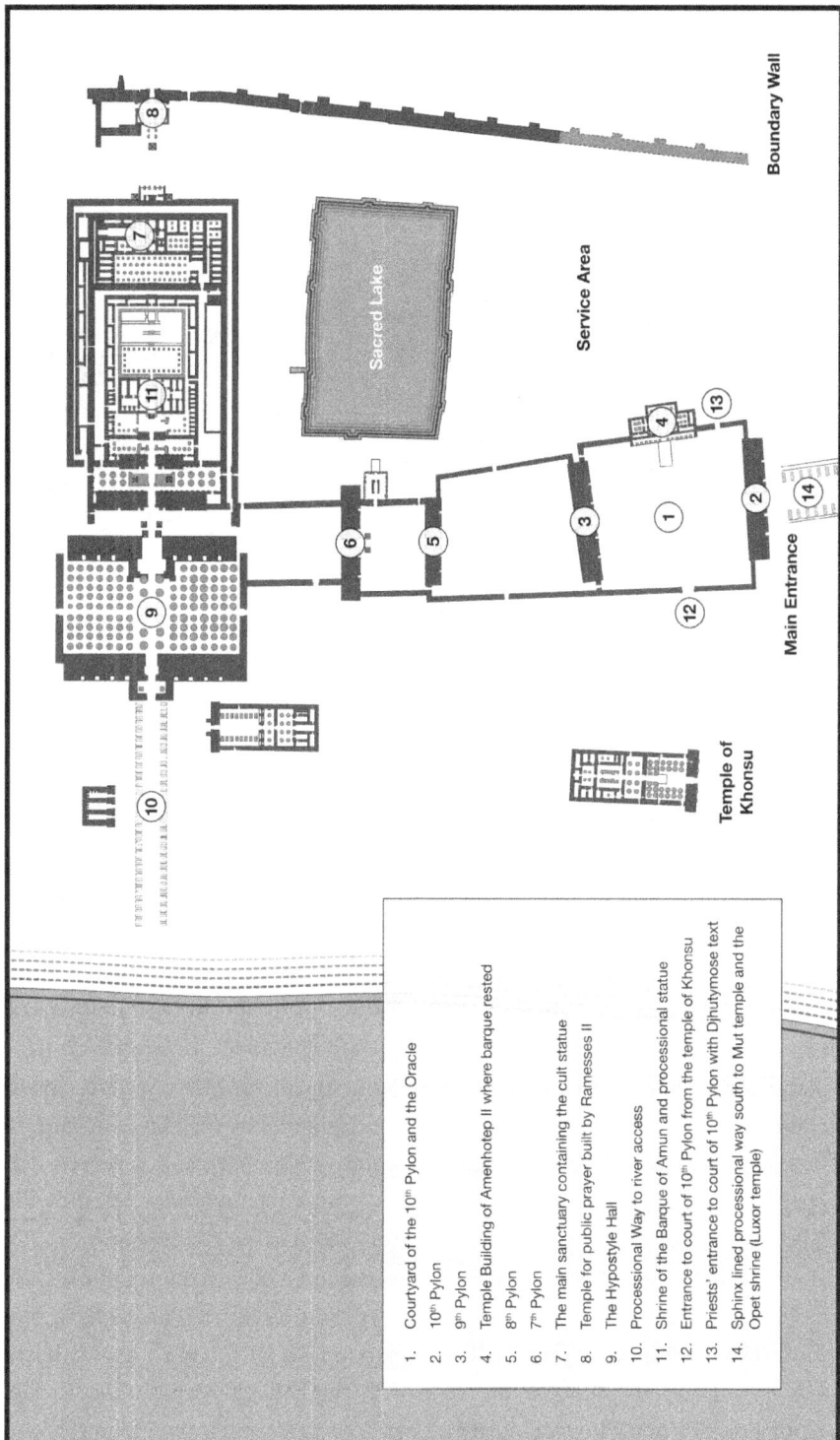

Figure 1.2 Plan of the temple precinct of Amun-Re at Karnak in the 21st Dynasty (1070–946 BCE).

1. Courtyard of the 10th Pylon and the Oracle
2. 10th Pylon
3. 9th Pylon
4. Temple Building of Amenhotep II where barque rested
5. 8th Pylon
6. 7th Pylon
7. The main sanctuary containing the cult statue
8. Temple for public prayer built by Ramesses II
9. The Hypostyle Hall
10. Processional Way to river access
11. Shrine of the Barque of Amun and processional statue
12. Entrance to court of 10th Pylon from the temple of Khonsu
13. Priests' entrance to court of 10th Pylon with Djhutymose text
14. Sphinx lined processional way south to Mut temple and the Opet shrine (Luxor temple)

Figure 1.3 Southern end of the processional way in front of the temple of Luxor.

Recent geophysical and geological research has shown that before the fourteenth century BCE, the main channel of the Nile flowed much further east than at present. This explains the importance of the north–south axis of the temple, which for much of its existence was the main approach. The gradual westward movement of the river made possible expansion of the temple in that direction, including its most famous feature, the hypostyle hall (Graham and Bunbury 2005) (Figure 1.4). This was begun by Amenhotep III, who erected the Third Pylon, which now forms its back wall (Aufrère, Golvin and Goyon 1991: 96–8). Amenhotep also extended the north–south axis almost two hundred and fifty meters to the south, to the Tenth Pylon (Azim 1980), before which were placed two colossal statues of the king some twenty meters high (Aufrère, Golvin and Goyon 1991: 96–8). This gateway was designed to be the main entrance of the temple for the people of Thebes (Lauffray 1978: 144), and it served that purpose for more than two thousand years, until the temple was closed by the Christian emperors of the late fourth century CE (Azim 1980: 159–60).

Inside the gateway Amenhotep III directed to be placed statues of his chief architect and director of works, Amenhotep, son of Hapu, who had recently died. The statues were provided with inscriptions that invited passersby to ask Amenhotep to intercede for them with the gods. Evidently this official's reputation—as one who would pass on petitions to the king—had followed him

Figure 1.4 Temple of Amun-Re, Karnak, entrance to the hypostyle hall from the courtyard of the Second Pylon, giving onto the riverbank entrance of the temple in antiquity.

into the next life (Galán 2003: 222–5); the statues were rubbed smooth by the hands of those who sought his help over the centuries (Romano and Bothmer 1979: 91). Indeed, Amenhotep's reputation for wisdom and his effectiveness at divine intercession led to his being worshiped as a god even after the king he served had long been forgotten (Galán 2003; Wildung 1977b: 83–109).

Amenhotep III did not long outlive his like-named minister. His gateway remained unfinished after his son Amenhotep, who had renamed himself Akhenaten, withdrew support from the cult of Amun in favor of a radical form of sun worship, closing Amun's temples and those of all the other gods. The gateway was completed by Horemheb, a mighty subject who made himself king after the last heir of the ruling family had disappeared. Horemheb completed the twin towers of the Tenth Pylon to a height of about eighteen meters (Figure 1.5);

Figure 1.5 Temple of Amun-Re, Karnak, courtyard of the Tenth Pylon, facing south.

he built another gateway, the Ninth Pylon, about eighty-five meters behind the Tenth. This second gateway is not at right angles to the first, as it was designed to square with the earlier gateway behind it (the Eighth Pylon), thus creating two new courtyards along the north–south processional way of the temple (Aufrère, Golvin and Goyon 1991: 98; Lauffray 1978: 138 fig. 10, 144).

Horemheb had clearly designed the courtyard of the Tenth Pylon (see Figure 1.2) as a public space to create a liminal zone between the outside world and the temple proper (Lauffray 1978: 144; Porter and Moss 1972: 187 [582, 583]). The pylon gateways on either side were flanked by large statues of the king (Barguet 1962: 284). Next to the southeastern one, on the visitors' right as they entered from outside, were the intercessory statues of Amenhotep, son of Hapu, together with similar images of Horemheb's prime minister Paramesse, whom the king had made heir to the throne (Barguet 1962: 249; Galán 2003: 221–3; Porter and Moss 1972: 188). On the opposite inner side of the gateway was a stela inscribed with Horemheb's decree describing how he had reorganized the country's government and rooted out corruption after the chaotic times of Akhenaten and his successors (Murnane 1995: 235–40). The courtyard was bounded by high stone walls decorated with reliefs that showed the king making offering to the gods, as well as processions of their images in their characteristic boat-shaped shrines (Barguet 1962: 250; Porter and Moss 1972: 184, 187–8).

The eastern side of the courtyard incorporated a small temple built by an earlier king that was later used to house the processional image of Amun (Azim 1980: 154–6; Lauffray 1978: 143–4 fig. 11). South of this building, along the same wall, was a gateway that gave access to the temple grounds in the right angle formed by the north–south and east–west axes of the main temple (Kruchten 1987: 2–4; Lauffray 1979: fig. 106). This part of the house of Amun was dominated by the sacred lake, a constructed pool measuring 132 by 80 meters that represented the primeval waters from which creation had sprung (Lauffray 1979: 197–8). It was used by the priests for bathing, in fulfillment of their rigorous purity requirements, as well as for ceremonies in which the sacred barque of the god sailed on its waters (Geßler-Lohr 1983: 425–47). In this area were found vast storerooms containing the wealth of the estate of Amun and gifts to the temple, as well as materiel necessary for the functioning of the temple. It also housed the pens of Amun's earthly avatars, the sacred geese, as well as the residences and offices of the priests and the areas that serviced them (Lauffray 1979: 197–203).

On the opposite side of the courtyard, another gateway (Lauffray 1979: 138 fig. 108; Porter and Moss 1972: 184 [561]) led to the smaller temple of Amun's son, the moon god Khonsu, which had been founded by Thutmose III and rebuilt in the reign of Ramesses III (Lauffray 1979: 214; Otto 1966: 91). The walls of the courtyard and the pylon are covered with inscriptions commemorating oracles from the time of the high priests of the 21st Dynasty (Lauffray 1979: 144; Porter and Moss 1972: 183–6) (see Figure 1.2).

The principal actors: Amun-Re and his priesthood

Amun was an ancient god, celebrated as one of the eight primeval beings that existed at the beginning of time. They were imagined as original elements of the universe, gendered male and female. At first there was only chaos, darkness and unendingness; then a wind blew over the waters of chaos, creating dry land and life. That wind was Amun, the hidden one (Otto 1966: 118–19). Thus Amun existed before the national creator and sun god Re and partook of the same creative power; he was therefore known as Amun-Re (Hornung 1982: 91).

Because Amun was also the city and family god of the kings of the Middle and Early New Kingdom, he was "lord of the thrones" as well as "king of the gods." He oversaw their foreign conquests, bringing about both Egypt's military and cultural supremacy (Otto 1966: 73–90). His power of rulership pervaded the spirit of every other god, and he was also the good and compassionate ruler who helped those in dire need who appealed to him and who righted the many injustices suffered by ordinary folk. Amun may have been a dynastic god who played an important role in the official ideology of rulership, but he was also a god who was popular with ordinary people. Ramesses II, although not a native of Amun's city of Thebes, was saved from certain death at the battle of Kadesh in 1274 BCE after he prayed to the god. Perhaps in acknowledgment of his rescue, Ramesses constructed a place of public prayer behind the sanctuary at the eastern end of the east–west axis of the temple (Assmann 2002: 231–2, 241–6, 263–71). This was known as the chapel of "Amun of the hearing ear," a place where ordinary members of the public could bring their concerns to the god (Sadek 1987: 46–7). Although Ramesses II's experience (as well as other sources) shows that all Egyptians could pray to their gods in appropriate circumstances, there was no institutional framework for such activity.

Since at least the mid–Old Kingdom (c. 2400 BCE), direct interaction with the gods was the exclusive preserve of the king and the highest-ranking male priests—the *hemu netcheru*, or "gods' servants" (in Greek, *prophetes*) (Sauneron 2000: 57–60). They were responsible for the care and feeding of the image of the god kept in the closed sanctuary of the temple (Meeks and Favard-Meeks 1997: 126–9), where its spirit chose to reside through the ministrations of the *sem* or *setne* priest, a magic and ritual specialist among the god's servants (Gardiner 1947: I, *39–42; Ritner 2003b: 453). Two or three times a day (Barta 1980), the officiating priest entered the god's sanctuary, woke up the image, and clothed and fed it. After the divinity had spiritually consumed its essence, the food reverted to the god's earthly servants, who consumed it themselves. The principle of "reversion of offerings" was, in fact, the economic basis of temple life (Fairman 1954: 180–1). All the inhabitants and employees of the estate of Amun were supported, either directly or indirectly, by this institution (Teeter 2007: 322–3).

In order to participate in the daily cult, a priest had to be selected by the god and the temple hierarchy from the larger body of priests, the *wabu*, or "pure ones" (Abdallah 1984; Nims 1965: 96; Ritner 2009: 121). Purity, both physical and spiritual, was a prerequisite for any kind of temple service. However, the duties of a *wab* priest could involve anything from agricultural labor to arranging the offerings and implements for the daily cult or carrying the processional image of the god (Caminos 1974: 17; David 2007: 111; Gardiner 1948: I, *53–55; Sauneron 2000: 70). When the lucky or well-connected were selected to be initiated—"introduced" to the god in his sanctuary (Kruchten 1989: 12–19;

1995: 6)—they gained entrée into the upper reaches of the social elite (Kruchten 1989: 177–85), with its fine houses, political connections and vast real estate holdings (Černý 1965: §IV; Haring 1997: 12–20, 372–7). Furthermore, an office in the priesthood did not mean a lifetime of celibate denial. The servants of the gods worked in shifts (Quirke 1992: 94–7). Each priesthood was divided into four "crews" (Roth 1991: 3) that worked for one month in each of the three seasons of the Egyptian calendar year. Although by 1000 BCE aspects of the Egyptian priesthood were becoming increasingly professionalized (David 2007: 107), this schedule left ample time for the four prophets of Amun to pursue other career options, such as politics or the army.

The shift-work arrangement in Egyptian temples not only acknowledged that the priests had other responsibilities but also ensured that there would be no break or slackness in the service of the god. Proper performance of the daily cult was tied to the maintenance of cosmic order (Teeter 2007: 310). If the god's spirit left its shrine, disaster would ensue for the temple, the city and the land. The image could not be moved and no unauthorized person was allowed into the sanctuary (Hornung 1982: 135; Kruchten 1989: 45ff., 251–2). However, although this regime ensured the preservation of world order (*maat*), it prevented the rest of the population from seeing the god or interacting with it.

The barque of Amun

To facilitate public revelation of divinity, more portable images of the god could hold its spirit (Hornung 1982: 135–6). These were generally carried in procession, in boat-shaped shrines; boats were the usual form of transport for Egyptians as well as for their gods, who traveled through the sky rather than across water (Brand 2001). From the Early New Kingdom onwards, all major temples had a special shrine for the sacred barque—the model-boat shrine and its image—in front of the main sanctuary. Responsibility for care of the image as well as for carrying it in procession was given to the *wab* priests rather than the prophets. In the temple of Amun, a parallel hierarchy of *wab* priests formed around the processional image (Kruchten 1989: 251–2; 1995, 63–4).

Though only a miniature boat, the processional shrine of Amun was a magnificent object. No example has survived, but its appearance can be reconstructed by using images and written descriptions. Made of wood, the whole was adorned with gold and silver leaf and inlaid with semiprecious stones or colored glass (Górski 1990: 101–4). The deck of the boat was decorated with images and emblems of the god and his divine associates, as well as flowers and green boughs. The prow of the boat was decorated with the head of Amun's other earthly incarnation, a curly-horned ram (Brand 2001; Robins 2005: 10).

The barque of Amun probably originated in the Middle Kingdom, when his identification with the sun god Re—who traveled across the sky in his solar boat—was made (Brand 2001). As noted above, the barque was carried in procession by the *wab* priests of the temple. Over time the barques of the gods in the domain of Amun grew in size to better reflect the glory of the god and the increased wealth of the temple. The boat itself was a scaled-down version of a vessel used for transportation by Egypt's upper classes, with a raised stern equipped with a rudder (Landström 1970: 70–89, 98–115). However, this boat lacked a mast and sail, and instead of a central cabin there was the shrine of the god, which took the form of the ancient *perwer*, a sacred structure that went back to prehistoric times, surmounted by a canopy. Since Amun is the hidden god, the shrine containing his image remained closed; it was fitted with a fine veil that partly concealed it and whose movement indicated the presence of the divine spirit. The boat's supernatural crew was represented by small images of reverent, watchful gods deployed fore and aft, at the rudder and the prow of the boat (Brand 2001; Karlshausen 2009: 181–94); these figures were probably made of gilded metal. The wooden hull of the boat and the shrine were also gilded, as were the shrine and the figureheads on the prow and stern, both in the form of a horned ram. These visible manifestations of the god were given inlaid eyes, and other details were picked out in colored glass or semiprecious stones (Górski 1990: 101–4 fig. 1).

In earlier times when the gods appeared in their processional boats, they were dragged on wooden sleds, but Amun was raised on the shoulders of his worshipers (Brand 2001) to be more visible in the crowded streets of Thebes, the new capital of imperial Egypt. This innovation made necessary a new mechanism for transportation that can in large part be reconstructed from highly detailed representations of the god's portable shrine. The model boat was placed on a small dais or base, which rested on a plank that was shaped like the traditional sled but was equipped with carrying poles. Originally there were probably only two poles, but as the barque became larger and more elaborate over time, the number increased to three and then four, finally reaching their maximum number of five during the reign of Ramesses II (Legrain 1917: 1–13).

The boat itself became more and more elaborate, with more small figures on deck, intricate decoration on the shrine, and embroidery on the veil that covered it (Karlshausen 1995: 121–7). In the mid-18th Dynasty, four bronze scarab beetles were added to the plank to secure the keel of the boat, and in the late 18th Dynasty, images of the king and the ancestor gods were placed between them on each side (Karlshausen 1995: 127–30; Lacau and Chevrier 1977: 156). During the reign of Sety I or Ramesses II, the most significant modification of the barque's design was made: a second, larger shrine that enclosed the first, attached to the plank rather than the boat to form a secure armature around the whole installation (Traunecker, Le Saout and Masson 1981: 77–8).

As the boat became bigger and heavier (Figure 1.6), the number of carrying poles matched the number of additional men required to lift it. From three bars and eighteen bearers, in the early to mid-18th Dynasty, to four bars—first with six bearers, then eight per bar—the barque required a total of twenty-four and

Figure 1.6 Modern perspective drawing of the barque of Amun, based on materials of the fourth century BCE (28th Dynasty). Reproduced from Traunecker, Le Saout and Masson (1981), with permission of Claude Traunecker.

then thirty-two men by the late 18th Dynasty. Then, under Ramesses II, the number of poles increased to five, with six men each, making thirty bearers, and finally eight, requiring forty men, under Ramesses III. By the time of Herihor, the dimensions of the barque—or at least the number of carrying poles—had shrunk from five to four bars, and the number of bearers from forty to thirty-two (Legrain 1917: 1–13; Traunecker, Le Saout and Masson 1981: 77–81).

It may be estimated that this later form of barque was around 3.25 meters long and that its total height when on the shoulders of the bearers was approximately 4.8 meters (Legrain 1917: 1–13; Traunecker, Le Saout and Masson 1981: 77–81). The documents from the reign of Ramesses II also state that the similarly designed barques of Mut and Khonsu had three carrying poles and twenty-four men each (Kruchten 1987: 7–9; Legrain 1917: 2). In other words, the barque of Amun was almost twice their size. The gilding and decoration would have made it extremely heavy, perhaps upwards of six hundred kilograms (Legrain 1917: 12), making carrying of the barque by its bearers an act of endurance as well as devotion.

The Great Festival of the Oracle of Amun: An imaginative reconstruction

The following description is an imaginative reconstruction based on documents and inscriptions from southern Egypt in the eleventh to ninth centuries BCE. Detailed information on the sources used can be found in the following section.

It is early morning on a bright, hot summer day in the courtyard of the Tenth Pylon, the entrance to the most esteemed of places—the domain of Amun-Re, king of the gods—around the turn of the first millennium before the Common Era. At the end of the sphinx-lined ceremonial way from the temple of Amun's consort, Mut (Aufrère, Golvin and Goyon 1991: 99 fig.; Eaton-Krauß and Murnane 1991; Porter and Moss 1972: 191), the great double doors of cedar of Lebanon, with their crosspieces and hinges of gilded bronze (Arnold 2003: 152), stand open. The great space of the courtyard is thronged by the people of Thebes, who are happy and excited about celebrating the holiday with not only a viewing of the great gods of their city but also an opportunity to see Amun pass judgment on some difficult issues. These issues have been of concern to the inhabitants of his domain, the people of the city and the southern part of the land of Egypt.

It is just three hours after sunrise when the astronomer priest, who keeps time during religious ceremonies (Sauneron 1962: 127), loudly announces the approach of the gods. A hush falls over the crowd, and those who are not part of the elite or temple personnel drift toward the edges of the paved courtyard or take up positions outside the outer gate and along the processional way from the temple of Mut. The sun shines brilliantly on the brightly painted reliefs of the courtyard walls and sparkles off the great cedar flagpoles that tower over the Ninth and Tenth Pylons (Azim and Traunecker 1982). Suddenly the flags begin to stir as the divine spirit approaches (Hornung 1982: 35–37).

An eruption of excited rejoicing is heard beyond the outer gate as the barque of Mut approaches from her temple to the south. She enters through the pylon gate in a cloud of frankincense and myrrh, her shrine borne aloft by twenty-four *wab* priests and escorted on each side by two prophets (Kruchten 1987: 9–10). Going before her, bent in reverence and walking backwards, another *wab* priest waves his gilded bronze incense burner (Kruchten 1987: 7–8)—which is shaped like an eternally offering hand (Beinlich 1978)—from side to side as he burns precious myrrh, one pellet at a time (Schäfer 1986: 228). Mut's barque sweeps up and around the east and north sides of the courtyard, taking up a position to the west of the inner gateway. Almost immediately, the similarly sized barque of her son Khonsu issues forth from the southwest gate of the courtyard; it has come from his temple, which lies parallel to the east–west axis of the temple of Amun. This second barque glides around the south and east sides of the courtyard, taking up a position to the east of the central doorway of the Ninth Pylon, which remains closed.

All at once, as the wind begins to blow the flags more vigorously, on the other side of the door is heard drumming, clapping, the shaking of sacred rattles, the singing of women and shouts of rejoicing—everything that would be done to announce a king (Simpson 2003: 23). Then, as the doors of the Ninth Pylon slowly open outward, the great barque of Amun-Re, king of the gods, begins to move slowly through the doorway, accompanied by all the perfumes of the Horn of Africa, wafting through the air. Raised on the shoulders of thirty-two *wab* priests (Kruchten 1987: 9; Traunecker, Le Saout and Masson 1981: 81), the shrine on its boat, topped by a canopy decorated with protective cobras and falcons, appears in the gateway. The priest preceding the boat wields a four-barreled incense burner of gilded bronze, a special design used only before the processional barque (Traunecker, Le Saout and Masson 1981: 38). A parade of women musicians follows the god into the courtyard, beating small drums and shaking the sacred sistrum rattles that calm his anger (Roberts 1995: 57–62). They sing and ululate joyfully as they take up their positions behind and beside the three sacred barques, which are now positioned in a line across the courtyard, with that of Amun slightly in front.

An expectant silence falls on the courtyard as the audience takes stock of the awesome presence of the god. Then, as the astronomer priest announces the approach of the First Prophet, the door in the southeast corner of the courtyard bursts open and Amun's foremost servant strides out. While the *wab* priests are barefoot and clothed in simple tube-shaped tunics suspended from straps (Kruchten 1987: 9), the prophet is dressed in a shirt of the finest linen, set off by a beautifully pressed pleated linen kilt, carefully tied at the front to show its delicately fringed edges. On his feet are finely tooled sandals of red leather (Nicholson and Shaw 2000: 306; Veldmeijer 2010: 19) inlaid with gilded designs, its elaborate toes curling up over the foot and joined to a crosspiece at the instep (Von Beckerath 1968: pl. 1). However, although he is dressed like a high official or a prince, the priest could not be mistaken for either of those. The sunlight gleams off his meticulously shaven and oiled head, and over his left shoulder hangs the skin of a leopard, its head at the front and its tail at the back—the ancient sign of the *setne* priest, the ritual expert and channeler of the divine spirit (Helck 1987: 22–3).

The priest moves across the vast expanse of the courtyard to its center. There can be seen a large paving stone, engraved with the name and titles of a high priest and the incised outline of two feet (Goyon 1978–81). Before standing on the stone's carved footprints, the First Prophet directs one of the *wab* priests to remove his sandals. He is then surrounded by six priests, two of whom wash his feet, two who pour water on his hands, and two who sprinkle water over his head and body from the elongated, hook-nozzled *qebeh* vessels used for all ritual purification (Goyon 1979–81: 278–80; Naville 1892: pl. 11.1). Although the First Prophet would have begun his day with rigorous cleansing, including a plunge in the sacred lake, every interaction with the god entails further purification (Fairman 1954: 128–9). The cleansing completed, the First Prophet moves away from the washing stone to stand directly before Amun, who is flanked by his wife and son, Mut and Khonsu.

As he gazes at the gods, it must seem to the high priest that their forms shimmer and tremble in the heat haze, for their bearers shift slightly to accommodate the weight and the great ostrich-feather fans that surround the divine barques (Kruchten 1987: 8) are wafting in the breeze. As he looks upon the physical embodiments of the gods sculpted on the prows of their barques—the hawk Khonsu, the beautiful woman Mut (Kruchten 1987: 8–9) and the sacred ram, whose very writing in the sacred script denotes awe and terror (Behrens 1986: 1243; Klotz 2006: 143, 167), fear and trembling—they seem to stare back at him even more intently. And then, after moments that seem like hours, the bearers of the barque of Amun appear to collapse slightly under its weight; it angles downward but then suddenly rights itself, the prow lifting slowly and majestically upward and forward as the bearers regain equilibrium. There is a very slight but audible sigh of collective relief—the god has acknowledged the First Prophet by greeting him. The oracular session may now begin (Kruchten 1987: 104–5).

The First Prophet begins to speak to the god, his right hand raised with the palm facing his interlocutor, a gesture familiar in Egyptian public speaking (Dominicus 1994: 77–80). His voice is loud, deep and resonant. It reverberates around the walls of the courtyard, commanding all mortals, if not the gods, to give it their full attention. "Amun Re, King of the Gods, my good Lord, is there a matter that has happened in the land before this great festival during this year that should be reported?" (Kruchten 1987: 54, 66). Once again the god gives the upward-and-forward gesture of positive acknowledgment.

The First Prophet continues: "Amun Re, King of the Gods, my good Lord, here are two documents. One states that there are matters that should be investigated in connection with Amenemope, son of Wennefer, inspector of divine offerings of the altars of Amun in the Hall of the Ancestors before the Great Seat. The other document states that there is no matter that should be investigated in connection with Amenemope, son of Wennefer" (Černý 1962: 45; Kruchten 1987: 54–5). As he speaks, the First Prophet indicates two *wab* priests standing slightly behind him to his left and right, each holding a small papyrus scroll. "My good Lord, will you choose between the two documents?"

Once again the god indicates agreement. The First Prophet signals the two priests holding the documents to step before the divine barque of Amun. As he does so, total silence falls on the crowd; attention shifts from the First Prophet to a figure who now detaches himself from the crowd at the southern end of the courtyard, near the entrance gate of the temple. A small man, clad in a more modest version of the shirt and kilt worn by the Prophet, walks slowly toward the center of the courtyard, back bent, hands stretched out with palms facing the ground in a gesture of obeisance and submission (Dominicus 1994: 33–6). Although his face is partially obscured by his ceremonial wig, his eyes are huge with fear and his complexion gray. When he reaches the center of the courtyard, he throws himself face down (Dominicus 1994: 33–5) on the limestone paving to await his fate.

Amenemope has every reason to be terrified. The Hall of Ancestors is the room directly in front of the main sanctuary of the temple. This is where, during the daily cult ceremony, the food offered to Amun-Re as well as to the other resident divinities and royal ancestors reverts to humanity, beginning with the officiating Prophet and those attending him, who share a symbolic meal at the end of the service (Fairman 1954: 180–1; Gardiner 1935: 101–6). Only the finest and most carefully prepared foodstuffs are fit for the table of the god. As well as the produce of his own estate, they include gifts from the king and the elite, whose generosity to Amun ensures that he will be generous to them and to the land of Egypt. The food of the god represents spiritual merit for those who give it, as well as for the rest of humanity (Derchain 1965: 10–19).

To peculate the daily offerings of the god would be not only a grave moral offence but a criminal one (Vernus 2003: 98–104). In the estate of Amun—that is, the realm of southern Egypt—human and divine economy are identical. Amun also rules as an earthly king, with the First Prophet as his minister. If found guilty, Amenemope would lose not only his position as provisioner of the altars but probably also his life. His property would be confiscated, leaving his wife and children destitute (Kruchten 1987: 106–9, 222–8, 242ff.). Although the provisioner of the altars has vigorously denied all the accusations against him, his accusers, headed by the God's Father Djedkhonsuiuefankh, are too well-connected. The God's Fathers, an intermediate rank of priests between *wab*s and Prophets, are a group who owe their position and upward mobility as much to political maneuvering as to holiness (Kruchten 1989: 188–90).

While the evidence against Amenemope is slight, he has not received a favorable hearing from the earthly magistrates who sit at the door of the temple (Sauneron 1954: 118–23). Thus he is here at the Festival of the Divine Oracle at the behest of his accusers as much as by his own volition. Although Amun once had a reputation as defender of the poor, times have changed (Assmann 2002: 229–46), and Amenemope and his family are fearful of the outcome. As he moves to the center of the courtyard, his wife and two young children cluster around the statue of the ancient sage Amenhotep, son of Hapu, rubbing the statue's feet and knees as they pray for him to intercede with Amun-Re.

Once again time seems to stand still. The two *wab* priests stand before the god, holding their scrolls in front of them. Then the priest bearing the first document, which requests an investigation, moves toward the god, holding out the document to him. At first nothing happens, but then, very slowly and gradually, the bearers at the front of the boat begin to collapse under its weight and its great mass slides downward. A gasp rises from the crowd—the god has refused the document! (Černý 1962: 43–4; Kruchten 1987: 105–8). Next, the priest holding the document rejecting the need for an investigation advances toward the barque. This time there is no hesitation. The god's vessel surges forward and upward.

Has Amenemope been justified? Is he true of voice before the god in this life, as he hopes to be after his death, before Osiris? This is a very serious case. The persons making the accusation are well-connected members of the priestly hierarchy, with influence extending to the First Prophet himself. Although the god has spoken, those involved are well placed and highly trusted. So, following established legal procedures, the First Prophet requests further confirmation of the god's decision.

When the priests with the documents have returned to their former positions, the First Prophet once again addresses the god: "My good Lord, may the question be repeated?" (Černý 1962: 43; Kruchten 1987: 87–8). Once again the god registers his approval. The presentation of the documents is repeated, and the response of the god—rejecting the first and approving the second—is swifter and more emphatic than before. Pivoting to address the crowd gathered behind him at the main gate of the temple and the doorway leading to the priests' quarters, to its left—and being careful not to turn his back on the god—the First Prophet declares, "The great god, Amun Re, King of the Gods, has attested that that there is no matter that should be investigated in connection with Amenemope, son of Wennefer" (Kruchten 1987: 173–4).

The Prophet then turns again to face the god, this time raising his arms before his face with the palms facing outward, the gesture of prayer (Dominicus 1994: 28–32). He raises his powerful voice in praise of the god, chanting:

> Hail to you, who made everything, who created all that exists,
> Father of the gods, who bore the goddesses,
> Who settled them in the towns and districts,
> Who begot males, who bore females,
> Who made everyone live,
> A pilot who knows the waters, that is Amun,
> A steering oar for the helpless,
> One who gives food to the one who has not,
> Who helps the servant of His house prosper.
>
> Amun, lend your ear to the lonely in court,
> He is poor, not rich.
> Might Amun appear as vizier,
> To let the poor go free;
> Might the poor appear as vindicated
> And may want surpass wealth.

Amun Re, who knows compassion.
Who hearkens to him who calls him,
Amun Re, king of the gods,
Strong bull, who glories in his power.
            (After Foster 2001: 121; Lichtheim 1976: 111–12; Ritner 2009: 127)

The oracular session is now over. The First Prophet backs away from the god toward the priests' entrance to the courtyard. Amenemope is on his feet, his arms raised in a gesture of rejoicing (Dominicus 1994: 58–61; Kruchten 1987: 12) (Figure 1.7). The sound of animated conversation rises from the crowd. Amenemope's family raise their voices in relief and praise of the god, his wife and mother ululating in joy at his deliverance. As he embraces his family, friends and members of the crowd congratulate him with handclasps, placing around his neck floral garlands that are a part of the festival (Sadek 1987: 176–7, 181).

Amenemope leaves the court of the oracle in triumph, now ready to enjoy the rest of the holiday. He has obtained a final judgment from the god; it can never be appealed or overturned. At some point in the near future he will receive a formal document of his acquittal, a magnificently lettered scroll with a painted vignette showing the judgment of the god, with the barque, the First Prophet and the acquitted man picked out in handsome colors and gold leaf. Other,

Figure 1.7 Temple of Amun-Re, Karnak. Twentieth Dynasty commemorative inscription of Nesamun in the courtyard of the Tenth Pylon. The inscription records a favorable decision of the oracle. After the First Prophet (upper right) poses the question to the god in his barque and the god gives a favorable answer, the questioner is seen in an attitude of rejoicing (lower right). Redrawn from the original by Robyn Gillam.

more influential or wealthier recipients might obtain permission to have a copy engraved on the walls of the courtyard (Kruchten 1987: 35; Parker 1962: col. pl. 1), but Amenemope will be content to keep it safely with him and pass it on to his children. Back in the courtyard, the scene is a little more subdued. The crowd is breaking up and many are leaving the temple grounds through the pylon gate. In the corner near the courtyard, Amenemope's accuser, Djedkhonsuiuefankh, remains, in earnest, hushed conversation with other high-ranking priests.

At this point there are two possible trajectories for the gods in their barques. They and their bearers could stay a while in the small temple of Amenhotep II, incorporated into the courtyard as a resting place along the gods' processional way (Kruchten 1995: 62, 167–8, 334; Lauffray 1978: 140–3). However, today's consultation has fallen within the Opet Festival, a great celebration during which the god and his family travel to his southern temple along a sphinx-lined processional way (Murnane 1980a). While the day is hot and the way is long— just over two kilometers (Favro and Wendrich 2014)—the *wab* priests bearing the gods will travel a little way before stopping at another resting place of the god (Kruchten 1987: 260–1) around noon.

Once the First Prophet and others who officiated at the ceremony have departed, the bearers of the barque begin to cross the courtyard, followed by the singers and musicians. As the crowd prepares to follow the gods out of the temple courtyard, the atmosphere is subdued, a result of the huge expenditure of energy entailed in the ceremony. Then suddenly the barque of Amun appears to lurch sideways, dragging the *wab* priests beneath it toward the southeast corner of the courtyard. Ejaculations of surprise and alarm arise from the crowd, who stop in their tracks. The god surges forward to the corner of the pylon and stops dead in front of Djedkhonsuiuefankh, almost pinning him to the wall as he is about to go through the priests' gate. There is little doubt among those watching what this means. As well as exonerating the man accused of diverting his offerings, Amun has decided to indicate who the real culprit is. Although the God's Father loudly demands to know what all this is about and insists he has done no wrong, his protests are ignored. Heavily armed police, present in the courtyard in anticipation of a guilty verdict for Amenemope (Kruchten 1987: 229), lead him away as his family cries out in alarm and his friends quietly melt away.

Djedkhonsuiuefankh, as a highly placed member of Amun's clergy, will no doubt get his own session before the oracle in an attempt to save himself. However, things do not look good for him. It is very difficult to refute the will of the god when he acts in such an emphatic and completely unscripted way.

This does not happen often, but when it does, it shows clearly that Amun is extremely displeased with the human stewardship of his estate. A few minutes later, Amenemope hears the extraordinary news as he partakes of a celebratory meal with his family under one of the great shade trees along the processional way (Cabrol 2001: 171–82). Like his namesake, a man who long ago wrote a book of wise sayings (Fischer-Elfert 2001), he does not rejoice in the fall of his accuser; instead he recalls that Amun is the keeper not only of justice but also of vengeance. As the First Prophet Menkheperre put it,

> Great of wrath, he is more powerful than Sakhmet,
> Like the fiery blast in a stormwind ...
> Who will withstand your displeasure,
> Or will dispel [the fury of] your wrath?
>
> (Ritner 2009: 127–8)

Sources for the Great Festival of the Oracle of Amun

The above narrative is a historical fiction. The identity of the First Prophet is left deliberately vague and the other characters are imaginary, although they bear names very common in this period and their functions are attested in the sources cited here. No such oracular consultation ever took place, but the description draws on documents from the 21st and 22nd Dynasties and the later New Kingdom. One of the main aims of the narrative is to illustrate the operation of the processional oracle at the time of its greatest power and magnificence, during the rule of the high priests of Amun in southern Egypt, between the eleventh and ninth centuries BCE.

Oracles were used for a wide range of purposes in the regime of the high priests. Although their status was primarily legal (Kruchten 2001b), they also had social, cultural and predictive value. Some specifically political oracles known from the regime of the high priests are the confirmation of twenty years of rule for Herihor by Amun (Černý 1965: §5); the confirmation of Menkheperre, son of Pinedjem I, as high priest of Amun after a rebellion in Thebes; and the confirmation of Osorkon, son of Takelot II, under similar circumstances (Ritner 2009: 124–9, 353–8). However, most oracular judgments by Amun concerned legal issues around the disposal of property or the attainment of priestly offices, which also enjoyed incomes derived from real estate (Černý 1962: 38; Ritner 2009: 130–5, 138–43, 162–6).

Oracles were also a way of soliciting the blessing of a god, as shown by a singular group of documents known as "oracular amuletic decrees," in which the god gives the recipient—often a newborn—life, prosperity and well-being; sometimes the deceased are promised eternal life (Černý 1962: 39–40; Kruchten 1987: 57ff.; Ritner 2009: 74–6). When Masaharta, the eldest son of Pinudjem I, fell ill at the northern fortress of Teudjoi, one of his brothers asked the local god, Amun of the Camp, if he would survive (Ritner 2009: 122–3). While this oracle can be seen as a request connected with human welfare, in this case it also has political overtones (Kitchen 1996: 259–60). Given that the 21st Dynasty high priests in particular had such close control over the domain of Amun, it is not surprising that the categories of oracular request often overlap.

One of the chief values of the oracular documents of the 21st Dynasty high priests is that they preserve an outline of the actual procedure much more clearly than do most of those of other periods. While it is clear that all important oracular decisions of the gods of the domain of Amun and other major temples were recorded in an official document on papyrus, only two of these have survived. The first is a decree for Nesikhons, the deceased wife and niece of Pinudjem II, found in her burial (Ritner 2009: 145–58). This, the most well-preserved oracular document to survive, begins with a long hymn describing the nature of Amun and his relationship with the land of Egypt and its political structures. It then goes on to proclaim Nesikhons a god, to protect her surviving family members from harm by her spirit and to guarantee her funerary estate. Unfortunately there is no indication of the ceremonial procedure entailed in obtaining the oracle. The papyrus is for the most part a transcription from a hieratic writing-board also found in the tomb, likely the document laid before Amun for approval (Ritner 2009: 145). Besides, the status and entitlements of the dead throw little light on the uses of the oracle in everyday life.

The other document, the so-called Saite Oracle papyrus, dates long after this period, to the fourteenth year of Psamtik I of the 26th Dynasty (650 BCE), and was purchased on the antiquities market in Luxor (Parker 1962: 1–2). This document is indeed an official legal record of an oracular event, complete with a beautiful illuminated vignette showing the ceremony and the names, filiation and titles of fifty witnesses, including the prophet of Montu, Amenemhat, who wrote the document (Figure 1.8). It records how Pemou, the son of Harsiese, successfully requested of Amun that his father, a *wab* priest of Amun, be permitted to transfer to the temple of Montu, the ancient Theban war god (Parker 1962: 1–11). Unfortunately the document was not found sealed in a tomb and is not in the best of condition. Most of the decree and the witnesses' names can be read (Parker 1962: 12–34, pl. 2–16), but the vignette itself—one

Figure 1.8 Vignette of the Saite Oracle papyrus, Brooklyn Museum, showing the four prophets of Amun (center) interceding with the god in his shrine (left) for the questioner (on the right).

of the best surviving depictions of an oracle—is in fragmentary condition, although enough can be made out to decipher the main action of the scene (Parker 1962: 3–6, pl. 1). Still, it is in much better condition than the numerous inscriptions scattered around the court of the Tenth Pylon and elsewhere in the temple of Karnak, the more elaborate of which were copied from similar documents (Porter and Moss 1972: 183–9; Kruchten 1987: 6, 35). Although the Saite Oracle papyrus is a vital source for the study of this subject, it is clear that the ceremonial procedure changed somewhat over the centuries, so it is not always useful in helping to reconstruct the earlier decrees. Nevertheless, it gives us the best idea of what the ceremony looked like.

The main inspiration for the narrative above is the inscription of Djhutymose, the chief steward of the estate of Amun, who was accused of some kind of mismanagement of this vast holding during the tenure of Pinudjem II (Kitchen 1996: 277). This long and complex document is found on the other side of the priests' entrance to the courtyard of the Tenth Pylon, once protected by a little porch and inviting the admiring attention of his associates (Kruchten 1987: 4–5). It is also provided with a vignette showing the first part of the ceremony, as it would have been in the original legal document (Kruchten 1987: 6–14, color plate). However, not only was the case long and complex, extending over several years and many oracular sessions (Kruchten 1987: 29–32), the inscription is also in very poor condition and large parts of it are completely illegible (Kruchten 1987: 32–4). Furthermore, the relief that accompanies the inscription suggests that presentation of the document involved some kind of box or shrine, as shown in the badly drawn and badly preserved vignette (Kruchten 1987: 10–11, 108–15, 228–9, 230 [fig.]). Jean-Marie Kruchten, who made an important and exhaustive study of this text, confessed that he found this aspect of the document completely incomprehensible (Kruchten 1995: 62–3), and for that reason our little story imagines a simpler procedure. It has also made the accused a less grand figure and confined his case to one oracular session.

The conception of the oracular session's being closed by a hymn to the god, praising the qualities he has shown in the judgment, is taken from a commemorative stela of Menkheperre, the father of Pinudjem II—now in the Louvre in Paris—that was found in the temple of Karnak in the mid-nineteenth century (Ritner 2009: 124-9). Although this object appears to have been reused as a grindstone, enough of it remains for us to see about half of the vignette at the top and to discern about three-quarters of the text (Von Beckerath 1968: pl. 1). Unlike the Djhutymose inscription, whose location connects it with the court of the Tenth Pylon, these oracles of Amun appear to have been delivered somewhere near the hypostyle hall of the main temple.

As noted above, the text begins with the arrival of Menkheperre in Thebes after a period of rebellion, when he is confirmed in his position of First Prophet by the god. It is only later, during the New Year festival, that the Prophet decides to ask if the leaders of the rebellion may be forgiven and allowed to come back home; when the god assents, the priest then breaks into a hymn praising his mercy and forgiveness of wrongs (Ritner 2009: 126-8). While a modern reader might understand this text as a clever way to introduce a more conciliatory approach to political rivals (Kitchen 1996: 261), its original intention seems to be to demonstrate the qualities of the god, who is ultimately responsible for everything that happens (Assmann 2002: 301-7). In our story, the quality displayed by Amun is his advocacy of the poor and downtrodden. Admittedly, this aspect of the god was not so much in favor at this period, but it was the subject of a number of earlier hymns found in scribal manuals and at the workmen's village in west Thebes from the late New Kingdom (19th and 20th Dynasties), some two centuries before this time (Posener 1971; Vernus 2003: 139-42).

We have combined a number of sources to create the hymn in the story. The opening comes from the Menkheperre text, emphasizing that the Amun of the oracles is the primeval creator of the universe (Ritner 2009: 124, 127). The rest is a combination of several New Kingdom hymns emphasizing Amun's support of the poor and insignificant, especially in legal situations (Foster 2001: 121; Lichtheim 1976: 111-12). Another excerpt from Menkheperre's hymn, which reminds us that Amun can be vengeful as well as forgiving, closes our story (Ritner 2009: 127-8).

It must be stressed that reference to the poor and insignificant should not be taken too literally. In the case of both our fictional protagonist and the authors of the late New Kingdom hymns, their humble situation was relative. The expansion of Egypt's overseas influence in the late Bronze Age necessitated expansion of its bureaucratic structures (Hayes 1962: §8). The wealth that poured into the royal coffers and temples gradually trickled down to an expanding group of educated urban-dwellers who staffed the offices and workshops of the palace, temple and army (Hayes 1962: §7). While more comfortably off than the humbler peasants and workers (Cooney 2007: 168–72), this expanding middle class still chafed against the power of the elite and the barriers they erected against further upward mobility. When the empire collapsed and the economy shrank, they resorted to any means necessary to save themselves. In the suburban workmen's community at Sut Maat (modern Deir el-Medina), near the royal cemetery of Thebes, they deployed political demonstrations, strikes, black marketeering and theft to survive (Vernus 2003: 1–50, 142–9).

Although the urban middle class became a casualty of the collapse of the Egyptian empire, those in upper-middle-management positions, like the hero of our story, Amenemope, also felt pressure from above. As noted above, the high priests of the 21st Dynasty tended to monopolize all the important positions and income in the domain of Amun, leading to increased social tension and competition among members of the other elite families and their followers (Kitchen 1996: 270–1, 275–6; Kruchten 1987: 95, 171–2). Although Menkheperre forgave the leaders of the rebellion against him and opened up a number of positions to people outside his family, the division and sharing of decreased economic resources remained a problem (Kitchen 1996: 56, 63, 276–7). Below the ruling elite, political factions formed that waged a clandestine war, using smaller players as pawns in their maneuvering and often attacking their rivals with charges of corruption. Although this was nothing new in Egyptian life, the vocabulary of oppression and helplessness found in appeals to the gods throws these social conflicts into dramatic relief. However, we must again remember that the "poor man" in this case is closer to the top than the bottom of society (Kruchten 1987: 246–9; Ritner 2009: 127, l. 15)—he is clothed in fine linen, not a ragged loincloth.

The appearance of the ceremony described in the narrative is based on its representation in the documents discussed above, and their interpretation by scholars. The vignette on the Djhutymose inscription shows the gods on the left-hand side of the picture. The barque of Amun is shown on a large scale, filling the whole vertical space, while the barques of Mut and Khonsu are shown as less than half the size, behind it on two small registers. Making allowances for the conventions of Egyptian art, we are to understand that the three barques are positioned next to each other, with the barque of Amun, which is giving the oracular responses, slightly out in front (Kruchten 1987: 7–10). In both the

Djhutymose inscription and the Saite Oracle papyrus, the vignettes show the officiating priests in the center of the composition and the applicant on the far right. We must assume that the applicant is standing behind the priests, as they are the intermediaries between the god and his human petitioners (Kruchten 1987: 66–7, 79).

In the Djhutymose vignette, behind the priest censing the god and those presenting the box with the documents, we see the First Prophet some distance further back, separated by an inscription, with the applicant standing right behind him. The First Prophet makes the speechifying gesture (Dominicus 1994: 77–80), suggesting that he is addressing the god (Kruchten 1987: 11–12). In the much later Saite Oracle papyrus, all four prophets of Amun stand right in front of the shrine of the god (not shown in a model boat), with the officiating Fourth Prophet censing the god (Parker 1962: col. pl. 4–5). Behind them in the vignette stands a lector priest, reading out the petition from a scroll. At the right-hand end of the picture are the petitioner and his son. Unfortunately this section of the document survives only in a few fragments, so we cannot tell exactly how they are posed, but both appear to have their hands by their sides (Parker 1962: pl. 1.9).

Although there are some differences, our two examples conform broadly to the composition of other depictions of the oracle. The figures of both the First Prophet and the applicant are badly damaged in the Djhutymose inscription (Kruchten 1987: color plate), but the First Prophet appears to be dressed like a king rather than a priest (Kruchten 1987: 11–12). The high priests of the 21st Dynasty were often depicted this way for political purposes; we cannot be sure if this reflected the way they actually dressed for ritual and ceremonial occasions. The earlier stela of Menkheperre has a vignette showing the priest standing before the god to ask his questions (Von Beckerath 1968: pl. 1). In this representation he is dressed in priestly regalia over the pleated linen robes of a king or high official, with sandals that reflect the current fashion for elaborate leatherwork (Nicholson and Shaw 2000: 306; Veldmeijer 2010). He holds an incense burner and the *aba* sceptre (Graham 2001) used for consecrating offerings made to the god. Unfortunately the head of this figure is missing, so we do not know if the First Prophet was shown with a shaven head, as in the Saite Oracle papyrus, or in a wig, as in the Djhutymose inscription.

The First Prophet in our narrative is imagined as being dressed like Menkheperre on his stela, but with a shaven head, because we must assume that he is exercising his priestly role in a state of bodily purity. The applicant or subject of the question prostrates himself before the god as before a king, for

Amun is the king of the gods (Otto 1966: 116–17; Dominicus 1994: 33–6) and ruler of the estate of Amun (Černý 1962: 36). He is imagined as being dressed in his best clothes as appropriate to his occupation, that of a middle-range official in charge of provisioning the altars of the estate of Amun. The favorable judgment depicts him in the traditional attitude of rejoicing (Dominicus 1994: 58–61), as found in most representations of processional oracles (see Figure 1.7; Kruchten 1987: 12, 94–5).

The deployment of the oracle in the courtyard of the Tenth Pylon is suggested by documentation of the walls of the courtyard and the extensive pavement revealed by excavations (Azim 1980; Kruchten 1987: 325–35; Lauffray 1978: 138, fig. 10; Porter and Moss 1972: 183–7). The paving stone with the incised feet, engraved with the name and titles of the First Prophet Menkheperre and his wife Isetemkhebe, daughter of the king of the northern half of Egypt, has been interpreted as a place of ritual purification, based on texts and representations of this period as well as comparison with similar installations elsewhere in the temple of Karnak (Goyon 1980). However, the main tool for reconstructing the oracular ceremony is not art or archaeology but texts and their interpretation.

Additional sources for the oracle of Amun

Although numerous texts document the processional oracle in the east-bank temples of ancient Thebes, another important source of information is the workmen's village of Sut Maat, over on the west side of the Nile at modern Deir el-Medina, in the desert foothills near the Valley of the Kings, where the workmen carved and painted the royal tombs (Haring 2001). The tombs and houses of the literate and highly cultured middle class that made up this community contained numerous papyrus documents, writing boards and graffiti (Janssen 1991; McDowell 1999: 9–13). In addition, a huge pit, originally dug as a well, was filled with thousands of texts written on limestone ostraca—one of the most extensive caches of documents from pharaonic Egypt (McDowell 1999: 17–18). Many of these documents provide evidence for processional oracles, as do others found near the funerary chapels in the cemetery. Much of our understanding of how processional oracles functioned comes from the work of the philologist Jaroslav Černý, who studied and published them from the 1920s onward as he worked with the French archaeologists excavating the village (Černý 1935, 1942, 1972; McDowell 1999: 253).

In considering the oracular texts and their descriptions of consultations with the gods, Černý focused on the words used to describe the procedure. In many of these texts, the intervention of the god in human affairs is described as a wonder or a miracle (in Egyptian, *bia*) (Černý 1962: 38; Kruchten 1987: 87–8) when the god "speaks" in answer to questions. As a person "goes before" or "stands before" a god, he or she may "call" the deity, "speak aloud" to it or "read" out a document (Černý 1962: 43). Such documents can also be "placed in front of" or shown to the god (Kruchten 1987: 89). The god "addresses" or "salutes" (*weshed*; later also "to approve") (Černý 1962: 43–4; Kruchten 1987: 23, 34, 45–7, 79). One of most common pieces of oracular terminology is the word *hōn*, used to indicate approval by the god (Černý 1935: 56); its basic meaning is "to approach," but later it also means "to comply with" (Černý 1962: 43–4).

Comparing two other parallel expressions for approval or disapproval by an oracle—they mean literally "walk forward" and "walk backward"—Černý identified the movements by which the god communicated its decision (Černý 1935: 57–8; 1962: 44–5; Kruchten 1987: 105). It has been further suggested that these movements also included an upward affirmative motion or a downward negative one (Kruchten 1987: 105n4, 108, 256n1). The god is also said to "stop" at a name read out from a list or at a particular person while moving along a line (Černý 1962: 43). In the former case the oracle would probably have made some kind of affirmative or acknowledging movement, and in the latter it would simply have stopped its forward movement in front of someone (Kruchten 1987: 73–4, 96) in a way similar to that described in our imaginary scenario. Documents or lists read out to the god were "repeated," as were petitions presented more than once (as in our story) in major legal cases (Kruchten 1987: 108–9). In an oracular session a god "made an appearance" (Kruchten 1987: 62, 247) and "rested" when it was over, reflecting the fact that the oracle was based on movements made possible when it was borne aloft (Kruchten 1987: 77).

A large number of ostraca—inscribed limestone flakes, the ancient Egyptian equivalent of scrap paper—from the great pit and around the tomb chapels of the workmen's village shed more light on the operation of processional oracles (Černý 1935: 42; McDowell 1999: 25–7, 107). Many take the form of short questions requiring a negative or affirmative answer. Here are a few examples:

My good Lord! Shall we be given rations [receive our wages]? (Černý 1935: 52)
Shall Sety be appointed priest? (Černý 1935: 43)
He will give the donkey. (Černý 1963: 59)
As to the cattle that woman is claiming, does she have a share in them?
(Černý 1972: 56)

Others are pairs of opposite statements that the god could chose between, as in "Shall I burn it?" and "Shall I not burn it?" (Černý 1942: 14, 1972: 52). One ostracon reads simply, "No!" (Černý 1972: 63–4).

Several oracular gods were used by the villagers, including several local forms of Amun, but the favorite was clearly the ancient king Amenhotep I, who had founded their community (Černý 1962: 40–2; McDowell 1999: 171–2). Images of oracular consultations and other religious processions show his statue being carried on the shoulders of the villagers—who acted as their own priests—without a closed shrine or a miniature boat (Černý 1962: 42; Foucart 1935: pl. 28–32). This minor deity is shown surrounded by flowers and fans, the women of the village accompanying him with music and song, as was done for the king of the gods (Černý 1962: 42–3; Sadek 1987: 135–40; Tosi 1987: 174–5). Combining the content of the ostraca with what we know of oracular procedure from other sources, it is possible to reconstruct what went on at oracular consultations in the workmen's village. The ostraca with the statements requiring an affirmative or negative response were likely read out to the oracle, who responded accordingly (Černý 1962: 42). In the case of pairs of statements, they would probably have been placed on the ground or held up on either side of the god, who would then choose one of them (Černý 1935: 57–8; 1962: 45; McDowell 1999: 172; Ryholt 1993). A variant procedure is suggested by the slips reading "No!" Perhaps a statement was read out or repeated and the god made a decision by moving toward one of two documents, one affirmative and one negative (McDowell 1999: 107–9).

The documents also give some indication of the affective response of the god to the petitions. In several of the official oracular records found in the great temple of Amun, the god is said to "greatly approve" a proposition (Kruchten 1987: 42, 45, 104–54). When a farmer in the vicinity of the workmen's village, identified as a thief by a local form of Amun, denied the charge, the god became "very angry" (Blackman 1925: 25). Černý suggested that this emotion may have been indicated by a violent shaking of the image (1962: 45), but this is a guess.

History and context of the processional oracle

The processional oracle as described above is directly attested in our sources between the thirteenth and seventh centuries BCE, as well as during the Graeco-Roman and Christian periods up to the seventh century CE (Černý 1962: 36–48). It appears suddenly in the reign of Ramesses II, a king who publically credited to Amun his own personal salvation in battle (Assmann 2002: 241–3, 255–71) and encouraged his subjects to seek the god's help by inaugurating a place of public prayer at the back of his main temple (Sadek 1987: 46–7). The king also used processional oracles to select persons for priestly duties, and others began to consult them, including the people of the workmen's village in western Thebes.

However, some time before, in the early to mid-18th Dynasty (fifteenth to fourteenth centuries BCE), several kings recorded that they had received personal counsel (in Egyptian, *nedjet-ro*) or direction from Amun. Hatshepsut and Thutmose IV both stated that they consulted the god and he advised them (Černý 1962: 35–6; Kruchten 2001b). An intriguing but difficult passage is found in a text of Thutmose III that describes a ceremony for laying out a building within the domain of Amun; this is done by marking off the area with measuring lines (Montet 1964). The god assumes the station for the measuring line, and as the king begins to measure out the building, Amun tells the king that he would prefer to do it himself (Černý 1962: 35). In another inscription the king describes this incident as a *nedjet-ro*, a phrase with the basic meaning of "consultation" or "advice" (Faulkner 1962: 144).

Elsewhere, Thutmose III describes how he was chosen to be king. This text informs us that, during his youth, while acting as a priest at a festival in the house of Amun, he was stationed in the great columned festival hall on a feast day (Černý 1962: 35). The god "made a circuit of the hall on both sides of it. The heart of those who were in front did not comprehend his actions, while [he was] searching for my majesty in every place. On recognizing me, lo, he halted [I threw myself on] the pavement, I prostrated myself in his presence" (Breasted 1906: §140 [60–1]). Although the term *nedjet-ro* is generally translated as "oracle" in the passages cited above, only this last one describes an incident that actually resembles the later ceremony—more specifically, the "stopping" gesture of the god when he picks a name or person out of a lineup (Kruchten 1987: 73, 96–7; 1995: 63). A later text of Ramesses IV (1151–1145 BCE) states that he was chosen by Amun to be king through an oracle (*khertu*). Sadly, although this source dates from the time of Amun's greatest popularity, specific details about the exact location and nature of the occasion are absent (Jansen-Winkeln 1999: 54–6).

Earlier Egyptian texts contain numerous references to the "plans" of gods as well as to the "finding" of instructions from them, be they in writing, natural phenomena or extraordinary events or things ("wonders") (Baines and Parkinson 1997). The word *bia*, often used to describe oracles (Kruchten 1987:

87-8; 2001b) and translated as parallel to the biblical "signs" or "wonders," appears to be related to words for heaven and its products, such as meteoric iron. Although *bia* denotes something of divine or heavenly character, it clearly has a much wider range of meaning than as a description of the later oracular ceremony (Graefe 1971: 124–5).

Indeed, a closer examination of the actual processional oracular ceremony and the term mostly commonly used to describe it, *peh netcher* (Kruchten 1987: 63–5), suggests a far more prosaic origin. Anyone who has studied the processional oracle cannot fail to be struck by the central role played by written documents (Černý 1962: 45). Given that the ceremony is structured in such a way that it could easily be carried on without them (McDowell 1999: 172–3) and that levels of literacy are generally thought to have been quite low (Baines and Eyre 1983), this in itself is remarkable. For some this confirms the elitist and exclusionary nature of Egyptian formal religion (Spalinger 1998, 2001). However, this does not accord with either the apparently public nature of the ceremony, presented in such extensive and spectacular venues as the court of the Tenth Pylon and the hypostyle hall at the temple of Karnak, or its popularity outside elite temple enclosures (Baines 2006: 282–93).

Aspects of the ceremony and its setting provide some valuable clues. Although Amun often traveled in a boat, as gods were wont to do, he was surrounded by the trappings of very high social status or royalty. He was even addressed as "my good lord" (Kruchten 1987: 43), as one would hail a king or other member of the elite. While the roles and character of gods in the Near Eastern and ancient Mediterranean world often closely resemble those of a king—in that a god's supreme position in the cosmos is analogous to that of the ultimate social superior—it may be argued that the connotations in this case are much more specific. Egyptian literature is filled with stories of kings as the ultimate arbiters of justice, to whom even the most humble can, in theory, address their appeals (Assmann 2002: 155–6; Boorn 1988: 316, 321; Parkinson 2002: 174–5; Simpson 2003: 25–44, 497–504). Below them were lesser representatives of justice: the judges and officials who heard complaints and judged legal cases (Tyldesley 2000: 39–46). However, although Egyptian courts were supposed to be open to all (Simpson 2003: 137), in practice there were any number of gatekeepers, from actual doormen to the officials who controlled access to the higher courts or to the king himself (Simpson 2003: 136).

Since the Egyptian government and courts were part of an extensive bureaucracy with a literate staff (Kruchten 2001a; Tyldesley 2000: 9, 11–12, 34–41), written documents were an essential part of the petition or appeals process.

Officials with the title "overseer of petitions" are known from the Old Kingdom (third millennium BCE) onward (Fischer 1978: 58–9). It seems, therefore, that it is no coincidence that Amenhotep III placed statues of his deceased first minister, a man who had a reputation for hearing petitions and passing them on, at his new public gateway to the temple of Amun, and that they remained there when the court was given over to oracular sessions in later centuries (Galán 2003: 224–5). Human courts often met at the gate of the temple or at the door to its festival hall (Kruchten 2001a; Sauneron 1954). Given its form and setting, the processional oracle ceremony appears to be modeled on the presentation of a petition to a high official or king. It has even been suggested that *peh netcher* means "petitioning" rather than "approaching" the god (Kruchten 1987: 26n2, 26n4). In any case, this hypothesis explains not only the judicial status of the ceremony but its peculiar format with its emphasis on written documents, which, while not necessary for informing an omnipotent deity, are an essential part of any official proceeding.

Surviving textual materials suggest that the processional oracle was set up in the reign of Ramesses II, at the same time as the place of public prayer at the rear of the temple of Amun (Sadek 1987: 46–7). While the oracle of Amun appears to be the original one that evolved out of earlier consultations of the god by kings (Černý 1962: 36), its interactive and public character led to its speedy adoption in temples all over Egypt (Kákosy 1980: 602–4), in ceremonies varying from the magnificent to the humble—such as those in the workmen's village in west Thebes (Černý 1962: 38–46).

Although the *peh netcher* remained the chief form of oracular enquiry for close to half a millennium (Kruchten 1987: 26), variant forms and other types of oracles evolved over time. Mention has already been made of the amuletic oracular decrees that guaranteed health, long life and other benefits for the recipients, who apparently wore them in lockets around their necks. Since the names in these documents often appear to have been added later, it has been suggested that they were blessed *en masse* by the god before being personalized (Edwards 1960: xi–xxiii; Kruchten 1995: 56). Posthumous documents such as the funerary decree for Nesikhons, which could not have been presented in person, were conveyed by a proxy, likely a close relative (Černý 1962: 39; Kitchen 1996: 65–6).

Herodotus, the Greek writer, who visited Egypt in the mid-fifth century BCE (Lloyd 2001), noted the popularity of oracles in Egypt (Waterfield 1998: 101–2, 136–7, 157–8, 165 [II 17, 18, 54, 111, 152, 155–6]) and spoke favorably of their reputation in the Greek world (Waterfield 1998: 20, 197, 117, 118

[I 46, II 32, 52–4]). The petitions with alternative answers mentioned above have been connected with the later practice, attested in Graeco-Roman Egypt, of the "ticket oracle," where the god chose between two answers presented to it in the sanctuary (Frankfurter 1998: 148–50). This method would have been more private and less costly than the processional oracle, but the actual mechanism remains obscure (Browne 1987: 68–9; Černý 1962: 47). Also, the earlier examples lack the demand for an answer found in the ticket oracles, which did not seem to occur any earlier than the second century BCE (Skeat and Turner 1968). Of course, the early existence of ticket, or speaking, oracles could have solved the problem of how the god "speaks" in the documents, although this can be explained in other ways, as for the processional oracle. Extended documents from this later period, often in obscure riddling language and containing instructions or prophecy said to have been spoken by the god or an avatar, suggest human intermediaries (Blasius and Schipper 2002: 120–2, Frankfurter 1998: 149–50); an example is the "Prophecy of the Lamb" (Simpson 2003: 445–9). A number of sanctuaries and shrines from the Graeco-Roman period feature concealed rooms behind the sanctuary walls or hollow statue bases that could have been used by priests speaking the words of the gods; apparatuses for speaking statues, featuring copper tubes, have also survived (Frankfurter 1998: 150–3).

Other kinds of oracles are known that were more divinatory in character. Documents from the Ptolemaic period describe how the movements of sacred scarab beetles could be observed in order to foretell the future (Jasnow 1997), a quality also ascribed to the Apis bull (Frankfurter 1998: 150)—the living incarnation of three major gods, Ptah, Re and Horus, that dwelt in the temple of Ptah at Memphis (Morenz 1973: 143–4; Vercoutter 1972). It is not clear if beliefs about the predictive significance of actions by sacred or possessed beings go back to earlier periods, but they may be related to the earlier descriptions of "wonders" (Kruchten 1987: 87–8; Parker 1962: 33–4). Prophetic messages and instructions could also be delivered through dreams, experienced either during normal sleep or in special incubation centers at the shrines of the gods (Sauneron 1959: 38–53; Szpakowska 2003: 50–2, 55–6, 142–7). Hor of Sebennytos, a priest who lived at Memphis in the early second century BCE, was a regularly inspired dreamer whose prophetic nocturnal visions were sought after by the kings in Alexandria (Ray 1976).

However, it must be pointed out that the predictive function of these later oracles and connected practices is a far cry from the legal and advisory function of the earlier processional oracles. Part of the reason for this was political. After the Roman conquest of Egypt, political pronouncements from the temples were considered treason, and major legal decisions were under Caesar's control. All oracular questions were subject to official scrutiny and, for that reason, recorded only in Greek (Ripat 2006). However, although many of the petitions of the Roman period request guidance on health and personal matters, a respectable number still ask about matters connected with commerce and property (Cosson 2002: 30–46, 70–2, 77–82). When, in late antiquity, the king of the Blemmyes— who ruled over Nubia, to the south of Egypt—"borrowed" the oracular statue of Isis from the temple of Philae, on the southern border of Egypt, for months at a time, we may be sure that the god advised on questions of far greater importance (Frankfurter 1998: 64–5, 105–6, 155).

Interpretation

According to the system of classification commonly used by scholars of religion, oracular activity is a type of divination. *Divination* may be defined as the use of magical means to discover information inaccessible by normal means of inquiry. Divination, which exists in all cultures, may fall under the rubric of religious activity—but not necessarily so, as in the case of the astrological forecasting and psychic activities popular in contemporary Western society. The practice falls into two broad categories. The first, or oracular type, occurs when a designated diviner enters an altered mental state and relays information that generally requires interpretation. The Delphic oracle, celebrated in classical Greece, is a good example of this type. The second type of divination is classified as interpretive and involves explanation of random or enigmatic data (Graf 2008). Examples of this form are the Babylonian method for predictive analysis of the livers of sacrificial victims—later adopted in the Graeco-Roman world (Maul and Bremmer 2012)—and the casting of yarrow stalks or, later, coins in the Chinese Daoist *I Ching* (Rollicke 2009).

However, as can be seen from the examples, this system of classifying divination is not perfect, as there is considerable overlap between the two types. In the case of the liver readings and the *I Ching*, the data have been so thoroughly analyzed that the randomness of the procedure is undermined, and if the mantic utterances of the Delphic oracle require such intensive interpretation, are they indeed oracular or divinatory? The Egyptian processional oracle is even harder to classify. Although the god does not communicate verbally, it is certainly thought to scan written documents; thus language can in some fashion be understood as the medium. Furthermore, the question is often repeated verbally during the procedure. Most important, can the movements of the men carrying the god be classified as random?

One question must remain uppermost in the mind of any modern researcher who investigates the Egyptian processional oracle: how did it work? The method of communication of the oracle, through its bearers and the resulting movement of the processional barque, may explain some of the modifications noted in the survey of its evolution given above. It is during the reign of Hatshepsut that we first see the addition of supports for the boat, in the form of scarabs on the carrying plank (Lacau and Chevrier 1977: 156), and in the reign of Horemheb, the addition of figures of the king and ancestor gods that would have made the barque's position even more secure (Karlshausen 2009: 44–5). Although regular processional oracles are not known in the 18th Dynasty, both of these rulers were chosen by the god, personally and publicly, to rule (Cabrol 2001: 748; Gardiner 1953). The innovation of the second shrine, which finally securely attached the boat to the platform, dates from the reigns of Seti I and Ramesses II, when the processional oracle is believed to have been institutionalized (Černý 1962: 36; Karlshausen 2009: 198; Traunecker, Le Saout and Masson 1981: 78). However, it must be admitted that this hypothesis does not explain why these locking devices do not appear in depictions of the barques of other gods that were known to have indulged in oracular activity.

While the basic movements of the god's image seem clear enough, the question remains: how were the movements decided and how was the decision communicated (Kruchten 1987: 187–8; McDowell 1999: 167)? Fortunately, ethnographic parallels from modern Egypt exist that go some way toward answering this question.

In Islam, as in Judaism (Hillers and Kashani 2007), it is customary to bury people before sundown on the day of their death (Esposito 2003; Tritton 2012). Apart from washing, there is minimal preparation of the body, which is buried in a simple, lightweight coffin or even just a shroud. Traditionally the body is carried to the cemetery by friends and/or family members. Between the nineteenth century and the present day, Westerners present at the funerals of holy or prominent men in Upper Egypt noted that when the pallbearers involuntarily altered speed or direction, this was interpreted as an expression of the will of the deceased about where he wanted to be buried, or what people or places he wanted to visit on the way to his rest. Pallbearers would recall how the body seemed heavy if the departed wished to stop, or very light if he wanted to move on (Legrain 1916: 167–9). One anecdote even relates that the deceased forced his cortege to travel back to his house to confront his—until then unknown—murderer (Kruchten 1987: 100; Sauneron 2000: 97–8). It has been suggested that the movements of the pallbearers exemplify a form of collective possession or subconscious suggestion (Nims 1965: 94). This practice continues to the present day; see Appendix A, page 217, for a first-hand account of a contemporary Egyptian rural funeral procession.

While there are many cross-cultural parallels to this kind of activity (Frankfurter 1998: 187–8; Chapter 2), interpretations made outside the field of religious studies are often extremely tendentious. We live in a world where questions about the ontological status of religious beliefs and practices are loaded with social, political and cultural baggage. Descriptions of statues with speaking tubes and secret passages recall all too clearly descriptions by early Christian writers of pagan priests who used such means to "trick" and "cheat" those who believed in their false gods (Frankfurter 1998: 150–1). The dismissal of other gods, especially those with statue cults, is a step on the way to a point of view that sees all religious belief systems as, at best, superstitious rubbish and, at worst, impostures to rob and oppress the ignorant and powerless. From this perspective, religion is but a way station on the road of human cognitive evolution (Dawkins 2006: 163–207).

It must be pointed out that such opinions, as well as their opposites, are a product of specific cultural, educational and economic positions (Berlinerblau 2005: 2–3). Those who take these positions align themselves in a culture war against religious establishments that are seen to be tainted by corruption and abuse and to be supporting socially backward agendas (Berlinerblau 2005: 130–4; Dawkins 2006: 311–40; Hitchens 2007: 15–36, 37–41, 43–61). In our world, religious affiliations—or the lack of them—are tied to political parties, media empires or educational systems. Such perspectives on religious thought and practice are not helpful for understanding a phenomenon such as the Egyptian processional oracle and its religious and cultural significance.

This, of course, leads us to ask questions that probe the "good faith" of the human actors involved in the processional oracle. Two documents from the workmen's village provide material for discussion. In one, a farmer, Pethauemdiamun, denied stealing clothing made from dyed cloth (a luxury item) when accused by a local god, Amun of Pa Khenty, who indicated his name in a list that was being read out. Declaring that he was in disgrace with his god, the farmer went to put the question to Amun of Tashenyt, who had a shrine not far away. However, this god also declared that Pethauemdiamun's protestations of innocence were false and instructed that he be taken before yet another local Amun in the presence of witnesses. Although the result of that oracular session is omitted from the document, we learn that the farmer twice more went before the original god, Amun of Pa Khenty, from whose storehouse the items had disappeared. On the second occasion he finally confessed his guilt, upon which he was given a hundred blows with a stick (Černý 1962: 40–1).

Another petitioner, also implicated in a clothing theft, wrote a letter to the god demanding that the matter be settled: "Look, you will cast off mystery today and come out in the course of a procession, so that you may judge the matters …" The letter would be delivered to the god by an employee of his house who had privileged access (McDowell 1999: 109–10). Yet another such letter promises a gift of imported beer and bread for the god in return for a favorable decision (McDowell 1999: 110). Scholars who commented on these texts earlier in the past century often assumed that the agency of the god expressed in such documents was a pious fiction, and that even if the author of the second document was "naive," the modern editor suspects "that the writer is indirectly but consciously addressing the oracle's priestly control" (Barns 1949: 69). Likewise it was assumed that the repentant farmer Pethauemdiamun visited the other local oracles to establish his innocence in an attempt "to curry favour by an appeal to local sentiment and local prejudices" (Blackman 1925: 69). More recent interpretations of these materials lean more toward perspectives taken from anthropology (Frankfurter 1998: 157–8; McDowell 1999: 109–10; Traunecker 1997: 35–6) and a greater degree of cultural relativism, emphasizing the affective emotional relationships people developed with their gods (Szpakowska 2010: 507–25; Weiss 2012).

Is the extensive use of the oracle of Amun by his priesthood during this period evidence of manipulation of superstitious credulity among the general population? The practice of giving the role of officiating priest to an unrelated individual when questions pertaining to a prophet's own family were brought before the oracle (Kitchen 1996: 19–20) could reflect careful following of legal procedures or else a perfunctory attempt to keep up appearances, so that the oracle would retain a vestige of credibility. However, if the oracle of Amun was a cynical sham designed only to prop up the power of the First Prophets and their families, how can we explain the unexpected and sometimes upsetting behaviors of the oracle—as when the god refused to come out of the barque shrine to participate in the Opet Festival because of the malfeasance of officials who had tried to frame Djhutymose (Kruchten 1987: 54, 73–4)?

It should be noted that the processional image of Amun that embodied

Amun-Re, king of the gods, the most celebrated avatar of the god, was the sole responsibility of the *wab* priests (Kruchten 1989: 188–90; 1995: 63; 2001), the lower-level religious functionaries who carried out all the sacred activities of the temple, with the exception of the daily cult in the main sanctuary (Kruchten 1989: 245, 251–2). They were not allowed to enter the main sanctuary, nor could they consume the reverted offerings of the god, which guaranteed eternal life (Kruchten 1989: 189–90, 201). However, their control of the processional image of the god allowed them to form a parallel hierarchy within the temple that had considerable influence. At the top of the ladder were those *wab*s who carried the boat of the god (Kruchten 1995: 62–3); in earlier times this honor had been given to highly placed officials from outside the temple (Černý 1962: 36). The prestige attached to this function is reflected in the names of these priests, such as Nespaherentahat, "the one who belongs to the prow," and Paenebiu, "he of the pole" (Kruchten 1995: 63). Indeed, in the only surviving papyrus scroll that records the liturgy of the daily cult of Amun, the ceremony is performed by the "great wab" (Moret [1902] 1988: 7–8) who, in parallel with the prophet in the sanctuary, enacted the same rite for the processional image (Kruchten 1989: 252–5). Was the extraordinary incident when the god refused to leave the barque shrine a demonstration of power by the *wab* priests to their superiors, the prophets (Kruchten 1989: 252–5)? Can we also see their influence in the unexpected acquittal of persons accused of wrongdoing by the ruling elite, as in the case of Djhutymose (Kruchten 1995: 63–4)?

The inscriptions that record the prophets' first introduction into the sanctuary of the god movingly describe genuine spiritual experiences (Kruchten 1989: 23, 142, 162). As for the *wab* priests, they could be seen as championing a public, non-elite form of religious experience in opposition to the elitist cult religion, or perhaps practicing a parallel form of worship that had grown up among an urbanized literate class during the New Kingdom (Gillam 2005: 67–9; Kruchten 1995: 63–4), one that complemented the temple-based religion rather than competing with it. The high priests may have made such extensive use of the oracle not because they wished to impose themselves on an unwilling populace, but in order to worship with them and to communicate according to their own cultural and social preferences.

2

Cross-Cultural Analysis

Robyn Gillam

As noted in Chapter 1, our analysis and historical discussion of the Egyptian processional oracle, it was a distinctive cultural and religious phenomenon, even in a world where divination and oracular consultation were commonplace. Most oracular consultations that conveyed the divine message came through spiritual possession of designated human beings or, less directly, through other types of divination. The processional oracle stood out, however, as a medium of communication in which the god's presence was felt directly by the persons carrying its statue. They were directed by its promptings to move in response to specific requests or, sometimes, in a spontaneous way as the spirit willed. Unlike the possessed individual, whose utterances often required interpretation, these gestures of the gods were clear and self-evident in their meaning.

Another distinctive attribute of the processional oracle was the role that written documents often played in the consultation. Although encountered in oracular sessions elsewhere, documents played a central role in this instance, especially in juridical oracles, where appeal to divine judgment took a decisive and transparent role. If we may take the gestures of the embodied god and the interaction with documents as a preferred medium of communication as the most distinctive attributes of the Egyptian processional oracle, then they may be used as a basis for cross-cultural comparison with some of the religious practices of Egypt's ancient neighbors, as well as some modern approaches that exhibit structural similarities. Such an enquiry could help establish the distinctiveness of this Egyptian Oracle, how it may have influenced (or been influenced by) neighboring cultures, and whether analogous practices elsewhere may throw more light on the performance and significance of the practice.

This last objective, especially in relation to modern analogs, is of particular importance. For example, without the knowledge of how the deceased communicate with the living at contemporary Egyptian funerals (see Chapter 1,

"Interpretation," and Appendix A), reconstruction of the ancient processional oracle would have been much more problematic. Related practices in sub-Saharan Africa and the African diaspora also provide useful models for the social nexus that produces such enactments.

Oracles in the kingdom of Kush

After the collapse of the Egyptian "empire" at the end of the New Kingdom in the eleventh century BCE, its former colonies in Nubia (northern Sudan) regained their independence. However, centuries of foreign rule had created an Egyptianized elite that retained close cultural and especially religious ties with southern Egypt (Morkot 2000: 72–90). Although documentation is sparse, it appears that between the eleventh and eighth centuries BCE, Egyptian temples—often in the same locations as indigenous sacred sites—continued in use, and social connections with their northern neighbors, who shared cultural and ethnic similarities, endured (Kitchen 1996: 288 §243).

Through the late ninth and eighth centuries BCE, as the theocratic state of the estate of Amun struggled to preserve its distinctness from a more aggressive line of kings in the north, a well-organized, wealthy and militarily powerful elite, deeply imbued with Egyptian religious practices and ideas of kingship, emerged in central Nubia. It was based in the earlier kingdom of Kush, a sometime enemy and trading partner of Egypt before it was conquered and colonized in the New Kingdom. From a shadowy and poorly documented context, the new kingdom of Kush suddenly emerged in the early eighth century as a fully fledged state. It had a pharaoh-like king whose rulership was legitimated directly by the god Amun, who was still worshiped at temples founded by the previous Egyptian colonizers (Morkot 2000: 133–66).

Before, during and after their conquest of Egypt in the early seventh century BCE, the Kushite kings were chosen, imbued with the divinity necessary to rule, and directed to perform necessary tasks by the god, through various methods of communication that included dreams, the processional oracle, and secret communication between the king and the god in temple sanctuaries. The dreams announced that the god had chosen its recipient to be king, while the processional oracle announced his selection to the community. The private royal oracle was received by the king in the sanctuary of the temple after he assumed office; it transmitted the divine essence of the god that made him fit to rule (Török 1997: 216–20, 241). The texts describing the election and enthronement of King Aspelta, who ruled in the late seventh or early sixth century BCE, provide us with a typical example of how this process unfolded.

After the death of Aspelta's predecessor, the royal entourage prayed to Amun, asking him to indicate whom he had chosen to be the next king. Following this, they assembled all the surviving male children of former kings in the festival hall of the great temple of Amun of Napata, the national shrine of Kush, for a festival appearance by the god in his processional barque. After first ignoring all the candidates placed before his barque, the second time around the god chose Aspelta. Following his selection by Amun at Napata, the candidate traveled to the other major temples of Amun for further confirmation by his oracles (Török 1997: 223–5, 227). When the king had been crowned and took his place on the throne at Napata, he was ready to receive the secret oracle guaranteeing his rulership: in the sanctuary of the god's temple, where he sometimes stayed for days. As with the processional oracle, the process was repeated at all the important temples.

After receiving both the processional and the secret royal oracles, the king was given a document that recorded them and certified the legitimacy of his rule; this document was somehow directly generated by the ceremony. It appears that the kings were buried with these documents, preserved in small, richly decorated cylinders, several of which have been found in their tombs. These closely resemble the cylindrical amulets that held the amuletic oracular decrees guaranteeing the welfare of newborn children and others in the Egyptian domain of Amun in the early first millennium BCE (Černý 1962: 39–40; Kruchten 1987: 57ff.; Ritner 2009: 74–6; Török 1997: 243; see also Chapter 1, "Sources for the Great Festival of the Oracle of Amun"). The secret communion of the god and the king clearly identifies with the personal counsel or direction from Amun to Egyptian rulers of the Early New Kingdom.

The legitimization process of the Kushite kings shows the pervasive influence of oracular practices around the Egyptian cult of Amun in the New Kingdom and the Third Intermediate Period. It is clear that Kushite kingship was deliberately modeled on the Egyptian original; it indeed appears to have been thought of as identical, directly licensing its officeholders to intervene in, conquer and directly rule its former colonizer to the north. The conception, execution and transmission of the Kushite ideology of rulership was completely Egyptianized. All the surviving documents that describe the election and installation of the kings are written in standard literary Egyptian and were published on the walls of the Egyptian-style temples where the kings and gods were represented.

The Kushite elite apparently spoke Egyptian and were highly educated in Egyptian high culture (Török 1997: 343–5). They not only formulated the theory, literature and representation of their state in an Egyptian milieu but also intermarried with the Egyptian elite. That they also held high office in Egyptian temples suggests that their grasp and use of their adopted culture were not regarded as in any way inferior to those of its originators (Morkot 2000: 217–22; Török 1997: 358–9). However, it is clear that the Kushites were in the process of reworking the earlier Egyptian theories and performances. After the fourth century BCE, Egyptian was no longer used by the Kushite elite; it was replaced in written sources by their native language (which is still not well understood). The later Kushite, or Meroitic, religion was also illustrated on the walls of temples, although its significance is not always clearly understood (Török 1997: 62–6, 409–16). However, from these materials and from travelers' tales preserved in Greek sources (Török 1997: 69–73, 276–7), it appears that selection of the king through the oracle of Amun was still an important event in Meroitic culture.

The oracle of Ammon in the Siwa oasis

The oracle of Ammon, as it was referred to by the Greeks, was situated in the westernmost oasis of the Libyan Desert, beyond the Nile Valley; it was also the most northerly oasis, within a few days' journey of the Mediterranean coast. Here it will be examined from the perspective of its geography and its cultural relationship with Egyptian oracles.

Egyptian contact with these western regions can be traced back to prehistoric times (Hope 2013). From the beginning of the historic period, Egyptian kings boasted of subduing and conquering these people, whom they referred to as the Tjehenu and the Tjemehu (Sagrillo 2013). In the second half of the second millennium BCE, there was both intensive contact with the westerners and occupation of the oases, when they were used by the Egyptian armed forces. Better information about these people during this period shows them to be pastoralists who were socially organized in large, kin-based groups or tribes. Among these were a group named the Libu, who later give their name to the whole region.

Towards the end of the Bronze Age, large groups of migratory seafarers known as the "Sea Peoples" attacked and destroyed settlements along the shores of the eastern Mediterranean. Although they failed to invade Egypt, they displaced the people to its west, driving them away from the fertile coastal areas, into the desert and toward the Nile Valley in search of a livable environment. Westerners defeated by the Egyptians were captured and settled in large enclosures, where they worked as forced labor. Over time they became recognized as a social or tribal group with military expertise. Following the period of political fragmentation in the 21st Dynasty, leaders of these military clans took on the royal title, for the most part controlling micro-states in northern Egypt. Their attempts to control the oracle of Amun in Thebes were unsuccessful, so they acknowledged his political and religious supremacy, as did the Kushites to the south. Although thoroughly assimilated into Egyptian society, they emphasized their origins and played up their connection to the southerly oases (Sagrillo 2013).

The first evidence of an Egyptian presence in Siwa is found in the sixth century BCE, under Ahmose II, or "Amasis" (570–526 BCE), a ruler of Libyan descent who built the temple of the oracle (Sagrillo 2013). An inscription on one of its walls records that he appointed a man named Sutherkhedis, indicated as "Libyan" by both his name and costume, as "governor," although he was really independent of the distant Nile Valley (Fakhry 1950: 26–7, 73). However, it appears that the king's sudden interest in this distant oasis was not entirely due to religious fervor or to fellow ethnic feeling. More pressing political reasons were the motivating factors. According to Herodotus, Amasis, who was not a member of the ruling family, became king as a result of the Egyptian army's revolt against the previous ruler, following a disastrous military expedition against the Greek colony of Cyrene (Aufrère, Golvin and Goyon 1991: 148; Fejfer 2013; Herodotus II, in Waterfield 1998: 161–3; Müller 2013).

Evidence from Greek sources shows that the oracle's greatest fame and prestige occurred between the sixth and fourth centuries BCE, corresponding to Persian rule of Egypt. It was consulted many times by elites in the Greek world, and archaeological evidence suggests that the oasis supported a mixed Greek, Egyptian and native population (Aufrère, Golvin and Goyon 1991: 148; Fakhry 1950: 28–30, 81–95; 1973: 179–206). The Cyrenians had their own temple to Zeus—with whom the Greeks equated Amun, as the king of the gods—but depicted him on their coins as a bearded man with the curving horns of the animal spirit of the Egyptian god (Boardman 1964: pl. 12d; Fejfer 2013). Visitors to the oracle originated from all over the Greek world via the city of Cyrene, which benefited the Cyrenians as well as the native Siwans, whose ruler controlled the oracle and its temple (Kuhlmann 1988: 155). The visit of Alexander marked both the greatest success of the oracle and the start of its decline, relying as it did on religious tourism controlled by Cyrene, which lost its independence shortly after that.

Although the oracle continued to be famous long after it ceased to be an international tourist attraction, the only descriptions of how it worked are embedded in accounts of Alexander's visit to the oasis. They are often frustratingly vague, and all of them are from much later than his lifetime, being very much second-hand accounts. However, two of the sources, those of Diodorus Siculus (50.3-4, in Oldfather 1933) and Strabo (17.1.4, in Jones 1982-97), Greek travelers of the first century BCE, are valuable because they also visited the place themselves. Both of them note that although the oracle was no longer celebrated, it was still in operation.

According to Diodorus, there were two temples of Ammon. The temple of the oracle was located on a hill inside a fortified complex that included the palace of the rulers of the oasis and a sacred spring. The other temple, close by, was located on flat land in the midst of a grove of trees, adjacent to another sacred spring (50.3-4, in Oldfather 1933). Both these temples have been identified in modern times, the temple of the oracle with the structure at Aghourmi and the other with that at Umm-Ebeida, less than a kilometer away. This second temple is later than the first, dating to the reign of Nectanebo II, the last native ruler of Egypt (Fakhry 1950: 69-79). Diodorus notes that the oracle, which was carried in a boat-shaped shrine by eighty priests and attended by female singers, expressed volition by forcing its bearers to go where it willed (50.1-7, in Oldfather 1933). This is probably what Strabo is referring to when he says that the responses of the god were given by nods and tokens (17.1.4, in Jones 1982-97). Pausanias, writing in the second century CE, mentions that the outer hall of the temple of the oracle was filled with monuments and inscriptions commemorating the oracle (9.16.1, in Levi 1971: 339-40).

Diodorus describes Alexander as asking the priest a question while watching the god's procession taking place in the forecourt of the temple (51.1-4, in Oldfather 1933). Other accounts describe the king as consulting the god alone, in the sanctuary (Fakhry 1950: 31; Plutarch, Alexander 27, in Perrin 1914-26). Allowing for Greek reinterpretations of the event, it appears that these accounts depict a standard Egyptian processional oracle. The private consultation can be compared with those made by Egyptian and Kushite kings (Kuhlmann 1988: 137). The temples themselves have a normal Late Period layout and decoration; even the problematic crypt is a common feature (Aufrère, Golvin and Goyon 1991: 154). The aniconic form of the image of the god is also common for the processional image of Amun in Egypt (Aufrère, Golvin and Goyon 1991: 152). However, it is possible to identify a number of adaptations to the local environment.

As was the case in the other western oases, water at Siwa came from underground springs—a crucial difference from the Nile Valley (Fakhry 1950: 2–5). This gave rise to a completely different conceptual framework, one in which the springs were the sustaining presence in the landscape. As in the other oases, Egyptian iconography and ideology were skillfully adapted (Kaper 2001). Each temple is adjacent to one of the springs. It has even been suggested that Amun-Re, the Egyptian king of the gods, was identified with Ammân, the Libyan god of springs (Aufrère, Golvin and Goyon 1991: 151–3), which suggests that the Egyptian Oracle cult was superimposed on indigenous religious observance. It also appears that the oracle was important to local life, as it persisted for a very long time, perhaps into the sixth century CE (Frankfurter 1998: 157). Although it no longer attracted wealthy religious tourists, the oracle remained important to local people on account of its connection to the springs that fed their rich garden agriculture. It is interesting that the fame of this oracle did not seem to lead to transference or imitation of its technique to its Hellenic audience. It is necessary to look elsewhere in the ancient Near East for possible evidence of that.

Oracles in the ancient Near East: Similarity and difference

Interesting oracular phenomena that invite comparison with the Egyptian processional oracle can be found in the ancient Near East, in the Levant, or eastern shore of the Mediterranean. This politically and culturally complex area lay between Egypt and the other great cultural heartland of this region—what the Greeks referred to as Mesopotamia, "the land between the two rivers"—in present-day Iraq and inland Syria. Since Mesopotamian civilization evolved earlier than that of Egypt and was a much stronger influence on the region, we shall first briefly examine oracular activity there.

The land between the rivers

Agriculture based on irrigation, rather than natural floodplains as in Egypt, was the basis of the earlier culture in southern Iraq. The first city-states appeared above the marshes into which the Tigris and Euphrates Rivers flowed before reaching the Persian Gulf in the land of Sumer. A complex society, characterized by social hierarchies, taxation and written records, appeared there in the fourth millennium BCE. Although these states were managed by human elites and their armies were led by kings, they were ruled by gods. The city-state was the estate of the god; humans worked for the gods and, through the king and priesthood, tried to nurture a reciprocal arrangement whereby the divinity would sustain and protect the city and the king in exchange for their goods and services (Redman 1978: 244–322). This model of state organization was copied all over the ancient Near East, including in Egypt (Knapp 1988: 47–59).

Mesopotamians understood that the gods communicated with them through signs and messages in many different ways. Dreams, visions and various natural phenomena could all convey those messages, as well as divinatory operations of many kinds, from observing the behavior of oil in water to interpreting the livers of sacrificial animals at festivals and cult performances. More modest forms of divination were practiced throughout society, although they could require expert interpretation (Cryer 1994: 141–214).

The most important forms of divination were practiced by experts in temples, which, as in Egypt, were major centers of learning and cultural production. This was also because it was the responsibility of the king to seek the advice of the gods, on whose behalf he governed, and to find out what might happen to the community in the future and how to prepare for it. The importance of such precautions is dramatized in the myth of Cutha (Pongratz-Leisten 1999: 5–11), in which a king and his land meet with a horrible fate as a direct result of not seeking omens to discover the will of the gods. The story was oft repeated to emphasize the importance of this activity, and kings took great pains to show their attentiveness to the divine will (Foster 2005: 344–56).

Among the many forms that Mesopotamian divination took, communication from the gods through movement of their images seems to be lacking, although there is some evidence for the use of written materials. From the late third millennium BCE, numerous documents in the form of letters or prayers were deposited in temples. These appeals for divine aid came from all levels of society, from the king to illiterate persons who made use of public scribes. These "letter prayers" appear to be simply written prayers composed as letters, because that is how one communicates formally with others in writing. When they were placed in the sanctuary of a temple, they achieved a close, continuous presence with the god (Foster 2005: 215; Pongratz-Leisten 1999: 202–3).

However, there are variant forms of this type of document that seem to demand an immediate response. They are first found in the northern kingdom of Mari, in present-day Syria, in the eighteenth century BCE, where they were written by kings seeking concrete advice on matters of state. The replies of the god did not come by mail but through ecstatic prophets who were possessed by the god, or through dreams, generally experienced by professional seers who spent the night in a temple (Pongratz-Leisten 1999: 202–4). In an interesting example, an official writes to King Zimri-lin to report the dream a man had in a temple, in which the god Dagan instructed the king on how to prosecute war with his enemies (Heimpel 2003: 266; Pongratz-Leisten 1999: 204, 205–7).

This practice was continued and further developed in the later kingdom of Assyria, located in present-day northern Iraq. Between the ninth and seventh centuries BCE the Assyrian kings waged constant war throughout the Near East, creating an empire that stretched from eastern Iran to Egypt (Kuhrt 1995: 478–501). They often presented themselves as specially chosen by the gods to rule, and they emphasized their proper worship of the gods and their just rule by constant verification, not only by divination but also through written correspondence (Parpola 1997: [36–44]). Returning from a successful campaign, the king would deposit a written report in the temple of the national god, Ashur, who in turn would reply in a long letter validating his royal conduct (Pongratz-Leisten 1999: 232–61, 273–4).

Just like his predecessors, the Assyrian king sometimes needed urgent advice from the god, which was solicited in a letter prayer (Pongratz-Leisten 1999: 270). Following earlier practice, the answer generally came via ecstatic prophecy or the dreams of professional seers. The replies of the prophets are generally expressed in the first person and the gods expressly identify themselves—for example, "I am Ishtar of Arbela, O Esarhaddon, king of the land of Assyria" (Foster 2005: 814; Pongratz-Leisten 1999: 223–5). Prophets—most of whom were attached to the worship of Ishtar, the goddess of love and war—could be female, male or transgendered; they brought on their ecstasy through meditation and weeping about the descent of Ishtar into the underworld, as well as by self-mutilation. Highly respected and influential figures in Assyrian society, they also delivered unsolicited prophecies that could be quite critical of the ruling elite (Parpola 1997: [45–52]).

While the second type of divine communication, via letter, has elicited considerable scholarly discussion, it seems unlikely that it represents transcriptions of the ravings of ecstatic prophets (Parpola 1997: [45]), especially since some of these divine communications are attributed to human authors. The communications are frequently not in the first person and their format is more like that of a conventional letter, often with literary overtones. There are also important differences in content. True prophecies refer to future events, whereas these formal responses of the gods generally refer to the past and serve to exonerate or legitimate the conduct of the king who wrote the initial letter or report (Pongratz-Leisten 1999: 270–4). It has been suggested that these particular compositions are literary and/or ideological rather than oracular and may be compared to speeches made by the gods to kings, inscribed on the walls of Egyptian temples. The presentation of these letters was part of a larger narrative created by the kings, in which their mighty deeds were punctuated by frequent divinatory inquiries interspersed with offerings to the gods. This conduct received divine sanction not only through its actual success but also through communication from the gods that supported and justified their acts (Pongratz-Leisten 1999: 272–85).

While Mesopotamian letter prayers may sometimes resemble the way documents were used in the ceremony of the Egyptian processional oracle, they are clearly purely Mesopotamian, both in origin and in conception. However, knowledge of this practice is essential to assessing the origin and character of oracular practices elsewhere in the ancient Near East.

Some oracular practices in the Levant

In ancient times the eastern shore of the Mediterranean between Egypt and Mesopotamia was covered by a patchwork of micro-states. Some rose to the status of major states with tributary nations or empires; others benefited economically from the trade routes that crisscrossed the northern Mesopotamian plain. The coastal trading cities were highly cosmopolitan. The states inland from the coast were strongly influenced by them, although it is also possible to see distinctive cultural characteristics. From the beginning of recorded history in the fourth millennium to the time of the Roman Empire, this area presents a complex mixture of cultural borrowing and innovation (Knapp 1988: 124–30, 183–212, 242–3). Although written records go back to the early Bronze Age, some of the best documentation of religious practices comes from the Roman period, in the first centuries of the Common Era, when both the archaeological record and literary sources are particularly extensive (Hajjar 1990). Study of both Graeco-Roman and earlier written sources suggests that all forms of divination were as widespread in the Levant as they were in Mesopotamia. Ecstatic prophecy and divine communication through dreams enjoyed particular popularity.

Our first source is a literary work, "The Syrian Goddess," written by the Greek-speaking essayist Lucian, who lived in the mid-second century CE and may have been of native Syrian rather than Greek descent (Lightfoot 2003: 205–7). The author describes the temple of the Syrian goddess—whom he identifies with Hera, the wife of Zeus—which was located at Hieropolis in Syria (present-day Manbij, near Aleppo). This goddess, also known as Atargatis, was worshiped all over the ancient world and seems to have been closely related to the Mesopotamian goddess Ishtar. Some five hundred years earlier, in a dream, the goddess had commanded the wife of King Seleucus to construct her temple. This great landmark has now disappeared, but it was once famous for a lake with sacred fish and a temple that was home to the sacred images of many other gods, including Apollo, the Greek god of prophecy (Lightfoot 2003: 1–85). As Lucian explains, Apollo communicated there in an unusual way:

> There are many oracles ... [b]ut these speak not, save by the mouth of priests and prophets: this one is moved by its own impulse, and carries out the divining process to the very end. The manner of his divination is the following: When he is desirous of uttering an oracle, he first stirs in his seat, and the priests straightway raise him up. Should they fail to raise him up, he sweats, and moves more violently than ever. When they approach him and bear him up, he drives them round in a circle, and leaps on one after another. At last the high priest confronts him, and questions him on every subject. The god, if he disapproves of any action proposed, retreats into the background; if, however, he happens to approve it, he drives his bearers forward as if they were horses. It is thus that they gather the oracles, and they undertake nothing public or private without this preliminary. (Strong 1913: 36 [76–7])

Lucian also states that he saw the statue detach itself from its bearers and float in the air, as well as shout through the locked doors of the sanctuary (Strong 1913: 37 [77]). Among the other notable customs and personnel connected with the temple, the author describes the Galli, men who dedicated themselves to the service of Atargatis through self-castration and dressing as women (Strong 1913: 15 [55–6], 22 [62–3], 27 [65–6], 43–4 [79–80], 50–2 [84–5]). They are known throughout the Graeco-Roman world, although they clearly originated in the Near East, where they were connected with the cults of a number of Syrian and Anatolian goddesses. They are also described as performing ecstatic dances and prophesying in poetic form (Hajjar 1990: 2259, 2307–9).

While the mechanism of oracular communication using the statue shows a close similarity with the Egyptian processional oracle, other aspects of the ceremony and cult do not. There is no record of an Egyptian processional image indicating that it should be taken out in procession, although it was known to have refused to go by making itself too heavy to lift (Kruchten 1987: 54, 73–4; see also Chapter 1, "Interpretation"). Furthermore, although the Egyptian processional oracle was on occasion capable of violent or sudden movement, its bearers do not appear to have moved in the violent and ecstatic way described by Lucian; it appears that the spirit of the god took possession of each of them in turn (Strong 1913: 36 [76–7]). The behavior of the priests at Hieropolis is more in line with that of the ecstatic prophetic Galli, who are clearly derived from the earlier prophets of Ishtar found in the Mesopotamian tradition (Hajjar 1990: 2259, 2269).

Apart from Atargatis and Apollo, the temple also honored the Syro-Phoenician storm god Haddad, as well as other Greek divinities such as Atlas and Hermes (Hajjar 1990: 2242; Strong 1913: 38 [77]). It appears unlikely that this center of worship was in use much earlier than the Hellenistic period (Lightfoot 2003: 8–9n9). Its multicultural character reflects the effect on local religious beliefs of interaction between the Greek kingdoms based in Mesopotamia and Egypt. Another, similar form of oracular divination is described by the Roman writer Macrobius, who probably lived in the early fifth century CE. In his work *Saturnalia*, embedded in a discussion of worship of the sun, is a description of the oracle of Jupiter of Heliopolis, located in Assyria (*Saturnalia* 1.23.10–16, in Davies 1969: 151–2). Fortunately, this god and his temple are well known outside this entertaining but derivative work.

Heliopolis, now called Baalbek, is named for the foremost deity of the Levant: Baal, the storm and rain god. Located in the Beqa Valley behind the mountains of Lebanon, the modern town is dominated by the imposing remains of the great temples the Roman emperors erected in the second and third centuries CE (Leisten 2013). Its god was worshiped all over the Roman world, represented by a distinctive iconography that shows him as a beardless man wearing a strange, sheath-like costume and holding what Macrobius thought was the whip with which he drove the chariot of the sun. Comparisons with pre-Greek depictions of Baal show that it is actually a thunderbolt, as befits the god of storms; this fits better with his identification with the Roman Jupiter and Greek Zeus (Hajjar 1977: 446–7, pls. 88–9, 90–1, 124; 1990: 2244, 2290).

The importance of Jupiter of Heliopolis (also known as Baal of Beqa) seems to have rested on his oracle, the operation of which is described in some detail by Macrobius. The image of the god was borne in procession by "leading men of the province," who had been prepared for this event by "a long period of abstinence"—probably from meat, wine and sexual intercourse—and with their heads shaven to ensure they were pure when in contact with the god (Hajjar 1990: 2244–7). They were moved by the spirit or breath of the god to go where he wanted. Macrobius explains this further with an interesting cross-cultural comparison of his own: with the oracle of the two goddesses of Fortune who were worshiped in the Italian port town of Antium, not far south of Rome. The images of these goddesses responded to questions by going backwards or forwards (*Saturnalia* 1.23.13, in Davies 1969: 151), like the Egyptian processional oracle.

The god at Heliopolis also had a more private oracle situated in his sanctuary; it could be accessed remotely by sealed letter, to which he might respond in writing or by signs. Macrobius gives a famous example, that of the emperor Trajan, who wished to find out if his invasion of Parthia, to the east, would be successful. He first tested the oracle by sending it sealed blank documents, and was surprised to receive a blank sheet of paper in return. In answer to his question, the god sent back a soldier's staff broken in pieces and wrapped in a linen cloth. This riddling answer was later interpreted to refer to Trajan's cremated remains, which were sent back to Rome after he died in the campaign (*Saturnalia* 1.23.14–16, in Davies 1969: 151–2). Although emperors continued to consult Jupiter of Heliopolis and the other gods of the region (Leisten 2013), inscriptional evidence suggests that the Baalbek oracle attracted questioners from many places and all levels of society (Hajjar 1977: 348–77).

It is particularly interesting that Macrobius refers to the Egyptian connections of this foundation, explaining that it originated from Egyptian Heliopolis under a king named Senemur (*Saturnalia* 1.23.10–11, in Davies 1979: 151). Although this statement has not been universally accepted, modern scholarship has investigated the idea and its possible explanation for the form of the oracle. The argument that the peculiar costume of the god is based on that of the Egyptian deity Osiris can be easily dismissed, as it has a number of regional analogs and probably originated in Anatolia (Hajjar 1977: 446–7). However, the site of Baalbek itself may have an Egyptian foundation, from long before in the late Bronze Age, when pharaonic influence stretched to the plains of Syria.

In his commemoration of the great battle at the city of Qadesh—located on this plain not far from the northern end of the Beqa Valley—Ramesses II describes a town named Ramesses-beloved-of-Amun in the Valley of the Pine, the Egyptian name for the Beqa Valley (Lichtheim 1976: 63n11). It has been argued that this town, either founded or renamed by this king, featured worship of both the king and Amun-Re, both gods with solar features. It has even been suggested that its foundation may date back to the reign of the sun-worshiping monotheist Akhenaten, some forty years before. Like others in the ancient world, the Egyptians tried to consolidate their rule over foreign peoples by introducing their own gods and identifying them with local deities. Perhaps the cult that they set up, combining the local rain and storm god Baal and their own solar divinity, endured for centuries, transmitting the story of its origin as well as the distinctive form of the oracle (Wettengel 2003: 231, 245–9). However, while the processional oracle does appear to closely resemble the Egyptian version, the written oracles show a much closer resemblance to the Mesopotamian letter prayers, as well as the procedures connected with the Greek oracles and their enigmatic responses (Hajjar 1990: 2248–50).

Divination in ancient Israel

Inland, at the southern end of the eastern shore of the Mediterranean, lay the land of ancient Israel, which existed independently from the beginning of the first millennium BCE until the late Hellenistic period (Berlin and Brettler 2004: 2060–2). Much of what we know about ancient Israel comes from the biblical text that achieved its present form in the mid-first millennium CE, the earliest versions of which date from the second century BCE. The text itself was extensively edited and rewritten over generations, beginning in the fifth century BCE (Berlin and Brettler 2004).

The Hebrew Bible is a collection from different kinds of sources. It consists of stories about the origin of the world and the people of Israel, an extensive collection of laws and customs given by God to the people, hymns, sacred poetry, wise sayings, stories about prophets and prophetic writings, and connected narratives of the history of the united and divided kingdoms of ancient Israel and their aftermath (Brettler 2004). According to these narratives and archaeological evidence, the kingdoms of Israel and Judah existed in the early first millennium BCE before they were destroyed by the Assyrian and Babylonian empires in the eighth and sixth centuries BCE respectively.

When Judah, and its capital, Jerusalem, was destroyed by the Babylonians in 586 BCE, its upper classes were relocated to the city of Babylon, but they were allowed to return to Jerusalem and rebuild their temple when the Persians conquered the Babylonians (Berlin and Brettler 2004; Kuhrt 1995: 648, 660). The biblical text is based on their traditions and priorities and raises questions about how much they were able to retain from their pre-Babylonian history. It is not, of course, historical in a modern sense but uses these stories to create narratives that carry theological arguments and seek explanations for why events had unfolded the way they did (Pfoh 2009: 29–39).

Archaeological evidence for the pre-monarchic period and the united monarchy is extremely sparse, with one highly contested reference to "Israel" in an Egyptian text of the late thirteenth century BCE (Simpson 2003: 356–60,

562–6). The kingdoms of Israel and Judah are better attested, and the northern kingdom was clearly the larger and more prosperous (Pfoh 2009: 161–87). Outside sources, especially the Assyrian royal annals, confirm the destruction of the kingdom of Israel and an attack on Judah by king Sennacherib (Kuhrt 1995: 462–72), which is discussed further below. The post-Babylonian resettlement of Judah is also documented in records of the Persian period (Briant 2002: 584–7, 976–7).

Two stories about the period before the building of the temple described how God's spirit could inhabit a personal shrine, the Ark. In 1 Samuel, chapters 5 to 6 describe how, during a war between the Israelites and their neighbors the Philistines, the latter captured the Ark. However, the Philistines were struck by plagues and disease, so they asked their priests and diviners how to send it back to where it had come from. They were advised that, after supplying the god with an indemnity offering, they should place it in a cart drawn by two non-working milking cows and send it off down the road. If the god headed straight back to his own territory, he had caused the plagues; if not, there was some other cause. It so happened that the Ark headed straight for Israelite territory, but those who looked at it when it returned were struck blind. In 2 Samuel chapter 6, King David wanted to bring the Ark into his city of Jerusalem, but he became concerned after a man named Uzzah, who touched the Ark to steady it, was killed. He decided to leave it where it was for three months before taking it into Jerusalem. David and his court danced before the Ark as it moved in procession, accompanied by musical instruments. As it approached Jerusalem, the king leaped and whirled "with all his might before the LORD" (2 Sam. 6.14, in Hebrew Bible in English 1913).

These stories describe cultic practices that recall both the Egyptian processional oracle and Mesopotamian and Levantine divinatory practices. The concept seen in the first story of a decision based on the direction of the processional shrine, independent of human volition, suggests Egyptian practice, as does the danger associated with proximity to it seen in both narratives (Cryer 1994: 282, 306–7). Likewise, the killing of Uzzah in 2 Samuel 6:6-8 is associated with refusal of the shrine to move any further, which may be compared with the situation described in the inscription of Djhutymose in Chapter 1, "Interpretation." However, the propitiation of the god by music and ecstatic dancing seen in the second story, and by the offerings in the first one, suggests practices around Mesopotamian and Syro-Phoenician divination described above.

In the Book of the Covenant, a collection of laws, immediately following the proclamation of the Ten Commandments in Exodus 22, we read:

> (6) If a man deliver unto his neighbour money or stuff to keep, and it be stolen out of the man's house; if the thief be found, he shall pay double. (7) If the thief be not found, then the master of the house shall come near unto God, to see whether he have not put his hand unto his neighbour's goods. (8) For every matter of trespass, whether it be for ox, for ass, for sheep, for raiment, or for any manner of lost thing, whereof one saith: "This is it," the cause of both parties shall come before God; he whom God shall condemn shall pay double unto his neighbour. (Exod. 22.6-8, in Hebrew Bible in English 1913)

While this passage has generated much discussion (Cryer 1994: 286), there is little agreement about the procedure that is being suggested in either instance (Vannoy 1974). In the first instance, when goods placed with a neighbor for safekeeping are not recovered, it must be resolved before God whether he is innocent of the crime or not. In the second instance, any dispute of ownership between two parties can be resolved in the same way. In other words, no independent human agency is capable of empirically ascertaining the truth of the matter. It has been suggested that the mechanism for resolving these situations was either a purification oath, which was common in the ancient Near East, or by some ceremony before or inside a shrine or temple. However, the similarity of the phraseology to oracular legal documents from the New Kingdom village at Deir el-Medina in Egypt (see Chapter 1, "Interpretation") suggests that such cases may have been resolved by the oracle of a processional god, as described in the stories about the Ark discussed above.

Our third example is a striking passage in 2 Kings, which narrates the later history of the kingdoms of Israel and Judah. Chapters 18 and 19 describe the invasion of Judah by King Sennacherib of Assyria. When the Assyrian army besieges Jerusalem and lays waste to the surrounding countryside, Sennacherib's spokespersons try to demoralize the Judahites with messages that their god has deserted them and their king is untrustworthy. Although the prophet Isaiah relays God's message to the king not to be frightened by this blasphemous message, Sennacherib sends a letter to Hezekiah, explaining that none of the gods of the surrounding kingdoms has been able to save them.

> (14) And Hezekiah received the letter from the hand of the messengers, and read it; and Hezekiah went up unto the house of the LORD, and spread it before the LORD. (15) And Hezekiah prayed before the LORD, and said ... (16) Incline Thine ear, O LORD, and hear; open Thine eyes, O LORD, and see; and hear the words of Sennacherib, wherewith he hath sent him to taunt the living God ... (19) Now therefore, O LORD our God, save Thou us, I beseech Thee, out of his hand, that all the kingdoms of the earth may know that Thou art the LORD God,

even Thou only." (20) Then Isaiah the son of Amoz sent to Hezekiah, saying: "Thus saith the LORD, the God of Israel: 'Whereas thou hast prayed to Me against Sennacherib king of Assyria, I have heard thee'" …

(35) And it came to pass that night, that the angel of the LORD went forth, and smote in the camp of the Assyrians a hundred fourscore and five thousand; and when men arose early in the morning, behold, they were all dead corpses. (36) So Sennacherib king of Assyria departed, and went and returned, and dwelt at Nineveh (2 Kgs 19.14-20; 35-7, in Hebrew Bible in English 1913).

The actions of the king in God's sanctuary have an obvious ritual character. It has been suggested that Hezekiah is performing an execration ritual against Sennacherib by activating the connection between the potent personal traces left by his letter writing and the power of the god, who is invited to see and hear his words as the document is spread out before him. This results in not only the destruction of the Assyrian king's army but, later, his own elimination at the hands of his sons (Heckl 2008: 159–63).

On the other hand, the combination of prayer with the presentation of a document, as well as the poetic divine response via the prophet Isaiah, suggests a close connection to the Mesopotamian letter prayer, especially as it was practiced by the Assyrians. The embedding of this incident in a narrative that juxtaposes human acts with divine interventions—as with Isaiah's "oracle" in response to the earlier message in chapter 18 (Cogan and Tadmor 1988: 234)— and its careful literary construction also invite comparison with the Assyrian royal narratives mentioned above (Pongratz-Leisten 1999: 270–5). However, there is an even more striking cross-cultural parallel. While Mesopotamian letter prayers are always specially written as appeals to the gods, in Egypt, materials that were simply factual information or actual legal documents were regularly presented to oracles (Kruchten 2001a). In the biblical rendering, when the god is presented with a document not expressly created for the purpose but for information purposes, there appears to be greater similarity to Egyptian juridical oracles than to the Mesopotamian letter prayer, even though the answer comes through a prophet rather than through the unlikely movement of a stationary shrine in a sanctuary.

Although the biblical tradition presents strongly redacted, highly literary material, it clearly retains some memory of oracular procedures that were influenced by both Near Eastern and Egyptian cultures. While ancient Israel was heavily influenced by the prophetic traditions of the Levant, it also seems to have employed practices that may reflect the Egyptian processional oracle, and especially its legal uses. Apart from its remoter connections through the

Exodus story, the kingdom of Judah in particular was closer to Egypt than to anywhere else in the Levant. The Second Book of Kings 18.7-8 tells us that Hezekiah was being punished by the Assyrians for rebelling; Judah also formed an alliance with Egypt and its Kushite masters, and there was frequent contact between the two states (Redford 1992: 334-8). Written documents that survive show that Judah's scribes used Egyptian numerals and were familiar with its cursive writing system (Calabro 2012). Although it is not primary material in the form of texts or eyewitness accounts from the time it describes, the Bible is still an interesting and informative window into the complexity and fluid nature of religious observance and cross-cultural influence in the ancient Near East. It also illustrates the particular difficulties of distinguishing the sources of those influences.

Modern parallels to the processional oracle: Analog or survival?

In Chapter 1 we referred to spontaneous changes in the direction and speed of pallbearers at traditional Egyptian funerals and pointed out their important role in interpreting ancient written and pictorial records of the processional oracle. These kinds of events, which still take place (see Appendix A), may be closely compared with a rite known as "carrying the corpse," which is widespread throughout West Africa and in the African diaspora in the Americas (Mintz and Price 1992: 55-6).

In Ashanti, in central modern Ghana, carrying the corpse is undertaken when there exists some suspicion about the cause of the deceased's death, whether it be by actual foul play or by witchcraft (Rattray 1927: 167). In some cases the body may be carried around wrapped up in a cloth, in which it moves or bends in answer to verbal questions. The body may also be carried on a bier, responding by causing its bearers to move (Rattray 1927: 168). A police report prepared by English colonial authorities in the late nineteenth or early twentieth century, investigating the suicide of a man (referred to as A—) accused of murder during one of these proceedings, includes statements by those who carried the corpse, to the effect that they did not act of their own volition:

> No, till I found myself in A—'s yard I did not know where I was; I felt weak as if something was pushing me, and not till I got to A—'s yard did I remember things clearly. When we first arrived at A—'s yard we walked round and round and could not stand until people came and held us by force. The corpse kept

knocking the fence in the yard ... A — asked the body, saying, "Am I the person who caused your death by witchcraft?" The body ran at him and knocked him. He asked the same question again and again the corpse rushed at him. (Rattray 1927: 169)

When one of A—'s sons, who was carrying the body, was asked if he had acted in a premeditated way, he replied:

> He is my father and I would not want to do that ... I knew I was going to knock my father but I could not help myself, as my whole body became weak ... I believe he is the one who caused this woman's death which is why he shot himself. I know in truth I did not want to bring any harm on my father, but I could not prevent the dead from knocking him, so I know my father must have caused its death. (Rattray 1927: 170)

The rite of carrying the corpse as performed in African slave communities in the Caribbean has been described in European accounts. They also record more spontaneous acts that took place during funeral processions, such as sudden halting of the corpse at the preferred burial place or stopping at the house of a debtor (Abrams and Szwed 1983: 163–6). Carrying the corpse is still practiced in the Americas, including the Ndyuka Maroon community in Suriname (Thoden van Velzen and Van Wetering 2004: 79–82, 171–3). It also exists alongside a form of divination extremely similar to the Egyptian processional oracle.

The so-called Maroon communities found in the Caribbean and Central and South America are descended from runaway slaves, who, having been able to evade capture in remote locations, were eventually recognized as independent political entities by the colonial authorities. These communities date from the seventeenth through early nineteenth centuries. They are generally believed to reflect the culture and practices of the societies in Africa where they originated, at the time when their ancestors were taken, although they do not exist in isolation from the modern world (Thoden van Velzen and Van Wetering 2004: 4–15). Ndyuka religion may reflect African practices of centuries past, but it is also marked by Amerindian and Christian influences (Case 2001; Thoden van Velzen and Van Wetering 2004: 34–6).

The Ndyuka have many points of contact with the numinous world. Everywhere there are informal human mediums, as well as professional shamans who often assume positions of spiritual leadership. Afaaka, or "carry oracles," are found in most Ndyuka villages, but they are not consulted on a regular basis. In moments of crisis or other times of special importance, the village elders take the sacred bundle—made up of numinous objects often connected with the ancestors—and place it on the heads of two bearers, to which it is attached by a plank. It is thereby moved from the temple into the village square, where it is questioned by the elders, who interpret the involuntary movements it forces the bearers to make. From time to time the principal gods intervene in society through an oracle, often based at an important religious center and curated by government administrators, priests and elders (Thoden van Velzen and Van Wetering 2004: 24-9, 51).

During the 1960s, H. U. E. Thoden van Velzen and W. Van Wetering, two Dutch anthropologists, were able to make an extended study of the Gaan Tata oracle, which represented one of the paramount gods, Gaan Tata. It operated out of Diitibiki, one of the most important spiritual centers of the Ndyuka, under the auspices of the Gaanman, a community leader and administrator appointed by the colonial government. The anthropologists observed both the practice and social context of the oracle. The oracular event never happened without a preliminary consultation between the priests, elders and Gaanman, and it normally took place on weekends, when the elders and priests were not at work. Elders of the surrounding communities were expected to be present at these sessions, in the main square of Diitibiki, sitting on their ceremonial stools while the rest of the community stood and watched. Consultation about the oracle began at sunrise, but it did not appear from the temple until early afternoon.

The oracle was performed by persons with clearly defined roles. The whole ceremony was directed by the Gaanman, who took the role of Chief of the God's Work ("high priest"), assisted by three to five God's Laborers ("priests"); the oracle was carried by God's Bearers. The interpreters of the god's movements were often village headmen or elders. The whole meeting was presided over by a Speaker who announced the god's decisions to the community, as the decisions were often discussed and interpreted in low, inaudible tones. The session often began with the god circling the bundle: one of the bearers would walk in a circle while the other remained stationary. At such an event, the god responds to spoken questions in the affirmative by moving forward and in the negative by moving back; it indicates persons of interest by moving toward them or nudging them; and wild or chaotic movements show displeasure. A rush toward the edge of the forest shows the approach of danger. Some very slight movements could indicate that questions should continue or can even be interpreted verbally by the bearers. The reactions of the god to those around it could also be based on its sense of smell (Thoden van Velzen 2014, personal communication; Thoden van Velzen and Van Wetering 2004: 57-65).

The Gaan Tata oracle originated in the late nineteenth century; its rise is connected with the persecution of witches, who were identified through the carrying the corpse rite, a practice that functions in a very similar way. Thoden van Velzen and Van Wetering have suggested that this particular oracle represented a form of political intervention by influential members in a society that was ostensibly egalitarian. Its rise, decline and reappearance were connected with competition between different cults and the social interests they represented (Thoden van Velzen and Van Wetering 2004: 33–55, 69–71, 130–8 and *passim*). While the practice may be interpreted differently (Price 1975: 42), it is notable that the oracular session is so highly curated, to an even greater degree than that of Amun-Re under the theocratic high priests of 21st Dynasty Egypt, to which it bears a superficial resemblance.

However, not all the carry oracles of Maroon Suriname operate in the same way. Although the Saramaka, a neighboring Maroon society, received an oracle from the Ndyuka in the nineteenth century (Price 1975: 38), their use of it is strikingly different. As with other forms of divination used by the Saramaka, their oracular session is preceded by open discussion among members of the entire community of the issues to be raised, and everyone can question the oracle. It has been suggested that the community itself is the diviner, and that the model here is one of consensus rather than the hierarchical decision-making seen in the operation of the Ndyuka oracle. The use of the oracle among the Saramaka may be seen as part of a process of change from a violent militaristic society to a more peaceful, cooperative one (Price 1975: 40–3).

Conclusions

This cross-cultural survey has described the use of the processional oracle in societies adjacent to Egypt and subject to its cultural influence. It has also looked at cultures in the ancient Near East with analogous practices that also display the interactions of local and Mesopotamian religions, and at modern Egyptian funerals and analogous practices in West Africa and the African diaspora. This latter material is of particular importance, as the customs found in Egyptian funerals have been vital to reconstructing the practice behind ancient accounts of the oracle. Without the connections to its modern equivalents, identification of the processional oracle in Diodorus's description of the oracle at Siwa would not have been possible, and neither would linking it with descriptions of oracular procedure at the temples of the Apollo at Hieropolis

(Manbij) and Heliopolis (Baalbek), or the activities described in the Hebrew Bible.

David Frankfurter, in his study of late survivals of Egyptian religion, sought to characterize the Gaan Tata oracle as a descendant of the Egyptian processional oracle (1998: 155–6). However, even if Ndyuka religious rites were a direct survival of earlier African cultic practices (which they are not), that would not prove that these rites stem directly from an Egyptian original. Both the carry oracle and carrying the corpse are found in west Africa, in Ashanti and Togo (Thoden van Velzen 2014, personal communication), as well as in Maroon Suriname, and carrying the corpse is practiced in both western Africa and modern Egypt, but it is not attested at all in ancient times. It may be possible that this funerary ritual was carried out in ancient Egypt but was not recorded in the written record because it was a non-elite practice.

The importance of modern descriptions of relevant activities in understanding the oracle also points to a problem with our ancient sources. Since literacy was restricted in the ancient world, all the records of ancient ceremonies that we have discussed are from an elite perspective. The oracle of Amun used by the Kushite elite probably had little relevance to the religious life of most people in that society, except for its role in their political leadership. The oracle of Amun at Siwa, promoted by the city of Cyrene to the ruling class of the Greek-speaking world, was described as deserted by the Greek travelers Diodorus and Strabo, who visited it in the first century BCE, although it was clearly being used by local people, according to their own descriptions. The descriptions of the oracles of Hieropolis and Heliopolis by Lucian and Macrobius also refer to their fame in relation to royal patronage, attested by the imposing ruins of the temple at Baalbek.

In our Egyptian material there was a strong contrast between the documentation of the oracle of Amun-Re, in his great temple at Thebes, and the village oracle at Deir el-Medina across the river, although this was also a literate community. The interests and concerns of this small community are reflected in the oracular questions and procedure. The accounts of religious activities among West Africans and the African diaspora are located in small-scale, largely illiterate communities (Thoden van Velzen 2014, personal communication). Their transmission of religious knowledge and practice, as well as its social meanings, is bound to be quite different from those found in the hierarchical ancient societies that we examined above. Cross-cultural analysis provides interesting clues to interactions and communications between ancient societies, but it also cautions us not to see similarity as identity. Analog and reflection are more useful models than direct borrowing or outright diffusion.

3

The Virtual Temple of Horus and Its Egyptian Prototypes

Robyn Gillam

Integral to the performance of the virtual and live Egyptian Oracle is the virtual temple of Horus, whose role in this activity has been briefly described in the Introduction. To date this environment has been used in several different ways: as a guide and teaching tool for understanding the Egyptian formal temple, as a setting for live performances filmed in blue screen and, most recently, as the environment in which a live audience experiences the Egyptian processional oracle. In this chapter we shall examine the ancient temples used as the basis of the virtual reality (VR) model and its construction, before moving on to an examination of the ancient temples themselves. We begin with a brief overview of the historical development of the Egyptian temple and how these temples fit into it, and then take a more detailed look at their historical, social and geographical settings, along with their physical and conceptual layouts.

The ancient prototypes of the virtual temple

We found most of our source material in documentation of the funerary temple of Ramesses III at Medinet Habu, near Luxor in southern Egypt, and the temple of Horus at Edfu, located some ninety kilometers south of Luxor. Apart from their good state of preservation, both these temples display a particularly clear and coherent layout, due to the fact that they were both constructed in a relatively short time span.

The temple at Medinet Habu was completed in only seven years, between the fifth and twelfth years of the reign of Ramesses III (1182–1151 BCE) (O'Connor 2012: 259). The temple at Edfu was begun by Ptolemy III Euergetes in 237 BCE but not completed until 57 BCE, in the time of his descendant Ptolemy XII Neos Dionysos, the father of Cleopatra the Great—a period of 180 years (Watterson 1998: 25–7). However, as will be explained below, although widespread rebellion against these Graeco-Macedonian rulers delayed its construction, inscriptions in the temple, as well as the consistency of its layout, suggest that it was built according to a master plan. It should be noted that most Egyptian temples, especially those in important centers, were added to, reconfigured, demolished and rebuilt over many centuries. Although the basic principles of layout and conceptual framework are remarkably consistent, the details of how such structures were configured are often difficult to recover (Spencer 2010: 270; Wilson 2010: 782).

These temples owe their preservation to both historical accident and the positions they occupied in the landscape. Study of the transformations they underwent is important in the wider study of understanding how ancient structures are reused and repurposed in the light of cultural and environmental change (Blake 1998; Onstine 2012). The large footprint of these buildings and their associated structures ensured that they would play a significant role in any landscape they were a part of. Including its outer wall and subsidiary buildings, the Medinet Habu temple measures approximately 340 by 240 meters, an area of more than 8 hectares. The temple itself measures 150 by 40 meters, excluding the First Pylon gateway, which is 68.25 meters wide (Hölscher 1934: pl. 2).

The temple of Edfu, including the outer enclosing wall but minus most of the related structures, which do not survive, is 140 by 50 meters (again excluding the pylon gateway), with an interior area of 7,000 meters (Watterson 1998: 49). The First Pylon, the largest of the entrance gates at Medinet Habu, was originally 24.1 meters high. In front of every temple gateway there towered great wooden flagstaffs of cedar of Lebanon, more than 30 meters high, from which fluttered flags in white, red, green and blue (Murnane 1980b: 11). The pylon at Edfu is 40 meters high and the surrounding wall 13 meters (Watterson 1998: 52–3). The outer hall, the tallest space in the building, is 15.75 meters high (Kurth 2004: 65).

Whatever the original purpose of Ramesses III was in surrounding his temple with massive fortified and bastioned walls, soon after his death, when the country descended into political and social chaos, it became a walled town. The areas set aside for staff residences were expanded and the settlement continued to grow over the centuries. At first the town owed its survival to the proximity of an ancient temple of the ancestor gods that had been incorporated into the king's temple complex, but almost a millennium and a half later it became a Christian monastic community. Over the centuries the back of the building, where the shrines of the gods had been, was demolished and its stones reused. However, the construction of a church inside the second courtyard of the temple led to unusually good preservation of the colored reliefs on its inside walls, which the monks simply plastered over. When the town was deserted more than a thousand years ago, ideal conditions were created for preservation of the front part of the building (Murnane 1980b: 2).

The temple at Edfu, unlike Medinet Habu, lay not out in the countryside but in the heart of the ancient city of Wetches-Hor, or Djeba (modern Edfu) (Watterson 1998: 45–7). The town was never abandoned, and when the temple was finally closed after the banning of pagan worship by Emperor Theodosius in the late fourth century, its surrounding grounds were soon taken over by townsfolk in search of land on which to build their houses and businesses. They also welcomed the protection from natural and human disruption that its great stone walls offered. Over time a constant deposition of river silt, dust and rubbish raised the ground level of the town surrounding the temple until the houses were built high up its walls, near the roofline. People threw their rubbish into the space inside the building until it was full almost to the ceiling (Kurth 2004: 21–36). Although this treatment of an ancient sacred space may seem disrespectful, it created the "best preserved temple in the ancient world" (Kurth 2004: 1). Conservation of these ancient buildings was achieved when, on account of their size and age, they began to be treated as part of the natural landscape by the people who continued to live around them. At Medinet Habu, this process was aided when the site was deserted by its human population. At Edfu, however, the very density of occupation sufficed to preserve the temple, by literally burying it in rubbish.

European travelers and scholars first began to investigate these buildings in the eighteenth and nineteenth centuries. Both were cleared out in the mid-nineteenth century under the direction of August Mariette, the first director of the Egyptian Antiquities Service. People who had lived in the Edfu temple had to be relocated, and the Coptic Christian buildings inside the Medinet Habu temple were largely destroyed (Kurth 2004: 36–41; Murnane 1980b: 3–4). Since the 1930s the temple of Medinet Habu and its grounds have been systematically excavated and its reliefs and texts copied and published by the Oriental Institute of the University of Chicago (Oriental Institute 1930, 1934, 1957). Many scholars have worked in the temple of Edfu since its clearance and it is currently being studied by the German-based Edfu Project and the French Archaeological Institute in Cairo. Despite extensive publication and analysis, the building and its texts are so vast that much remains to be done (Kurth 2004: 41–4).

Egyptian temples: Types and development

The temple of Horus at Edfu is a cult temple—a center for the worship of a god and its maintenance, located in the middle of the urban community and surrounding area recognized as its home (Wilson 2010: 782). The temple at Medinet Habu is a mortuary temple, dedicated to the cult of the deceased Ramesses III or, more precisely, a form of the god Amun, with whom the king's spirit had merged (O'Connor 2012: 209–10). While it might be assumed that the cult temple is the original form of Egyptian temple from which the mortuary foundation was derived, the reverse is in fact the case.

Evidence for veneration of gods in local and community contexts in the late prehistoric period and the third millennium BCE consists mostly of the scant remains of improvised structures, often built around natural formations. They show little evidence of rectilinear ground plans or axial structures (Roth 1993, 38–9; Wilson 2010, 783–5). The earliest substantial structures that can be identified as temples are connected with the tombs of the kings of the Archaic Period and Early Old Kingdom (3150–2625 BCE). These establishments were attached to large tracts of agricultural land that provided the food offerings that formed the basis of the cult of the deceased king and, as explained below, were fundamental to all human and divine transactions (Wilkinson 1999, 114–24).

By the 4th Dynasty (mid-third millennium BCE) there was a small cult area near the royal tomb in the desert and another on the edge of the valley, where the cults of the deceased kings could be carried on for generations (Posener-Krieger 1976: ix, 637–40). These temples display the axial symmetry that became a central feature of Egyptian sacred architecture (Roth 1993: 45–6, 50–1). Common features include open courtyards, often surrounded by colonnades, as well as columned porticos and halls terminating in a sanctuary area with multiple statues of the king (Verner 2001: 206–9, 224–34, 247–50, 275–8, 285–90, 293–7, 313–19, 327–9, 334–8, 344–7, 352, 355, 364–8). For the better part of a millennium these royal cult temples were the only substantial temples (Wilson 2010: 785–7). When more permanent community shrines to the gods began to be built, it is not surprising that they resembled the royal mortuary temples. The earliest surviving axially symmetrical temples date from the Middle Kingdom, in the early second millennium BCE. The layout was simple, based on a tripartite arrangement of portico, hallway and sanctuary area. These buildings were often square or wider than they were long (Vandier 1955: 614–40, 650–4).

That the king's cult temples should predate substantial temples for the gods is not all that surprising when we realize that the Egyptian ruler occupied a unique and pivotal position in society and the cosmos. As the chosen earthly incarnation of Horus, the ancestor god of all rulers of Egypt, the king was during his lifetime the partially divine intermediary between the gods and humanity (Assmann 2002: 301, 407). The gods gave the king rulership on the condition that he upheld world order (*maat* in Egyptian) by maintaining the earthly part of the cosmos that they had created. Apart from maintaining social order and securing the borders of Egypt against its enemies, one of the main tasks of the king was to present the gods with gifts in the form of products of the land they had placed under his rule, especially food offerings. The gods received these offerings when they inhabited cult statues in their temples, which it was the responsibility of the king to maintain. Thus the gods and the king had a symbiotic relationship. Without the gods, the king could not rule; without the king, the gods could not receive worship and offerings. In fact it was the king, who incarnated divinity in the world, who made possible the interaction of gods with humanity and their appearance in the world through their temples (Assmann 1995: 17–23; Spencer 2010: 260).

The temple of Ramesses III and other New Kingdom mortuary temples

By the time Ramesses III built his mortuary temple, almost a thousand years of development in temple architecture had taken place. After the Middle Kingdom, following a period of foreign domination, chieftains from the southern city of Thebes expelled the invaders in the mid-sixteenth century BCE and went on to control large territories in the Levant and northern Sudan (also known as Nubia) (Bourriau 2000).

Much of the wealth that the kings of the New Kingdom (1570–1070 BCE) acquired through this empire-building was channeled into temples, where it not only supplied the offerings the king owed the gods as part of their cosmic bargain but also augmented the temples with new additions to the gods' earthly homes, and sometimes complete rebuilding (Hayes 1962: §111). Finally the temples of the gods outshone the burial complexes of the kings, which were now concealed deep in hidden rock-cut tombs to guard against robbers (Reeves and Wilkinson 1996: 15–17). Nowhere was this more the case than in the temple of Amun—or Amun-Re, as he had become—the city god of the first New Kingdom rulers who became a national god. As noted above, the temple of Amun at Karnak is one of the largest religious structures on the planet (Myśliwiec 2000: 14–27; Van Dijk 2000: 273–4). This came about because the kings of the New Kingdom, and those who came after them, sought to please the god and give glory to themselves by enlarging his earthly home. This was done by adding more and more of the basic elements of temple design to the front of the building, in the form of additional colonnaded courtyards, passageways, columned halls and imposing two-towered pylon gateways (Hirmer and Lange 1968: 488–96; O'Connor 2012: 225–7; Vandier 1955: 862–943). Thus developed the Egyptian formal temple, the basic design of which endured into the early centuries of the Common Era.

Another reason for the longitudinal expansion of the temple was to provide an imposing processional way for the portable image of the god that went out into the world during the numerous public festivals (Gillam 2005: 68–9; O'Connor 2012: 219; Van Dijk 2000: 274). These became increasingly important during the New Kingdom and afterwards and provided the venue for oracular events (Černý 1962: 36–40). This made necessary another addition to the layout of the temple: a special shrine for the processional barque, the model boat in which the god appeared in public. In the temple of Amun at Karnak, this was placed directly in front of the old sanctuary (Legrain 1917: 13–32; O'Connor 2012: 216–19, 226–7) where the cult statue was housed. Barque shrines were found in the temples of most gods at this period (Colin 2003; Karlshausen 2009: 244–8). The festivals in which Amun took part wove the god and his activities into the wider landscape of ancient Thebes and its environs, establishing relationships with other gods in the city and neighboring towns, as well as the human community and the natural environment. Nowhere was this more the case than on the west bank of the city, where the cemetery, which included the royal tombs and mortuary temples, was located (O'Connor 2012: 210–11).

One of the most important festivals celebrated in the Theban area was the Feast of the Valley, which took place in early summer, in the second month of the season of *shomu*, or "harvest." During this celebration, Amun left his home in the Karnak temple and crossed over the river to visit the goddess Hathor, who dwelt in the desert cliffs that towered over the western shore directly opposite Karnak. He spent the night near her shrine (Schott 1952: 6), celebrating a sacred marriage that ensured the rebirth of nature as well as rejuvenation of the spirits of the dead, especially those of the deceased kings. The image of Amun was supposed to visit all of the dead in the cemetery, but it always made a special stop at the mortuary temple of the reigning king, whose spirit had merged with that of Amun-Re (O'Connor 2012: 210–11, 214–16).

Hathor was an ancient divinity closely associated with kingship; her very name signified "house (or mother) of Horus." She was also worshiped as a goddess of fertility, erotic love, childbirth, music and dance. As she presided over both birth and resurrection, she was an important guarantor of life after death for all Egyptians (Hart 1986: 76–82; Pinch 1993).

Although Amun had always been imagined as a creator god, he was originally thought of as the wind or breath of life that moved across the waters of chaos (Klotz 2006: 63–4; Otto 1966: 118–20). Later on, in the early Middle Kingdom, his creative character was linked to that of the sun god Re, who brought about existence by providing light (Hornung 1982: 91). In adding to the meaning of his creation, Amun's worshipers also added to his prestige, by connecting him with this ancient royal god from the north of the country (Kahl 2007: 61–3; Kemp 1989: 197–200). This linked Amun to the solar cycle—the movement of the sun from south to north and back through the year, as well as its daily appearance and disappearance, which had always suggested birth, death and rebirth to the Egyptians. Thus Amun-Re, like Hathor and Osiris, the father of Horus, became a god of the afterlife.

Within the hidden tombs of the kings, transcriptions of sacred books re-presented the death and regeneration of the sun in the underworld every night and his triumphant rebirth. Through his identification with Amun-Re, the king was assured eternal life in the sun. Osiris was king of both the underworld and the dead, as well as the father of Horus, the once and future king (O'Connor 2012: 210, 260–4). In the course of the New Kingdom, Egyptian thinkers came to imagine the union of Re and Osiris as the essence of the potential for rebirth and eternal life (Assmann 1995: 28). The identification of the king with Amun-Re, Re and Osiris guaranteed his participation in this endless cycle of renewal. It also meant that he was deeply enmeshed in the pattern of Amun's festive visitations, as both a living and dead participant.

Thus Ramesses III's temple, the last in the series of such New Kingdom mortuary foundations (Hirmer and Lange 1968: 508), shared features with these other temples and with the temple of Amun at Karnak, with whom his spirit had merged (O'Connor 2012: 209–10). Each mortuary temple was dedicated to a cult of a form of Amun merged with a particular king. The product of this spiritual union was the god venerated in the central sanctuary at the back of the

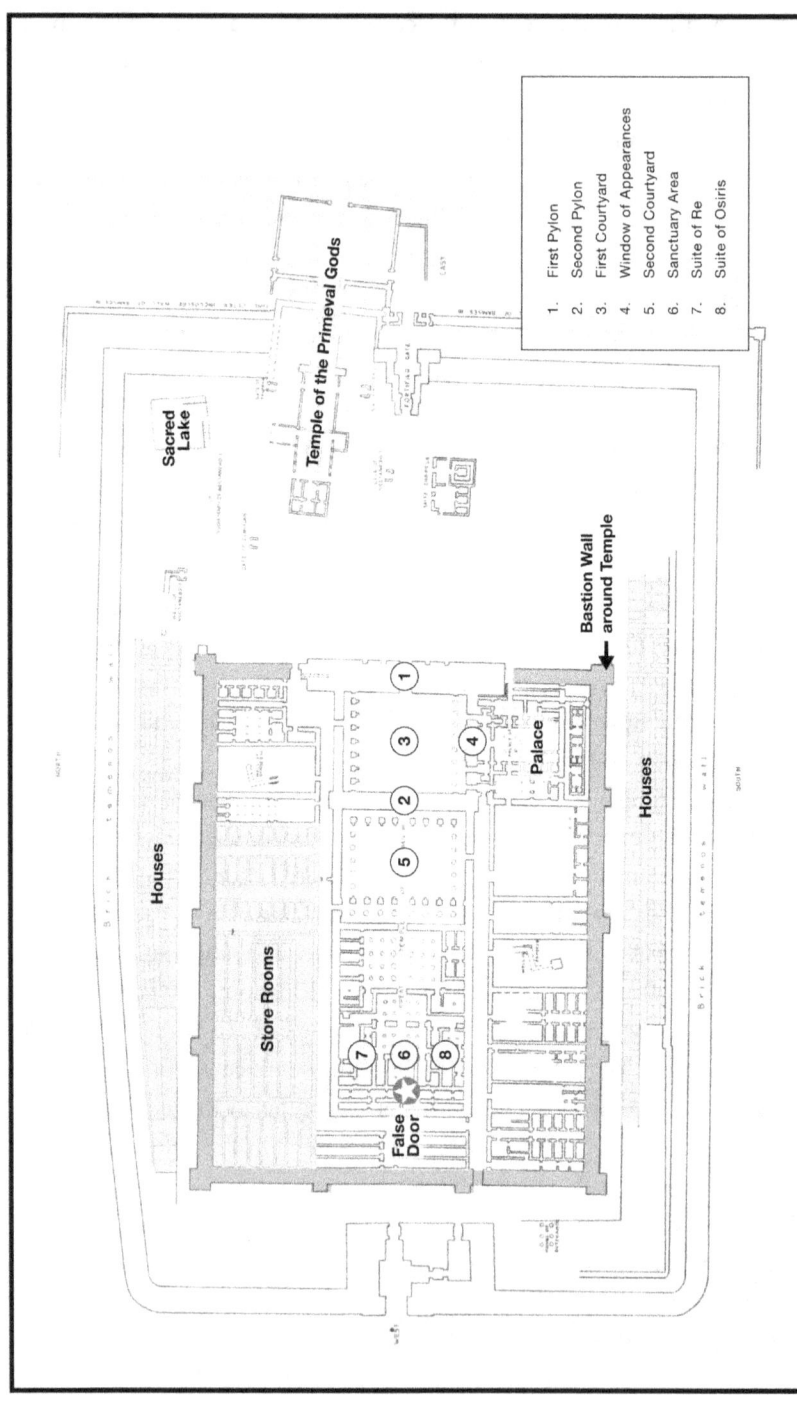

Figure 3.1 Plan of the temple precinct, Medinet Habu.

temple. The mortuary temples were oriented east–west in order to position their owners for resurrection in the solar cycle (Assmann 1995: 44–5).

On the back wall of the sanctuary of the Medinet Habu temple was a false door, as in the tomb chapels, that allowed the *ba* spirit of the king to move between his tomb in the Valley of the Kings and his temple (Murnane 1980b: 64; Spencer 1982: 58–61), where he received spiritual sustenance from the food offerings. In front of the sanctuary was a special shrine for the barque of Amun, which resided there when it visited during the Feast of the Valley (Murnane 1980b: 63; O'Connor 2012: 214–15). Two suites of rooms lay on either side, also in front of the sanctuary. The one to the south was dedicated to the cult of Osiris, who was clearly identified with the king, and the one on the north side to Re-Horakhty, a god who combined Horus and Re as the sun appearing on the horizon in the morning (Murnane 1980b: 49–60). Part of the latter suite included an open courtyard where the rays of the sun could directly reach those performing the cult for this god (Murnane 1980b: 50). Reliefs on the walls of these rooms depict the journey of the sun through the underworld and the identification of the king with this god. The combination of these two suites with the sanctuary area ensured that the composite divinity that was Amun and Ramesses III enjoyed eternal life through the lunar, agriculturally linked passion of Osiris and the daily and yearly solar journeys of Re-Horakhty (O'Connor 2012: 210, 260–3). These elements were also found in the New Kingdom sanctuary of the main temple of Amun at Karnak,

Figure 3.2 Temple of Medinet Habu. First courtyard, looking through the second courtyard to the sanctuary at the back of the temple.

which also stressed the identification of this god with the king (O'Connor 2012: 226–7).

In front of the sanctuary area, but still within the central part of the temple, were three columned halls, each slightly smaller as one moved toward the sanctuary. The second hall gave access to the Re-Horakhty and Osiris suites; the first was surrounded by shrines for other gods who visited during festivals or played various roles in the cultic life of the temple. There were also storage rooms for the cultic and other equipment used in the temple. Although the arrangement of spaces along the axis of the processional way was strictly symmetrical, the arrangement of rooms on either side was not. The layout of the Osiris rooms actually mirrored the mazelike earliest temples.

The temple of Ramesses III at Medinet Habu had two courtyards. The second inner courtyard, which opened into the main temple on its western side, was surrounded by a colonnade behind which have been found beautiful colored reliefs of two of the most important festivals celebrated in the temple (Murnane 1980b: 26). On the south side, in line with the Osiris chapel and proceeding into the temple, runs the procession of the Festival of Sokar, a celebration of the old earth god of Memphis, the original capital of Egypt, which marked the end of the Nile flood season and germination of freshly planted seeds (Gaballa and Kitchen 1969; Murnane 1980b: 28–32). Since Sokar had long been identified with Osiris, its significance for Ramesses III and his continued existence in eternity is obvious. On the other side, moving out of the temple, is depicted the Festival of Min, which took place at the end of the planting season and the start of the harvest. Min was a very old fertility god, known from prehistoric times, who presided over a celebration in which the king cut the first sheaf of grain, thereby demonstrating the renewal of his power (Refai 1998). As the deceased ruler, he was identified with Osiris as the grain that is cut, threshed and comes back to life (Murnane 1980b: 32–8). These two popular festivals were portrayed for their relevance to the continued life of the king and his cosmic function. They also remind us that the courtyard of a temple was the place where the general population was permitted to celebrate festivals, as they were not allowed to enter the main part of the temple (Wilson 2010: 791).

The reliefs at the various entrances of the temple show that those who enter it must be pure. At the western end of the courtyard and colonnade is an image of the king being washed by the gods (Medinet Habu IV pl. 298; Murnane 1980b: 26–7). At the entrance of the First Pylon, the king himself warns against unauthorized entry by those who are impure (Medinet Habu IV pl. 247 C&H). These images are found near the center of the colonnade and at either end.

Figure 3.3 Temple of Medinet Habu. Second courtyard, showing the southern colonnade with reliefs of the Festival of Sokar.

At the eastern end of the courtyard, on the back of the Second Pylon, we find images and texts about the king's successful military campaigns (O'Connor 2012: 258–9 fig. 6.11). They bring us to the main theme of the first courtyard.

The first courtyard, immediately behind the main pylon gateway, was fronted on its southern side by a small palace. The façade of the palace that faced onto the courtyard consisted of a balcony with an elaborately framed window, inset into a columned portico, in which the king appeared to people assembled in the courtyard. The rest of the building, behind the window, consists of a columned hall with a dais for a throne and a small suite of residential rooms. It appears to have been enlarged at some point, perhaps after Ramesses III's death, when the complex was fortified (Murnane 1980b: 2, 23–5, 69–72). It has been suggested that the original palace was not a functioning unit but a dummy building, like those found connected to the early tombs. The palace may also reference one known to have existed in the temple complex of Amun at Karnak (O'Connor 2012: 230–2). Like that installation and probably also quite small, it was a place for the king to sleep, eat and change his costume during extensive ritual performances (Gillam 2005: 87).

The administrative and economic importance of the Medinet Habu complex is indicated by large numbers of documents surviving from the reign of Ramesses III and later (McDowell 1999: 22–3). One of the most important of these is Papyrus Harris I, now in the British Museum, which seems to be a statement or will drawn up shortly after the king's death (Grandet 1994: 119–23). It details generous donations that Ramesses III made to these gods (Grandet 1994: 43–8). The gifts to Amun and his family include the king's own funerary complex, with attached lands. The beauty and lavishness of the gifted temple, as well as its cultic significance, point to its central importance in the estate of Amun (O'Connor 2012: 244).

On the opposite, north side of the first courtyard was another colonnade, with columns in the form of statues of the king. These were common in royal funerary temples and normally showed the ruler in the form of the mummified god Osiris, but here they represented the king as a warrior, equipped with a dagger. This fitted well with the reliefs that decorated most of the courtyard, which showed Ramesses III's remarkable victories over several groups of foreign peoples that tried to invade Egypt during his reign (Murnane 1980b: 21–2). Although the theme of royal power coordinates with the palace façade, the defeat of enemies was also a suitable theme for the outer portions of a temple building (Wilson 2010: 794).

Earlier temples in the Old and Middle Kingdom had little decoration on their walls, but by the late New Kingdom most stone temples were covered in elaborately carved and brightly painted images and hieroglyphic inscriptions (Wilson 2010: 787). On the exterior of the outer wall of the Medinet Habu temple is an amazing series of reliefs and texts displaying the king's wars against would-be invaders, and on the back of the First Pylon, images of him hunting wild animals (Medinet Habu II, pls. 116–17; Murnane 1980b: 11–18). Although they mostly chronicle actual events, the reliefs also have a larger, metaphysical significance. The temple is a miniature replica of the universe where cultic acts essential for the perpetuation of *maat*, the cosmic order, were performed. As such it had to be protected from the forces of chaos. Although the creator wrested the elements of creation from chaos, the formed universe as we know it was thought to merely float on its surface or be surrounded by it, like the yolk in an egg. Only eternal vigilance, energy and regeneration of the creative spirit and its avatars could prevent chaos from overcoming what had been created (O'Connor 2012: 232, 241).

Apotropaic depiction of defeated enemies was not enough. Another perimeter wall, equipped with bastions, surrounded the temple, palace and service buildings. In addition, the entire complex, including parks, residential areas and the sacred lake, was surrounded by a massive mud-brick wall, originally more than 18 meters high and 18.6 meters thick, protected by fortified gates in the east and the west (Murnane 1980b: 6–8, 35). The best-preserved gate, on the eastern side, is constructed of stone; it resembles a type of fortified tower then common throughout the ancient Near East. It has been argued that these and other features of the structure suggest that it had a religious, apotropaic function rather than a defensive one (O'Connor 2012: 235–7, 251–7). Be that as it may, within a few decades of its builder's death, the temple was fortified and then besieged in armed conflict, which destroyed the Western Gate (Murnane 1980b: 2).

The Eastern Gate, which was served by a canal and its own jetty, was primarily intended for ceremonial processions of the king and the gods who visited during the great festivals. Presumably crowds of worshipers were permitted on these occasions to follow the procession through the gate and the pylon into the first and second courtyards. However, the main public entrance into the complex was at its western end, where goods and personnel entered. The back of a temple was also the site of public worship (pp. 26, 47, 49), as it was the point outside the building closest to the sanctuary—the place where the spiritual energy of the god could be most easily accessed (Wilson 2010: 794–5). In a funerary temple like Medinet Habu, it was the place where the departed king's spirit traveled in and out of the sanctuary through the false door (Murnane 1980b: 64).

Although the temple at Medinet Habu is unique for the good preservation of its ancillary buildings and its brightly colored reliefs, the destruction of the sanctuary area and most of its decoration makes its interpretation a work of inference and comparison as well as direct observation. While the Medinet Habu temple provides us with useful comparative material, for a complete and fully self-documented structure we must now turn to the temple of Horus at Edfu, the structure that provides the basic template for our virtual temple.

The temple at Edfu as a library and teaching tool

From the mid-first millennium BCE onward, the walls of Egyptian cult temples (no royal mortuary foundations survive) began to be covered with extremely detailed texts and representations of the gods, their cult and rituals, and scripts for the performance of these routines. As well as hymns and the dedicatory and historical inscriptions found earlier, there also began to appear the actual texts, whether full or excerpted from sacred books, as well as lists of similar works held in the temple libraries. If the Egyptian temple of this period is not exactly a book—as suggested by German scholar Jan Assmann (1992: 9–10; Zinn

2011: 188)—it is certainly a descriptive catalog. And this is not just a figure of speech. The Book of the Temple, a papyrus document that was excavated from a Roman-period temple in the Faiyum, in northern Egypt, gives general directions for how to lay out and decorate a temple (Wilson 2010: 793). Other works, some of which are listed and quoted in the temple at Edfu, explain why the temple is constructed the way it is, how its different parts are related, and how the whole thing works (Zinn 2011: 183–5).

Of course, the priestly scholars who wrote these texts did not make them easy to understand. They presented them in unusual and deliberately difficult hieroglyphic writing (understood only by skilled scribes like themselves) and expressed themselves in terse, allusive language (Baines 2007a: 334; Finnestad 1985: 20–1). This makes it doubly difficult for modern readers, who can only access its connotative context in a fragmentary way, if at all. Still, what can be gleaned from the texts and pictures on the walls of the Edfu temple provides us with a more or less coherent and enlightening key to understanding how an Egyptian temple worked and what it re-presented. It should be also be pointed out that, although Egyptian priestly scholars wrote many general works on temple design, study of individual buildings reveals that the basic template made sense only when interpreted in relation to specific natural and human environments (Wilson 2010: 793); we have already seen this principle at work in the temple at Medinet Habu.

Horus of Edfu, or Djeba (Watterson 1998: 45), was a form of the divine ancestor and motivating force of the Egyptian kings. His original home, in the prehistoric settlement of Nekhen (in Greek, Hierakonpolis), lay some fifteen kilometers to the north and was also located on the western side of the river (Kemp 1989: 37–41). The city of Edfu had existed since at least the mid-third millennium BCE and there was a New Kingdom temple on the site of the present structure. The present temple of Horus was apparently begun by Nectanebo II (361–343 BCE), one of the last native rulers of Egypt, who contributed the large black granite shrine in the sanctuary that holds the god's statue, although he may have simply placed it in the earlier temple. Work on the existing structure was begun by Ptolemy III Euergetes in 237 BCE (Watterson 1998: 46–7).

The temple complex at Edfu was, like the temple of Ramesses III at Medinet Habu, originally surrounded by a high mud-brick enclosure wall of roughly the same height (a portion of its southwestern corner still survives). Inside this enclosure would have been found many of the same installations that survive at Medinet Habu, including the sacred lake and extensive storage areas, traces of which still exist (Watterson 1998: 48–51). The Edfu temple did not have

Figure 3.4 Temple of Horus at Edfu. Sanctuary of the temple, showing the monolithic stone shrine that held the god's image that was the subject of the daily cult. The processional barque in front of the shrine is a modern replica.

a ceremonial palace but it did have a temple to the sacred falcon, a live bird worshiped in the temple as an avatar of Horus, who appeared in circumstances where a human ruler would originally have appeared (Fairman 1973: 46–7; Watterson 1998: 97–103).

The temple itself had the same basic layout (see Figure 3.5) as the one at Medinet Habu, although it was half as long again; however, its plan was far more compact and tightly organized. The proportions of the pylon were more elongated than the First Pylon at Medinet Habu, and it was considerably taller, with towers forty meters high (Watterson 1998: 52–3). There was only one courtyard, although it was rectangular rather than square, and longer than the combined area of the two courtyards and Second Pylon in the earlier temple. It was surrounded by a colonnade on three sides, with a screened colonnade giving onto the outer columned hall (Watterson 1998: 56, 67). According to the text in the temple describing the building (see below), the courtyard was known

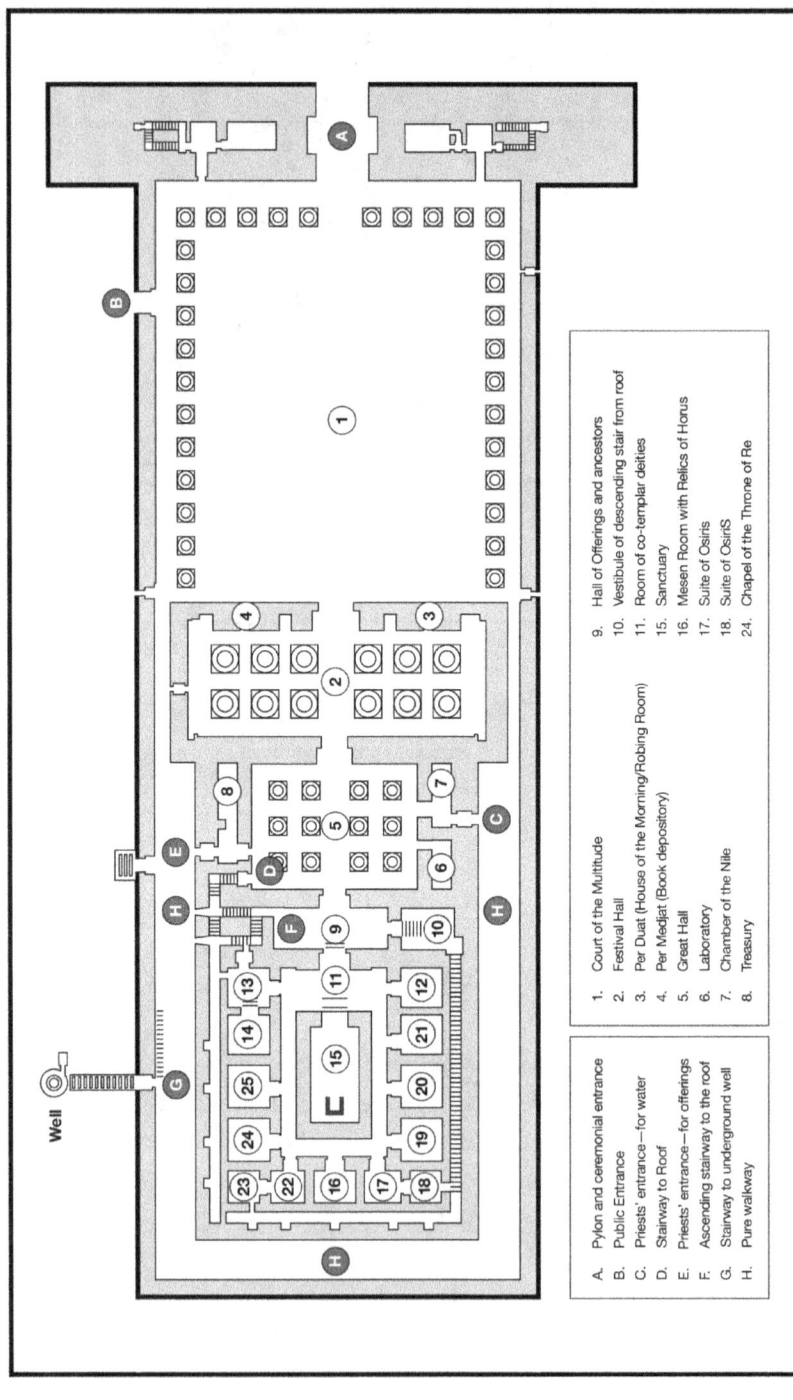

Figure 3.5 Plan of the temple of Horus at Edfu.

as the "court of the offerings" or the "court of the multitude" (Kurth 2004: 34, 60), because this was where food, drink and other items to be presented to the god were displayed on festival days. Members of the general public were permitted to gather here on festival days and make their own contributions to the god's bounty, as well as witness his public appearances (Murnane 1980b: 22; O'Connor 2012: 242; Wilson 2010: 791).

The main public entrance to the temple lay near the southeastern corner of the courtyard, a doorway that was connected to a pathway leading to the main river docks (Kurth 2004: 66; Watterson 1998: 51). The enclosing wall at Edfu was much closer to the temple than at Medinet Habu. It surrounded the main, northern part of the building on three sides before joining the wall around the courtyard. The narrow passageway between these walls was called the Pure Walkway (Kurth 2004: 65; Watterson 1998: 65–6), perhaps because it was reserved for the priests, whose own entrances to the temple were located on its east and west sides (Kurth 2004: 65–6). All the surfaces on the inside and outside of this wall, as well as the outer walls of the main temple building, were covered with texts and representations (Watterson 1998: 65).

The ancient description of the temple notes that the outer columned hall was higher than the rest of the main temple building, and wider (Kurth 2004: 65). It was well lit by the upper half of the screened colonnade (Watterson 1998: 67) and probably contained memorials of prominent local people, whose spirits could share in the offerings that devolved from the gods and the royal ancestors before they were actually consumed by the temple staff (Spencer 2010: 268, 272). Such spaces are often referred to as "festival halls" in other temples and

Figure 3.6 Temple at Edfu. Courtyard facing façade of the main temple, showing the screen wall separating the courtyard from the festival hall. The Pure Walkway is located between the back and side of the main temple and the surrounding wall.

may have been open to high-ranking members of the community as well as the priests (Spencer 1984: 84–5).

The whole of the inner part of the temple is referred to as the Great Seat (Watterson 1998: 48), although this term more specifically applies to the sanctuary itself and the shrine within it where the god rests, which sits at its heart (Goyon 1972: 33–57; Kurth 2004: 37ff., 60–1). The sanctuary consisted of a self-contained box-like building (Finnestad 1985: 12; Sauneron and Stierlen 1975: 104) that was surrounded on three sides by a narrow passageway, the "Mysterious Corridor" (Sauneron and Stierlin 1975: 36, 104–5; Watterson 1998: 70–2). Around this were arranged thirteen rooms, four on either side and five at the back. Directly behind the sanctuary was the *mesen* room, where especially powerful images of Horus as a falcon, along with the weapons that he used to defeat chaos, were housed (Finnestad 1985: 53; Kurth 2004: 58–60; Watterson 1998: 72–3). Adjacent to this on the east was the chapel of Hathor and, on the east side, the suite of Re and the chapel where food offerings were displayed. On the west side was the Osiris suite and rooms for gods associated with him.

The central hall in front of the sanctuary was where the images of the gods who shared the temple with Horus were kept (Kurth 2004: 57–61; Watterson 1998: 73). In front of this suite of rooms and opening into the central hall was the Hall of Offerings, where food and other gifts were offered to the gods, royal ancestors and honored dead before reverting to the god's living servants (Watterson 1998: 70). On either side of this hall were ascending and descending staircases that led to the roof.

In front of the Hall of Offerings was an inner columned hall, the Great Hall, off which service rooms connected to the priests' entrances opened on either side. On the west was the Chamber of the Nile, for storage of pure water, and the laboratory where incense and scented ointments used in the daily cult were prepared. On the other side was the treasury, where the precious objects, amulets and cultic tools where stored (Watterson 1998: 69). As the building inscription makes clear, the sanctuary and then the rest of the Great Seat were the first parts of the temple to be constructed. The outer hall, courtyard and pylon where added later, in succession (Kurth 2004: 49–53; Watterson 1998: 47–8).

Although mortuary temples were always aligned east–west, the direction in a cult temple was governed by where the god manifested in its local environment, most commonly in relation to the direction of the river (Wilson 2010: 794). Access to the Nile—the main artery of transportation in southern Egypt—was essential, for both the god's festival journeys and supplying the necessities for the cult and the people who performed it. Since the main channel of the river was generally bounded by natural levees (Butzer 1976: 15–18), docking facilities were usually found on feeder canals (Bunbury 2012: 16; Finnestad 1985: 16; Graham 2012: 21; Murnane 1980b: 6). Interestingly, Ptolemy III changed the orientation of the older temple of Horus from east–west to north–south, parallel to rather than facing the river. No obvious explanation is offered in the temple's copious inscriptions. It is likely that this orientation faced the temple toward the source of the Nile, also corresponding to the direction of the god's gaze from his sanctuary; the chapels of Re-Horakhty and Osiris were positioned on his left and right, corresponding to east and west rather than north and south, as at Medinet Habu.

According to Egyptian mythology, the source of the Nile was near the southern border of the country, at Yebu (in Greek, Elephantine) Island, just above the First Cataract, at modern Aswan (Hart 1986: 75–6). The whirlpools and eddies that formed around the island were the Nile flood—personified as the androgynous god Hapi—welling up out of the depths that connected with the waters of chaos (Ritner 2003a). The area was also the site of the great temple of Isis on Philae (in Egyptian, Pilak) Island, a structure that was also substantially added to by the early Ptolemaic rulers (Bagnall and Rathbone 2004: 242–5). Isis was also venerated at this period as the mother of Horus, protecting him from Set, the murderer of his father, Osiris. Since Osiris can be understood as the waters of the Nile flood (Assmann 2002: 409–11) as well as the father of the king, the changed orientation of the Horus temple can be seen to have continued significance in terms of regeneration—although in this case of the river and the land, rather than the setting and rising of the sun or the succession of one king by another.

The temple represented the cosmos and its daily cult the creation, but on an everyday level it was simply the house of the god. In fact, the Egyptian word for temple, *hut-netcher*, means just that (Finnestad 1985: 12–16; Wilson 2010: 769–79). It has been noted that the ground plan of the formal temple is very similar to that of the palace (O'Connor 1991), and these similarities can be easily studied at Medinet Habu. Both spaces have entrance halls and a columned hall where the king appeared, seated on a dais, or the god appeared when he left his temple during a festival. The balcony in front of the palace where the king appeared corresponds to the gateway of the temple, where the god appeared. Adjoining the throne room on each side were sleeping quarters and a bathroom. This whole area corresponds to the sanctuary of the temple, where during the daily cult ritual the god was woken up, fed and clothed every morning, as well as being offered meals at noon and in the evening, after which he was wrapped in cloths and returned to the shrine (Murnane 1980b: 69–73; O'Connor 2012: 231–2). The exclusivity of the back parts of the temple corresponds to the private parts of an upper-class house, although the homes of non-royal Egyptians did not exhibit the axial symmetry found in palaces and temples (Kemp 1989: 294–305; Roth 1993: 40–3, 45–8).

Like real houses, the house of the god had attached service areas outside the main building. These included silos for storage of grain and storerooms for other foods and materials, as well as food preparation areas, animal pens, abattoirs and areas for craft production (Kemp 1989: 277–81, 294–300). Like the king's palace, the larger gods' houses contained an institute of higher learning, known as the House of Life. The House of Life trained students in the literate arts as well as other areas of higher learning, such as architecture, painting, sculpture, music, dance and medicine, all of which were practiced in the service of the gods and the world order they had created. Each temple possessed an extensive library, the contents of which were listed on their walls and occasionally survive in fragmentary condition. At Edfu, books currently in use for the rituals and festivals being celebrated were placed in a depository called the House of Books (*per medjat*) in the outer hall of the temple, conveniently adjacent to the House of the Morning, where the acting prophet was purified before entering the sanctuary (Zinn 2011: 188, 191).

As in an upper-class house, only high-status individuals used the front door; everyone else used the service entrances. Only the god and the king used the main entrance between the pylons on great festive occasions (Murnane 1980b: 1; O'Connor 2012: 242), when other members of the procession may have been permitted to follow them through. Four entrances designated for members of the public were found at Edfu, on either side of the forecourt. Three side doors into the main temple building were designated for priests performing various functions (Kurth 2004: 65–6). The house of the god, like that of an upper-class person, was supplied with trees, gardens and pools, as we have seen at Medinet Habu (O'Connor 2012: 233, 235–6).

However, the idea of the god's temple as a house is only the shallowest of the many levels of understanding the Egyptians had of the sacred space. There were essentially three levels of meaning in the interpretation of a temple: functional, theological and integrative. The functional level is more or less self-explanatory; it refers to the activities performed in the temple as a whole and its various parts. The theological level refers to the deeper significance of those activities, which could be mythological, poetic or philosophical. The integrative level refers to understanding how the parts of the temple worked together as a whole on both a functional and a higher level. In later temples such as Edfu, the theological dimension is always the most important (Kurth 1994: 33). An important text for understanding the temple is inscribed in a band that goes right around the lower wall of the main building, celebrating the inauguration of the structure and its acceptance by the god as his residence during the reign of Ptolemy X Alexander I, around 100 BCE. It goes on to describe all the spaces in the temple, their dimensions and purpose, and how they are connected with one another (Kurth 2004: 1–3, 44–67). The measurements given for the rooms are so accurate that only small discrepancies between this plan and the actual temple can be discerned (Cauville and Devauchelle 1984; cf. Zinn 2011: 185–7).

On a ritual, performative level, the temple was articulated by the priests and other persons who acted within it (Finnestad 1985: 8–10, 13–14, 74–5, 101–2). On an architectural level it was articulated by the spatial forms that made up the physical building. On a discursive level it was articulated by the texts and images that covered its surfaces. The texts and images rigorously and exhaustively explicated the axial symmetry of the building as a re-presentation of an Egypt-centered universe in a minutely plotted layout. Everything flowed in two directions from the back wall of the central sanctuary, the same point where the god's power moved out of the back of the building toward the place of public prayer (or where the spirit of the divine king entered and departed). Here the two opposing streams of the decorative program and its main subject—the king's daily offerings to the god—met, with the scenes back to back. From this point flowed the meaning of each side of the temple, as Upper and Lower Egypt or the right and left banks of the Nile, extending outwards to the four directions to encompass the rest of the world. Everything on one side of the temple was thematically, artistically, conceptually and geographically mirrored in the other (Wilson 2010: 794–5).

The temple presented time as well as space, in terms of daily, monthly, seasonal and yearly cycles, even going back to the origins of the cosmos. The pylon gateway represented the horizon, or *akhet*, over which the sun rose and set every day. As the temple replicated in miniature the Egypt-centered cosmos, this gate signified the mountains that bounded each side of the Nile Valley in Upper Egypt, supplying the original image behind the hieroglyphic sign for "foreign lands." According to this viewpoint, Egypt and the rule of *maat* ended where the Nile flood could not penetrate (Finnestad 1985: 910; O'Connor 2012: 239–40; Wilson 2010: 791–2). The horizon was where the sun appeared in the morning and was also a powerful metaphor for rebirth and renewal. When the god in the sanctuary was woken up every morning at sunrise, according to the hymns inscribed there, he appeared on his horizon like the sun arising from the underworld (Blackman and Fairman 1941).

The daily ritual also related to the myth of Osiris and his rebirth. The acting priest assumed the identity of his son, who was responsible for his mummification and burial, which brought about resurrection. This was achieved by swathing the deceased in linen bandages and reviving him by anointing his limbs with precious ointments and imparting the breath of life with the smell of incense (in Egyptian, literally "that which causes divinity") (David 1981: 63–71; Moret [1902] 1988: 72–3). These operations were also central to the daily cult, along with the offering of food and drink and the gift of *maat* (Spencer 2010: 260; Wilson 2010: 799). Like Osiris, the god also waxed and waned with the moon every month, and his yearly resurrection at the end of the flood was guaranteed by the rites performed in the Osiris room, to the right of the main sanctuary, as at Medinet Habu (O'Connor 2012: 236, 260–4; Watterson 1998: 72–3).

The god also attained earthly life when he appeared periodically in public on his processional barque, along with his wife, Hathor, and their son Harsomtus— the Horus who unites the two lands, Upper and Lower Egypt (Watterson 1998: 52). In the later temples, the separate barque shrines in front of the sanctuary were dispensed with and the gods' processional boat shrines were kept in the enlarged sanctuary, where the cult was performed for all the divine images within, along with those in the surrounding rooms (Fairman 1954: 70, 80).

The temple as the place of creation of the world as we know it

The Egyptian idea of creation is mythopoeic and narrative but, like similar stories in other cultures as well as scientific hypotheses, it is based on observation of the human and natural environment. In this environment, creation is a recurring event—it has happened before and may well happen again. This way of understanding origins runs counter to most of our ideas about it.

It relates to the seasonal and agricultural experiences of people who lived up and down the Nile River Valley and in the Delta, rather than some abstract idea of time. It also relates to how they experienced the spaces in which they lived. Most people seldom traveled beyond the environs of their town or village, which was, for them, the world. Just as the cosmos was bounded by the hills on either side of the Valley, so the world that the creator brought into existence was that of the town and the surrounding countryside, with the temple at its center (Finnestad 1985: 49–51).

The creation of the universe and the temple at Edfu by a form of Horus is the subject of one of the most important texts in this temple, The Enumeration of the Mounds of the First Time, which is carved on the inside of the surrounding wall (Finnestad 1985: 24–5). The text begins by describing the chaotic flood, which at first threatening and destructive, becomes calm. Then a tangle of reeds appears in the water, and a falcon alights on them. In place of the falcon, Apy—a great winged sun—appears, and with light, space is revealed. Through the agency of Apy, the gods and the land, in the form of mounds rising out of the water, come into existence. These mounds are named as the places making up the region of Edfu, and the first floating reeds (*djeba*) as the shrine of Horus in his sanctuary in the temple of Edfu (Djeba). First the watery chaos and then the swampy wasteland are pacified. Agricultural land is created. The world ordered according to *maat* has been created (Finnestad 1985: 25–56).

Two important observations can be made about this description of the creation. First, the watery chaos clearly represents the yearly inundation of the Nile and the stages that it goes through, from threatening to pacific, before it recedes after fertilizing the fields (Finnestad 1985: 42). The second is that the world created is an agricultural landscape, consisting of land bounded by levees and divided by canals, with sites of habitation constructed on mounds above the flood. It is not a "natural" landscape but one created by human agency. Humans play an important part in creation, and as we have seen, they maintain it through an agreement of mutual gift-giving with the gods (Finnestad 1985: 44–5, 51, 78, 120–1). In addition, it is also obvious that the sanctuary at the heart of the temple is the site of creation. In the morning hymn at the front of the sanctuary, the god is said to alight on the floating reeds, which are his "seat," the sanctuary where his cult is celebrated every day. In other words, the enactment of the cult also repeats the first occasion of creation. This is presented in concrete form by the temple itself (Finnestad 1985: 52–6, 64, 99–101).

As explained in the building inscription, the spaces inside the temple expand as we move out from the center, beginning with the small area inside the black granite shrine that contains the cult statue of the god (Finnestad 1985: 64; Kurth 2004: 57–66). This is because the appearance of Apy, the winged sun, brings about not only the appearance of things within space but the space itself. As we look into the temple from the entrance to the pylon and move through the courtyard into the main temple building, we see the image of the winged sun carved over each doorway, right back to the sanctuary. What we are seeing is a kind of stop-motion animation of how the god's flight "brings to light" the cosmos, with its ever broadening space expanding through the sanctuary, the

Mysterious Corridor, the Hall of Offerings, the inner Great Hall, the outer hall and the courtyard, before it bursts over the pylon gateway in the first dazzling sunrise (Finnestad 1985: 111–12). The god's flight brings to light not only the space of the cosmos but also what is contained in it. It is summarized in all the entities shown on the interior walls of the temple, which are also illuminated every morning, when the doors are opened, by the sun in the outer world (Fairman 1954: 176). The interior of the temple reveals to us the world at the beginning of creation, while its exterior presents its finished state.

Inside the main temple building, the outer hall was illuminated by the open upper half of the screened colonnade whose central doorway opened onto the courtyard. The inner columned hall received light when the outer central doorway was opened, as did the central rooms of the Great Seat; additional light was provided by carefully positioned openings in the roof. However, the inner rooms at the back of the Mysterious Corridor received no natural light at all and had to rely on artificial illumination. The lighting of a candle in the *mesen* room (behind the main sanctuary) at the beginning of the morning ritual was the cultic equivalent of the appearance of light at the beginning of creation (Finnestad 1985: 12, 94–8). All the ceilings of the main temple building were decorated with stars and images of the sky goddess, representing not the night sky but the cosmos before the existence of light (Finnestad 1985: 12–13).

It has been suggested that the introduction of light into these spaces replicated the original creative act that caused them, and what they contained, to appear. The pillared halls and the courtyard presented a chaotic marshy landscape rather than a civilized, cultivated one. The columns, which occupied the space in a claustrophobic way, took the form of marsh plants such as papyrus and reeds. The floor of the temple was imagined to be a watery swamp, with a waterline painted on the base of the columns; the courtyard surrounded by such columns suggested a swampy pool. Thus the temple was not a static cosmic map but a dynamic entity where creation was ritually produced each day. No wonder it had to be so carefully protected (Finnestad 1985: 11–12, 84).

The main subject represented on the temple walls is ritual acts performed by the king for the gods (Kurth 1994: 51–2). These are to be found on the three central registers in the middle of each wall surface. Below is a procession of figures carrying agricultural produce, in the form of either the goddess of the fields or the androgynous male Nile god. These represent all the provinces of Egypt led by the king, fulfilling his part of the contract between humanity and the gods for maintenance of the cosmos. Placed at the foot of the wall, this bottom register represents the earthly, agricultural foundation of life. On the outer walls of the temple, bands of inscriptions between the upper and lower borders of the central ritual scenes relate to the stability of the temple, such as the descriptive building text discussed above (Finnestad 1985: 122–3; Kurth 1994: 55–7; Wilson 2010: 795–6).

The upper decorative friezes often consist of patterns that use the names of the king combined with protective or other meaningful signs to form a kind of rebus pattern. The purpose of this frieze was not just to protect the king but also to weave his name and being into the fabric of the temple (Kurth 1994: 56). At Medinet Habu this was accomplished by positioning the king's name in very large letters around doorways and on the tops of walls (O'Connor 2012: 259). Inside the Edfu temple, the uppermost decorative frieze made use of groups of hieroglyphic signs to indicate the use or higher purpose of the room in which they were placed. For example, the book depository in the outer hall had a frieze with a design that combined Thoth and Seshat, the god and goddess of writing, with the king's name; over the doorway was carved a giant scribe's palette (Zinn 2011: 193–4).

As noted above, protective motifs played an important role on the outside walls of the temple. Images of the falcon on the upper decorative friezes frequently had lion, bull or snake heads to more clearly convey their apotropaic function (Kurth 1994: 64). The images of the king and gods in the central ritual zone were depicted in a single gigantic frieze, on a scale calculated to repel the agents of chaos as well as to impress the general public (Finnestad 1985: 12, 136–41; Murnane 1980b: 7). Indeed, a number of such images, both here and in earlier New Kingdom temples, became the subject of a spontaneous public cult in which the image was embellished with gold and semiprecious stones and protected by a veil attached to the wall with temporary supports (Brand 2007).

Inside the wall, along the Pure Walkway, a number of the depictions of ritual performances referred to Horus's defeat of his enemy Set, who represented the forces of chaos (Watterson 1998: 65–7, 112–21) and especially the infrequent but violent rainstorms that occur in desert areas. Even waterspouts, in the form of lion-shaped gargoyles, were explicitly labeled as Horus in lion form, throwing his enemy, the rain, harmlessly to the ground (Kurth 1994: 32–4). Though the infrequent downpours could do little real damage to a stone temple, it must be remembered that they could completely destroy the mud-brick houses in which most Egyptians lived (Burke 2012).

The story of the defeat of Set by his nephew (in older versions, his brother) Horus was also an important theme of kingly legitimacy (Kurth 1994: 33–8), as well as relating to the concept of *maat* as legal justice. When Horus, whose spirit

Figure 3.7 Temple at Edfu. The façade of the pylon, showing emplacements for the flagstaffs, as well as scenes of the king dispatching his enemies before Horus.

was in every king, succeeded his father, Osiris, he was the legitimate ruler. When he defeated Set, the would-be usurper, order triumphed over chaos. When the gods, sitting as a legal tribunal, recognized Horus as the legitimate heir, justice was done. In Egyptian, all these concepts—legal succession, triumph of order and justice—were represented by one word: *maat*. Maat signified the cosmic ordering principle of the world and was one of the main themes of the temple, as can be seen on the front of the pylon (Kurth 1994: 32, 35, 37–8).

Since the later Ptolemies, unlike Ramesses III, had no great military victories to celebrate, their scenes of triumph over enemies are all conventional symbolic ones, such as those found on the front of the Medinet Habu First Pylon, which show the king grabbing a bunch of his enemies by the hair and clubbing them. This motif went back to prehistoric times (Kemp 1989: 38–43; Murnane 1980b: 19–20; Watterson 1998: 56). Around this emblematic scene are placed smaller tableaux that depict Horus's defeat of Set in the form of a hippopotamus (also found elsewhere in the temple) and his vindication by the tribunal of the gods (Kurth 1994: 38). This theme is reinforced in the magical protection against Set provided by the four great cedar flagstaffs that flanked the gateway on either side. These were identified in accompanying texts as Isis and Nephthys, the wife and sister of Osiris, who stab the rain god in the sky and render him harmless. This theme relates to the balcony over the central doorway, where the sacred falcon was displayed as the avatar of kingship, in a festival that immediately followed the one celebrating the resurrection of Osiris at the beginning of the growing season (Kurth 1994: 34–5; Watterson 1998: 100).

Thus the temple at Edfu shows itself, through its texts, visual decoration and arrangement of space, as a re-presentation of the cosmos, a house of the god, and a thriving economic and social center. At its heart were the ritual performances and festivals that made it an effective mechanism for perpetuation of world order, be it in a religious or a cultural sense. This is what we are attempting to reproduce in the virtual temple, with the aid of mixed virtual and live performances such as the Egyptian Oracle.

Part Two

The Performance

4

Technical Description

Jeffrey Jacobson

This chapter describes the Egyptian Oracle performance in enough detail to provide a coherent view of the performance. It includes discussion of the characters, the narrative, dramaturgy, use of space, software, hardware and how we arrived at key design decisions.

Most of the historical evidence underpinning the Egyptian Oracle can be found in Chapter 1. Chapter 3, "The Virtual Temple of Horus and Its Egyptian Prototypes," describes the setting for the drama and its historical underpinnings. Chapter 5, "Mixed Reality Theater and the Egyptian Oracle Project," describes the performance from a dramaturgical point of view and places it in the context of theater performances that mix physical and virtual space. Chapter 7, "Puppetry and Virtual Theater," describes the nature and history of mechanical and digital puppetry, of which the Egyptian Oracle is a part.

Setting and dramatis personae

The scenario depicted in the performance takes place in a temple of Horus in a town somewhere in Egypt in the fourth century BCE. As noted in Chapter 1, while there is evidence for the existence of the processional oracle into late antiquity, most of it comes from the late second and early first millennium BCE. We placed the ceremony at the beginning of the Ptolemaic period, because it was a time of cultural change and interaction led by Egypt's Hellenistic rulers, which is accessible to our audiences in schools, universities and museums. Our educational goal for participants to become more open to other cultures and to learn about ancient Egypt's tradition of religious theater. Although other types of oracular consultation are known at this period, the interactive character of the processional oracle best suits our basic pedagogical purposes, as well as the medium of virtual reality.

The Egyptian Oracle performance described in this book was intended to be a prototype. It was produced on a relatively small budget, assisted by generous donations of time and resources, including the pre-existing virtual temple of Horus (Chapter 9). Because of this, our oracle ceremony is much less grand than the oracle of Amun described in Chapter 1. We have only one priest, one sacred barque (boat) with minimal decoration and simplified construction, a minimum number of *wab* priests carrying it, and so on. Nevertheless, building it answered our basic technical questions and proved the efficacy of our approach. We successfully staged the drama in a mixed virtual/physical space, gained audience acceptance, and demonstrated the performance's worth as an educational tool (see Chapter 6).

The other, non-virtual actors in the drama are the live actress, audience volunteers who play small parts, and the audience that participates as a whole. We describe them all below.

The sacred barque of Horus

In the narrative, the spirit of the god inhabits the divine image in the shrine on the barque. In response to a humble query from the high priest, the god miraculously moves the barque and the priests carrying it are pulled along.

Figure 4.1a The virtual sacred barque of the god Horus.

Figure 4.1b The barque of Khonsu as depicted in the temple at Medinet Habu. Courtesy of the Oriental Institute of the University of Chicago 1930, 1934, 1957: pl. 193.

Its movements are a simpler version of the oracle's expressions of approval, disapproval and choice as described in the oracular texts (see pages 38 to 46).

Figure 4.1a shows the sacred barque as it appears to the audience, projected onto a video screen or wall (see "Physical setup"). We developed its appearance partly by selecting key features from the barque of Khonsu depicted in wall art at Medinet Habu (Figure 4.1b). We also referred to other scholars' reconstructions of ceremonial barques (Landström 1970: 120–1; Traunecker, Le Saout and Masson 1981: pl. 28). Dr. Gillam made the final judgments on which features were most essential and our artist, David Hopkins, did as much as he could. The image in Figure 4.1a has been modified from the original screenshot for illustrative purposes; it does not necessarily represent the current state of the software.

An important design decision was to depict both the barque and the *wab* priests carrying it in a stylized way. We wanted them to look as consistent as possible with the scene in the Saite Oracle papyrus (Černý 1962) and the artwork found at Medinet Habu (Oriental Institute 1930, 1934, 1957), such as the Festival of Sokar processional (Murnane 1980b: 26–39). We did not want to represent the Egyptian Oracle ceremony with any kind of false realism but instead to visualize its mythic form as the Egyptians themselves described it. It also avoids the "uncanny valley" effect (Mori 2012) in which the human figures are real enough to be creepy and disturbing. As we have it, the procession blends in well with its surroundings, the virtual temple of Horus.

The sacred barque and its carriers together form a single "puppet" with several basic movements that are under the control of its operator. (See page 126).

The high priest

Like the sacred barque, the representation of the temple's high priest, Petiese, is stylized (see Figure 4.2), much like the depictions of priests in the temple wall art and the Saite Oracle papyrus (Černý 1962). Specifically we made Petiese resemble the First Prophet Menkheperre as he appears on his stela, standing before the god to ask questions (Von Beckerath 1968: pl. 1). However, we gave him a shaven head, because we must assume that he is exercising his priestly role in a state of bodily purity. See Chapter 1 for background and details.

During scenes in which the priest appears, he does not walk but only turns to bow to the divine image of the god inside the shrine on the sacred barque. Most of the time he is standing facing both the audience and the actress, but he never turns his back on the oracle (Kruchten 1987: 7–8). This is why he walks backward as he leads the procession during the scene transitions. (See page 126 for a fuller discussion of the priest's movements.)

Figure 4.2 The high priest, Petiese.

The chief temple musician, Atumirdis

During Egypt's late period, many of the musicians in temples were women (Onstine 2001: 82–4). We created the character Atumirdis, the chief musician of the temple, to be played by a live actress. In full costume, with her voice amplified by the sound system, she is part of the Egyptian content, but she also occupies the physical space with the audience. As explained below, she plays a key role in the narrative as a character, acting as an intermediary between the audience and the virtual world, introducing them to the temple and helping them play their parts as members of the Egyptian populace. She also bridges the physical and virtual worlds by interacting with the animated high priest, Petiese. Most important, she facilitates communication between the audience and the virtual priest. Most of the time she stands to one side of the projection screen showing the temple, the priest and the sacred barque (see Figure 0.1).

Figure 4.3 Musicians. Relief from the tomb of Djed-nefer, 4th century BCE, Heliopolis. Maspero 1890: pl. 11.

Audience volunteers

Just before the show, organizers select a number of audience volunteers for small parts in the drama. Each part is described on a role card. Some cards are unique but others have multiple copies, so several people may have the same or very similar roles. For example, there is only one accused water thief but two disputing homeowners. The role cards are as follows:

- **Retiring mayor** (one card): You have served the people of the town for years and now wish to retire. Today the oracle will choose your replacement. When it is time, stand and accept the gratitude of the people and after the oracle chooses the next mayor, wish them luck.
- **Candidate mayors** (two or three cards): Today the town's mayor of many years is retiring. You are one of several potential candidates to replace him. Simply being considered as a candidate is an honor. When called to do so, move to the front of the room and place this paper on the ground in front of the oracle's boat and step back. If you are chosen, stay to receive your mark of office before you sit down.
- **Ascending priest** (many cards): You are a junior member of the priesthood and have excelled in your studies. Your teachers feel it is time to ask Horus if you should move up a level in the temple, taking on new responsibilities.
- **Homeowners with collapsed wall** (two cards): You have a lovely home, which shares a wall with your neighbors. They do nothing to take care of it on their side, and it finally collapses. You will be called to stand in front of the sacred boat, and Horus will decide whether you or they will pay for the repairs. When the Priest asks you questions, do not accuse your neighbors, but defend your own conduct.
- **Accused water thief** (one card): You have been accused of stealing water from the neighboring fields for your own field. This is a very serious crime, but you know you are innocent. You will be called to declare your innocence. Stand your ground but be respectful.
- **Asking for a blessing** (two cards): After the god has addressed public business, he may choose to accept personal petitions. You wish to ask for a blessing from the god for your child. To begin, make your request to the High Priest with great ceremony.

Last but not least, the entire audience is expected to play the roles of ancient Egyptians at the oracle ceremony. As you will see in the narrative below, they are immediately given a way to express their excitement, using Egyptian-style "applause." Later they are allowed to pose questions to the oracle. Generally they can feel that they are part of the show vicariously, through the volunteers mentioned above.

Physical setup

The dominant prop of the performance is a projection of the virtual Egyptian temple onto a wall or large screen—a theoretical extension of the physical room into virtual space. In all the scenes the priest is on the right side in the virtual space, while the barque of the god is roughly in the center or to the left. The live actress stands slightly to the left of the screen, where she can engage with both the priest and the audience. The puppeteer who controls the priest avatar is hidden away but can see the audience through a webcam at the front of the room (see Figure 4.4).

The projection screen can be a standard pull-down or fixed-location movie screen—the kind found in classrooms, auditoriums and movie theaters—or it

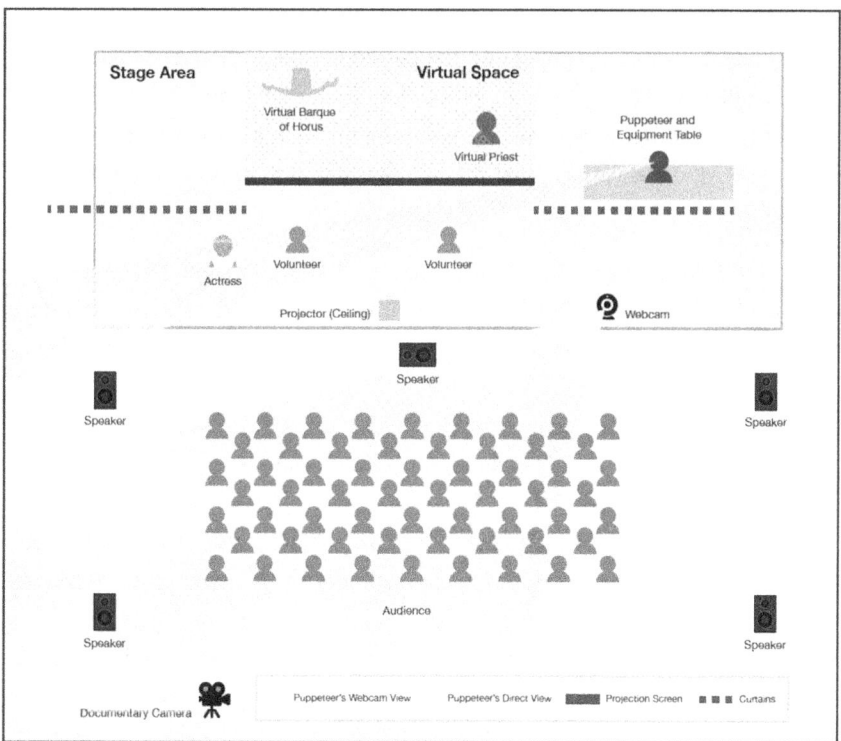

Figure 4.4 Physical arrangement of the equipment and participants.

can be a white wall or any other suitable projection surface. Ideally the projector is mounted on the ceiling, out of the way so that the actors can get reasonably close to it without casting shadows. The less projection distance required by the projector the better. Alternatively, the projector can be behind a screen made of rear-projection material; that eliminates shadows, but rear-projection screens are rare in public venues and require space behind the screen.

The curtains are partially drawn to cover the edges of the screen but are slightly in front of it. From where the puppeteer is sitting, he or she can see the space immediately in front of the screen, which is where the actress usually directs audience volunteers to stand during their parts in the performance. (It also allows them to see the puppeteer, but that does not seem to detract from the performance.) A webcam gives the puppeteer a second way to view the audience, as shown in Figure 4.4. It has a fairly wide angle of view and is motorized, so it can be rotated during the performance.

The equipment table shown in Figure 4.4 holds the following:

- the main computer, usually a laptop, generating what the audience sees on the screen (the puppeteer sees the same view on the computer screen);
- a controller, plugged into the main computer, that the puppeteer uses to manipulate both the puppet and the sacred barque; we used an Xbox 360 controller (Xbox 2013), as described later in this chapter;
- a second laptop that controls the webcam and displays what it sees; and
- the control panel (mixer) that the puppeteer uses to adjust the sound system.

A powerful but low-cost six-speaker surround-sound system (Nambiar 2011; Nambiar and Jacobson 2012) produces dramatic sound effects and music, including an ambient sound and music track to create a greater sense of immersion. The actress and puppeteer both wear mobile microphones so that their voices are amplified to be heard above the ambient sound. Finally, in larger venues the actress has a hand-held mobile microphone she can pass to audience members.

Figure 4.4 also shows the theoretical or illusory locations of the temple, priest and boat, treating virtual space as an extension of the physical space. We create the illusion of extended space partly through the placement of these elements. Similarly, Figure 4.6 illustrates the performance as existing in a single space that is partly real and partly virtual. However, it is the way the actress and the virtual priest interact with each other and with the audience that really ties the spaces together and makes the virtual space seem real.

Much depends on the skill of the puppeteer, who can make the digital priest point to an audience member or turn his head in that person's direction. To do this, he or she integrates three different views: the gap between curtain and screen, the webcam display and the monitor showing the audience's view. From those views, the puppeteer constructs a coherent mental image of the mixed physical and virtual space and everyone in it in order to orient the puppet correctly. He or she must simultaneously maintain a mental image of what the audience is experiencing *and* simulate the character of the priest. Like many other art forms, puppeteering is democratic in the sense that anyone can do it, even with digital puppets such as these. However, significant training is required to successfully carry out a performance such as this. See Chapter 7 for an in-depth look at the evolution of mechanical and digital puppetry and its implications for the Egyptian Oracle Project.

Narrative structure and key moments

In this section we provide an overview of the narrative for the overall performance and focus on key moments. We include samples of the narrative that have been simplified from the actual performance. The puppet's movements and the scene changes afforded by the software still leave plenty of room for variation in the script and the audience interactions. The full storyboard from which the actors worked is published in Jacobson (2011b: 44–58).

When we are gathering evaluation data during a performance, we ask audience members for permission to videotape them, to fill out a questionnaire afterward, and so forth (this is described in more detail in Chapter 6). After the role cards are distributed, and sometimes a few words from a host or sponsor, the play begins.

Introduction to the temple

The play begins with the audience facing the front of the temple, projected onto the background screen as a simple flat image (see Figure 9.1). The live actress introduces herself, saying, "Hello, and welcome to the temple of Horus. I am Atumirdis, the chief musician, and we are gathered here to celebrate the New Year." She wears a historically accurate costume and uses a small microphone that amplifies her voice through the sound system, combining it with the ambient soundtrack. The effect is to create an auditory illusion of a large stone temple.

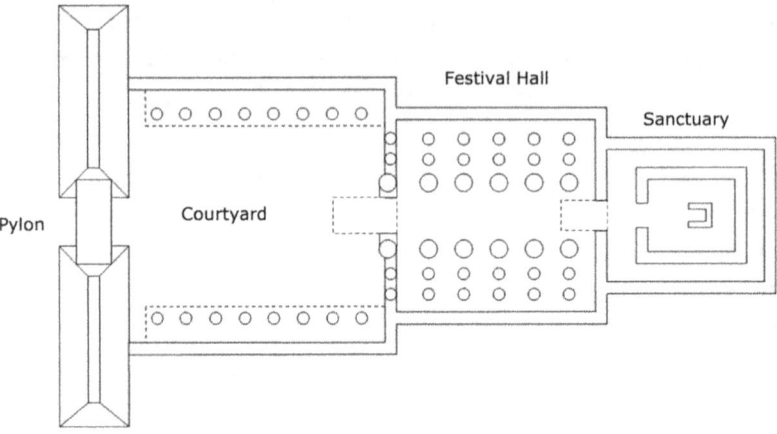

Figure 4.5 Virtual temple layout.

In the next three scenes Atumirdis takes the audience through the temple, describing what they see: first the pylon gate at the front, next the courtyard, and then the festival hall (see Figure 4.5). As each scene changes, the camera view moves forward and stops at a spot until the next scene change. Each transition is completely automated, triggered by the puppeteer activating a simple control. At this stage the audience is seeing the temple as an architectural space, depicted as one might see it in a film.

When the projection viewpoint is in the courtyard, Atumirdis shows the audience how to perform "Egyptian-style applause." The women put their hands in the air and ululate, and the men make a lower *aahhh* sound while beating their chests. The "applause" is directly analogous to the repeating of "amen" in Judaeo-Christian ceremonies and affirmations in other religious proceedings. This action is based on the *henu* gesture, an ancient performance often attributed to gods and ancestral spirits in Egyptian art and literature. A recent study (Stone 1998) that elucidates the gesture with modern ethnographic parallels is the basis for our reconstruction. It gives the audience a way to participate, albeit minimally, in the action later.

Breaking the fourth wall

In the fourth scene we see the procession come out of the inner sanctuary and into the festival hall. The high priest, Petiese, leads the sacred barque, which is carried by eight lower-ranking priests. The barque carries a shrine wrapped in a semi-transparent veil of the finest linen. In the shrine stands or sits the divine image imbued with the spirit of the god Horus.

This transition is completely automated, triggered when the puppeteer presses a key on the keyboard. As he leads the barque, the high priest walks backward, entreating the god to come forward. The procession stops in the middle of the projected view of the Festival Hall. The priest turns to face the audience and recites a prayer, an extract from the "Wisdom of Ani" (Lichtheim 1976: 137, 131):

> Do not raise your voice in the house of God,
> He abhors shouting;
> Pray by yourself with a loving heart,
> Whose every word is hidden.
> He will grant your needs,
> He will hear your words,
> He will accept your offerings.
> Libate for your father and mother,
> Who are resting in the valley;
> When the gods witness your action,
> They will say: "Accepted."
> Do not forget the one outside,
> Your son will act for you likewise.
> Offer to your god.
> Beware of offending him.
> Do not question his images.
> Do not accost him when he appears.
> Do not jostle him in order to carry him.
> Do not disturb the oracles.
> Be careful, help to protect him.
> Let your eye watch out for his wrath.
> And kiss the ground in his name.
> He gives power in a million forms.
> He who magnifies him is magnified.
> God of this earth is the sun in the sky,
> While his images are on earth;
> When incense is given them as daily food,
> The lord of risings is satisfied.

Figure 4.6 Priest puppet (in the festival hall) and live actress communicate across the "fourth wall" of the virtual stage.

At this point, the action on the screen is still film-like, but then the actress addresses the high priest by name. She asks him a question and he responds, beginning a dialogue:

> ATUMIRDIS: O honored servant of the god, what business will be brought before the great god Horus today?
> PETIESE: Ah, Atumirdis. Our great mayor who has served us so well, lo these many years, is ready to retire. Where is our mayor today?
> ATUMIRDIS: Will the mayor, who has the yellow card, please stand up and receive thanks from the community? We know how to do that, right?
> *The audience volunteer stands up. The men beat their chests and the women ululate.*
> ATUMIRDIS: Thank you for so many years of service! You may now take a seat.

This breaks the fourth wall between the virtual and the physical space, creating a mixed reality. Interestingly, this could also be implemented by using carefully timed video and good acting. One of our research questions for the future is whether and at what point the audience perceives the virtual space as an extension of the physical space. However, that perception is not strictly necessary. We know from live shows that a small puppet in front of a flat background can still support an engaging interactive narrative.

The oracle selects a new mayor

It is plausible that the oracle would select a mayor during this time in Egypt's history. In an ancient text Thutmose III described how the oracle chose him to be king (Černý 1962: 35).

When the first dialogue is over, the priest and actress begin another that includes audience volunteers. As with the previous dialogue, the one presented here is condensed for simplicity and economy of space. In the actual performance the actors and audience members ad-lib their lines and sometimes banter. Here the word *résumé* is an artifice we added to make sure the action is crystal clear to a modern audience.

> HIGH PRIEST: Now the time has come for a new mayor to be chosen. Will the candidates place their résumés before Horus?
> ATUMIRDIS: Who here wishes to be the new mayor? If you have brought your résumé, the mayor candidate card, please come forward. Place your résumés before Horus and stand over here to await his decision.

Two to four audience members have received the role card for mayoral candidate. Atumirdis brings them forward to stand to one side while placing the cards, which represent their résumés. The actress guides the candidate mayors to place their résumés at predetermined "strike points": places on the floor in front of the screen marked with tape. This helps the puppeteer know exactly where they are located.

Historically the Egyptians wrote the names of things or declarations on pieces of papyrus or chips of limestone (ostraca) and placed them on the ground before the oracle. The oracle might then select one by leaning toward it or show displeasure by leaning or moving away from it (see Chapter 1). Often the petitioners gave the oracle two things from which to choose.

> HIGH PRIEST: And now the great god Horus shall choose.

The puppeteer activates a control that makes the boat move and dip down toward the right or left side of the screen, pointing to one of the résumés. (The movement of the boat is similar to what is shown in Figure 4.9, below.) If the result is ambiguous, the actress declares one of the résumés to be chosen.

> HIGH PRIEST (*to the volunteer whose résumé was chosen*): Horus has chosen you for a great honor. You are now responsible for the welfare of the people. Let us all celebrate.
> ATUMIRDIS: Congratulations to the new mayor of the town! Let us celebrate

our new mayor with Egyptian-style applause! (*The audience applauds as described above.*)

HIGH PRIEST: In addition to the change in the town's leadership, members of our community will now receive a great honor. Will all of the young acolytes please stand.

Everyone with an "ascending priest" card stands, prompted by the actress if necessary. The puppeteer presses another control that causes the barque to move forward and up, a gesture of approval from the oracle. The actress leads another round of applause.

HIGH PRIEST: And now there are important matters to conduct in the courtyard.

Next there is a scene change from the festival hall to the courtyard, arranged as shown in Figure 4.7. This time the audience viewpoint moves to follow the procession from the festival hall to the courtyard.

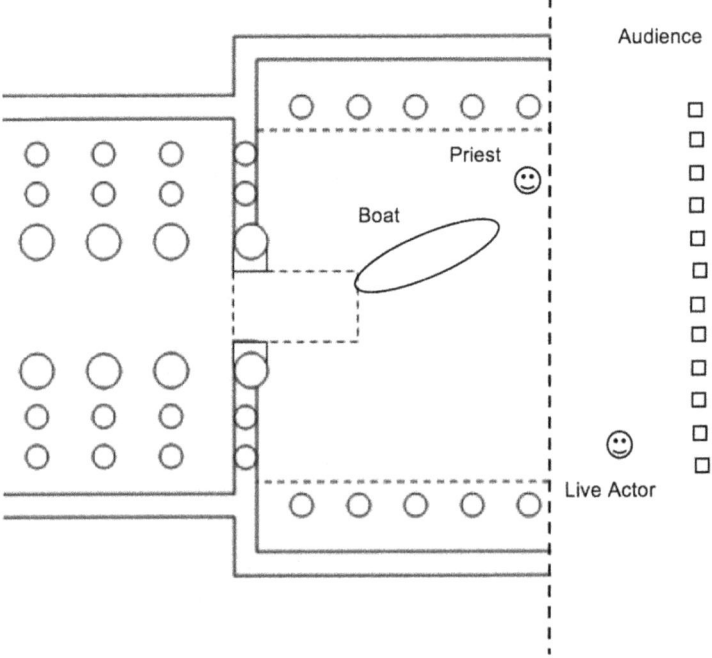

Figure 4.7 Layout of the mixed reality space in the sixth scene.

Dispute over a shared wall

Once in the courtyard, the high priest says, "Who has an audience before Horus?"

> ATUMIRDIS: An enormous hole has opened up in the wall between two houses, and neither of the owners will take responsibility for it. Today Horus will decide who will fix the wall. Can the two neighbors who are here please come forward?

During this time in Egypt's history, the oracle was used to resolve many types of disputes such as this (see Chapter 1). The two volunteers with the "disputing neighbor" cards come forth and Atumirdis guides them into position. One stands to the left of the screen and the other stands to the right. Petiese repeats the charges and interrogates the litigants (see Figure 0.1). The volunteers invent their own dialogue, generally simple denials and claims of good behavior. The priest responds in kind.

Finally the high priest says, "O great Horus, we await your decision!" The barque then moves to point to the left or the right as the puppeteer chooses (Figure 0.1).

> HIGH PRIEST: The great god Horus has ruled that *you* (*points to the chosen person*) will repair the wall and pay the damages. Everyone in the community will check their walls for weakness or damage. By the divine principle of *maat*—the harmony of all things—we must each follow the law and contribute to the community. (*Atumirdis leads another round of applause.*)

It is especially interesting and important that the volunteer shown in Figure 4.8 flinched away from the barque as it (virtually) approached him. It shows that he was either dramatizing for the rest of the audience or the barque had become real enough in his imagination that he began to react to it physically. This is clear evidence that he was experiencing some degree of presence (Slater, Spanlang and Corominas 2010).

The accused water thief

The next dialogue also takes place in the courtyard, where the oracle will determine the guilt or innocence of an accused water thief. Again, judgments of this kind were well known, similar to the case of Djhutymose, accused of mismanagement of the estate of Amun (see Chapter 1).

ATUMIRDIS: Next we have a very serious matter at hand. Someone here has been accused of stealing water from his neighbor to water his own crops! Who has a card with the water symbol on it?

HIGH PRIEST (*shakes his head*): He who steals water steals life. Let the accused stand up!

The volunteer with the "water thief" card comes forward to stand to the left of the stage, next to Atumirdis, facing the priest with the barque in the background.

HIGH PRIEST: Please, because this is such a serious crime, state your case.

At this point the volunteer denies the charge in his or her own words. The audience member shown in Figure 4.8 did especially well, with the following response: "The breach in the water system was not my doing! My field is just as dry as my neighbor's."

HIGH PRIEST: Only the great god Horus knows for sure. O great Horus, god of kingship, does this man speak the truth?

The god answers no by moving the boat down and backward (see Chapter 1; Kruchten 1987: 105n4, 108, 256n1). An alarming soundtrack indicates the god's displeasure (Figure 4.8).

ATUMIRDIS: Since this is such a serious matter, could we ask Horus again?
HIGH PRIEST: As this is of the greatest importance, we ask for confirmation. O great Horus, is the accused innocent?

Figure 4.8 The god does not approve!

The oracle answers affirmatively this time, by moving the barque forward and up (Kruchten 1987: 105n4, 108, 256n1). Important questions to the oracle were often repeated (Kruchten 1987: 108–9); see Chapter 1 for more explanation and examples.

>HIGH PRIEST: And with a divided answer, we request a final judgment. Did the accused speak truthfully of his innocence?
>(*The oracle signals approval once again.*)
>HIGH PRIEST: Horus has vindicated you! Go in peace, knowing that the gods see you for the good citizen you are. We honor you, Horus. Thank you for your wisdom. We will look elsewhere for the criminal who so endangers our society.

The puppeteer triggers the last scene change, which causes the process (and the audience's viewpoint) to move to the front of the temple. The audience is now at the foot of the monumental front wall of the temple, as seen in Figure 9.1.

Telling fortunes, blessing a child and choosing the next Isis

The last scene is the most dynamic and interesting, because it allows for more improvisation and audience participation. However, it is thus difficult to describe on paper—a written dialogue cannot capture the experience and in that sense would be misleading. Also, our descriptions of the previous scenes illustrate the dramatic structure of the performance, which is also difficult to capture for this scene. Therefore, we will describe the rest of the performance in a general way. For an earlier version of the sample dialogue and diagram, see Jacobson (2011b: 44–58) or, best of all, view the video at http://publicvr.org/egypt/oracle/longvid.html.

The puppeteer and the actress prompt the audience to ask general questions about life that can be put to the oracle. She demonstrates by asking the oracle to indicate whether her brother will recover from his illness, and it is predicted that he will. As the audience asks questions, the puppeteer and the actress ad-lib their responses.

Up to this point it was possible for the audience to imagine that the priest was guided by some kind of artificial intelligence. In the open-ended questioning, however, the puppeteer demonstrates that a human intelligence clearly guides the priest. References to specific members of the audience establish a direct connection between the high priest and the audience.

Figure 4.9 The spirit of Horus moves the sacred boat to choose a woman (center) for a great honor. This is the moment when many realize the priest is a puppet and not a program.

Next the priest asks all the "young maidens" in the audience to stand up so the oracle can select one to play the part of Isis in the play next year. Sometimes the actress will have them stand up at the front. The puppeteer triggers a control to make the boat point to the left or right of the screen, effectively toward one of the young women. If the choice is ambiguous, Atumirdis resolves it by selecting an individual and congratulating her (Figure 4.9).

Finally the high priest calls for a parent and child to come forward and receive a blessing, which he recites. Sometimes this is actually a parent-and-child pair, but often a puppet or doll takes the place of the child. Requests for blessings are called amuletic decrees, and the oracle's blessing was usually written on a small scroll or object that could be given to the applicant (see Chapter 1; Černý 1962: 39–40; Kruchten 1987: 57ff.; Ritner 2009: 74–6). Replicating that for the performance is one of our long-term goals.

Controlling the digital puppets

Like physical puppets, the priest and the sacred barque are designed to have movements and features intended for a particular narrative (see Chapter 7). We chose to make them dramatic and stylized, to match Egyptian sources, rather than make any attempt at realism. This is consistent with the physical appearance of the priest and the barque, which look as though they have stepped off the walls of the temple. Our goal is to represent the experience of the processional oracle in its mythic form. In this section we will describe what the movements are, why we made the design decisions we did, and how the puppeteer controlled the movements.

The puppeteer controls the virtual priest and the sacred barque with an Xbox 360 gamepad (Xbox.com 2013). We chose this device because it offers a number of simple controls that can be directly translated into puppet movements. It is rugged, low-cost and commonly available, which is important to the public-distribution goal of this project. While this particular device may be obsolete by the time this book sees publication, ones like it have been available for a long time and are likely to continue to be available in the future. In the following sections we describe precisely how the puppeteer uses the gamepad and some of the keys on the computer keyboard to control the sacred boat and the virtual priest. See page 000 for a discussion of why we used this type of controller and not live motion capture.

The sacred barque

The puppeteer controls the sacred boat by using the four-way rocker switch on the lower left side of the gamepad. The rocker has four positions that can be pressed only one at a time: LEFT, RIGHT, DOWN and UP. Each position triggers a sequence of movements by the sacred boat and an accompanying soundtrack. The triggered movements are as follows:

- UP causes the sacred boat to move forward and up, showing that the god is pleased, approving or saying yes.
- DOWN causes the sacred boat to move downward and back, showing that the god is displeased, disapproving or saying no.

The approval and disapproval movements are based on Černý's description from the oracular texts of the boat moving forward or backward (Černý 1935: 57–8; 1962: 44–5; Kruchten 1987: 105) and the suggestion of an upward affirmative motion or a downward negative one (Kruchten 1987: 105n. 4, 108, 256n1; see also Chapter 1).

- LEFT causes the boat to turn and be carried toward the screen to something on the left side of the screen.
- RIGHT causes the front of the boat to point to something on the right side of the screen.

The left and right movements were developed from accounts of the oracle moving the sacred boat toward or away from a person or thing. For example, a statement might be written on a piece of papyrus or limestone and placed on the ground. The oracle moving the boat toward it would indicate agreement with the statement. Or the oracle might select a person from a group for an honor or judgment. This evidence is discussed in detail in Chapter 1.

Complete implementation of the oracle would allow the puppeteer to move the boat to any location and cause it to lean in any direction. However, having the boat point to just two different places in front of the screen, left and right, creates enough semblance of choice to support the current narrative. This simplifies the choreography, which the actress and the puppeteer have to partially invent every time. Many scenes in the show are somewhat improvisational, and the actress often calls upon audience volunteers to stand up front. She may have to arrange them differently depending on the physical dimensions of the screen, the stage, and the volunteers themselves.

The priest

The joystick on the far left of the gamepad controls the priest's head much like the head control of a physical stick puppet, allowing for a reasonably good range of movement. The joystick on the right works differently, offering four distinct movements, and only one at a time can be selected. All motions begin at zero (no effect) and become more pronounced the further the puppeteer pushes the stick in the chosen direction.

- FORWARD brings the hands forward with the palms up, usually a gesture of supplication.
- BACK brings the hands up and toward the chest, curling in. This allows the puppet to refer to himself or appear to talk to himself.
- RIGHT creates a gesture with both hands to the audience's right.
- LEFT creates a gesture with both hands to the audience's left and upwards. The additional upward movement is there because the sacred boat is generally to the left of the priest. This is another example of how specifically wired to the narrative he is.

Each of the four buttons on the right of the gamepad creates a distinct movement in the priest:

- BUTTON A (green) places his hands on his hips.

- BUTTON B (red) brings the hands up, palms forward.
- BUTTON Y (yellow) raises the right hand to "point" with an open-hand gesture and sweep from the audience's left to right.
- BUTTON X (blue) returns the priest to a resting position, standing with arms at his sides.

When the puppeteer presses a button, it "loads" the movement into memory. On the front of the Xbox controller, where the index fingers rest, are two trigger switches. When the puppeteer squeezes the left trigger, it controls the amplitude of the movement. For example, pressing the B button initially does nothing, because when it cues the hands-up motion, the amplitude control (in the rest state) is at zero. By slowly squeezing the left trigger the puppeteer can make the hands rise from the at-rest position to fully aloft. By rocking the switch in and out, he can move the hands up and down. This is important for the right-handed pointing gesture (button Y). The rest or zero state of the movement is for the arm to be completely up. Squeezing the trigger causes the hand to move slowly from side to side, which allows the priest to point to any person in the audience.

Of key importance is the software's ability to blend several motions together. The puppeteer can turn the priest's head in any direction while the priest is gesturing with his arms. The puppeteer can also make the priest do one motion from the menu of buttons and one from the right-side joystick at the same time. The software blends the two animations together, resulting in a third. The puppeteer uses all these movements at his or her discretion; they are not specified in the narrative.

Scene transitions

As described above, there are several scene transitions, each one triggered by the puppeteer pressing a number on the computer keyboard:

- 0 Reset viewpoint to the beginning, facing the front of the temple.
- 1 Travel from the front into the courtyard.
- 2 Travel from the courtyard into the Festival Hall.
- 3 Focus on the offering table.
- 4 Move into position to interact with the priest. Pressing this button also brings the procession out of the sanctuary and into the Festival Hall.
- 5 Move everything from the Festival Hall to the courtyard.
- 6 Move everything from the courtyard out to the front.
- 7 Fade to black.

In transitions 5 and 6, the priest is leading the processional oracle, walking backward so that he never turns his back to the god (Kruchten 1987: 7–8; see also Chapter 1 for more discussion and context). In transitions 5 and 6, the audience viewpoint follows the procession.

Why not use live motion capture?

A valid question we are often asked is why we did not use live motion capture of the puppeteer to animate the priest. For example, we could have used a low-cost system such as Microsoft's Kinect (Han et al. 2013; Xbox.com 2013) to capture the head and hand movements of the puppeteer and simply have the priest shadow him. This has been done for a number of digital avatars or puppets in the past, with distinct advantages (Mazalek et al. 2011). We decided against it for several reasons:

- In the hands of an experienced puppeteer, the few controls we did have were more than adequate to convey the character of the priest.
- We wanted the puppeteer to be free to do other things in the middle of a scene, such as activate keyboard controls, consult the script or adjust the sound system.
- An affordable motion-capture system at the time would have produced fairly "noisy" data, which could lead to significant error. Using the gamepad the way we did made the priest's movements clearly defined and precisely controllable.
- The programming and animation would have been more complex and could have overrun our budget.

In the future, of course, we will consider live motion capture, perhaps for parts of the puppets. But for now, discrete movements work well.

5

Mixed Reality Theater and the Egyptian Oracle Project

Josephine Anstey and David Pape

This chapter views the Egyptian Oracle through the lens of mixed reality theater. Mixed reality theater typically involves a trans-disciplinary team that includes computer-based-media makers, actors and designers who design and deploy real and virtual spaces and entities in the production of a dramatic theatrical experience. In the first section we give a brief and necessarily partial overview of mixed reality theater productions, offering a few paradigmatic examples to both flesh out this concept and complicate it. In the second section we use our paradigmatic examples to discuss some dramatic implications of mixed reality theater and notions of virtual and physical space. In the third section we discuss how the oracle fits into this tradition, what dramatic techniques it deploys, and how it handles spatial issues.

What is mixed reality theater?

Mixed reality has been defined as a class of environments that straddles virtual worlds and the real world—a merging of physical spaces and objects with computer-generated elements (Milgram and Kishino 1994). This merging can be done in different ways, most commonly using projection or head-mounted displays (HMDs). In a projection-based approach, the computer imagery is projected on large screens, often in stereoscopic 3-D, and participants view real-world elements directly in front of or alongside the projections. In an HMD approach, views of the real world can be transmitted from a video camera (typically attached to the HMD to provide a first-person perspective) and combined in real time with rendered computer images, with the result displayed in the HMD. The concept of mixed reality, though it originated in scientific and engineering research, has become useful for describing the combination of computer technology and live theater performance exemplified by Steve Benford and Gabriella Giannachi's recent text *Performing Mixed Reality* (Benford and Giannachi 2011: 126–38).

Some aspects of the use of mixed reality in theatrical productions can be traced to technological developments in mass entertainment at least as far back as the nineteenth century. Panoramic paintings sought to immerse audiences in reconstructions of distant lands or historical events (Grau 2003); world fairs featured precursors to modern location-based entertainment with primitive motion platforms, moving panoramas or large projections, actors, and storylines (Bransford 1998). However, for this chapter we limit ourselves to the more recent applications of computer technology in primarily traditional narrative theater settings.

Beginning in the 1980s, George Coates Performance Works (GCPW) experimented with virtual scenography, first using analog projections in place of traditionally built sets in the 1982 production *Are/Are* (Dixon 2007: 338–43). Based in San Francisco, Coates formed the Science Meets the Arts Society to develop connections between high-tech companies in Silicon Valley and the arts. With 1991's *Invisible Site*, GCPW's productions moved into the digital realm, making use of stereoscopic virtual sets generated by high-end graphics workstations (Salter 2010: 69–70). These computer images were projected onto a large (thirty by sixty feet) scrim made of perforated aluminum that hung in front of the actors. Precisely controlled lighting revealed the actors without noticeably affecting the projections. This allowed the actors and the virtual sets to join together visually in one cohesive reality. The effects were further enhanced by the fact that the digital imagery was stereoscopic: audiences viewed the show using 3-D polarized glasses. The story of *Invisible Site* involved a virtual reality game under attack by a computer hacker. The actors appeared to be standing or floating inside video displays, cloudscapes and a giant birdcage, among other sets. In one scene a large virtual eyeball, under the control of an offstage joystick, followed a live actor. The drama was first presented at the 1991 SIGGRAPH computer graphics research conference, followed by performances at GCPW's regular San Francisco venue.

Later Coates productions continued to develop the mix of projected computer graphics and live actors. In 1996 Coates presented the show *20/20 Blake*, a three-dimensional re-creation of the poems and paintings from William Blake's *The Marriage of Heaven and Hell*, mixed with Blake's own life story (Parker-Starbuck

2011: 161–84). Because the imagery in the Coates shows was generated by computers in real time, it could respond directly to the actors' movements. If prerecorded animations had been used, the actors would instead have had to respond to the images, with their actions being driven by the fixed timing of the animation. But with the real-time element, the computers could function almost as virtual actors—a full-fledged part of the live performance. The moving eyeball in *Invisible Site* was a first example of this; in *20/20 Blake* a flock of birds appeared to hover over the stage and audience, then chased a live actor around the stage wherever he moved.

In 1992, Brenda Laurel's group created *Placeholder* (Laurel, Strickland and Tow 1998). The physical set comprised two gently illuminated circles built of rocks. Two participants donned virtual reality helmets and stepped into these "magic circles." There was no plot or dramatic arc; rather, the participants were encouraged to play in a rich virtual world inspired by Native American mythology. The virtual environment they encountered simulated the physical environment close to Banff, in the Canadian Rockies: a sulfur hot spring in a cave, a waterfall and a landscape of hoodoos (tall, thin rock spires). Each participant could communicate with (and see an avatar of) the other participant and could also communicate with a goddess—a voice part played by a live performer—who acted as a guide. The participants could explore the space and become smart "critters": Spider, Snake, Fish and Crow. Becoming one of these critters altered the participant's avatar and abilities; for example, Crow could fly. The landscape contained recorded traces of stories based on Native American culture, and the participants could add their own stories to the world. The interdisciplinary production team included media makers and computer graphics programmers who worked with a theater group to brainstorm the underlying concepts, which then informed the visuals, sound, interaction and staging of the experience.

In the late 1990s, the Institute for the Exploration of Virtual Realities (IEVR) at the University of Kansas produced several plays in which the performances were enhanced with virtual reality technology (Reaney et al. 2004). In 1995 they presented their first show, Elmer Rice's *The Adding Machine* (Mahoney 1995). A relatively small audience—its size was limited to ensure the quality of the visual effect—watched a combination of live and virtual actors in three-dimensional computer-generated environments. The computer images were generated by Power Mac computers and the live actors performed in front of offstage video cameras. The images were then chroma-keyed together and projected stereoscopically onstage. Paths through the virtual worlds were chosen by the crew, on the spot, during the performances. IEVR's 1996 productions *Wings* used a mixture of virtual reality technologies, combining backdrops on projection screens with additional graphics presented via see-through head-mounted displays worn by each audience member (IEVR 2013).

In 1999 the theater group Blast Theory and the Mixed Reality Lab at the University of Nottingham produced *Desert Rain* (Benford and Giannachi 2011). This mixed reality experience had a narrative plot that included a mission for the six participants, encouraging them to think about the connections between the first Gulf War and our attraction to technology, spying and media. Each performance lasted thirty to forty minutes. Built in a large, open factory space, the physical set included a darkened waiting room, six fabric VR cubicles with rain screens, a sand tunnel and a hotel room. The environment projected onto the falling water of the rain screens included a virtual representation of the same hotel room and a dark space that connoted the *Tron*-like electronic interior of a networked video game. On arrival, each participant was handed a card and assigned the mission of finding the person named on the card. The participants were given hooded rain jackets and taken to the cubicles, where they used a footpad system to navigate the virtual environment and chase down their targets. Once the mission was completed, a real actor walked through the curtain of rain and exchanged the target card for a swipe card. The participants were walked through the sand tunnel to the hotel room. Their swipe cards activated video interviews with their targets that presented multiple viewpoints of the war. The creative team included writers, actors, improvisers and mixed reality computer researchers.

In 2009 the Intermedia Performance Studio (a group that includes the authors of this chapter), in collaboration with a satirical theater group, the Real Dream Cabaret, produced the mixed reality drama *WoyUbu*. *WoyUbu* was a mash-up of two existing plays: Georg Buechner's prescient crime drama *Woyzeck* (begun in 1836) and Alfred Jarry's 1896 fantasy *Ubu Roi*. In this production, Woyzeck's endless mental struggle to survive in an exploitative dystopian world was complicated by the eruption of the *Ubu* pastiche of Shakespeare's royal plays. The chaotic *Ubu Roi* scenes read as Woyzeck's delusions. *WoyUbu* was produced in a large storefront with a dividing wall from the back of the space to the middle. The scenes from *Woyzeck* were played by two live actors on one side of the dividing wall, in a set that was physically minimal but featured large projections. The interrupting scenes from *Ubu Roi* were multimedia explosions of green-screened live actors, film, TV, puppetry, virtual reality, computer games and robots, created on the other side of the dividing wall and projected into the *Woyzeck* space (see Figure 5.1). Audience members could choose to

Figure 5.1 The *Woyzeck* side of *WoyUbu*, with the performers in front of large projections.

sit in tiered seats and watch *Woyzeck* or to participate in live mixing of the multimedia scenes in the *Ubu Roi* space. The creative team included computer graphics programmers, AI (artificial intelligence) programmers, roboticists, media makers, performance theorists, actors and musicians.

Dramatic implications and notions of space

In this section we discuss some implications of mixed reality theater that are particularly relevant as context for a discussion of the Egyptian Oracle. As it is an interactive project, we focus more on issues that arise in projects such as *Placeholder*, *Desert Rain* and *WoyUbu* and less on the type of mixed reality theater that puts spectacle in the forefront and has a passive audience, such as the work of Coates and IEVR. Specifically we consider strategies and challenges in three areas: deploying real and virtual actors, managing the role of the audience, and handling mixed real and virtual spaces.

Liveness and presence: Puppets, bots, avatars and actors

One critical set of issues for mixed reality theater is the status and impact of live performers compared with virtual actors or entities. Performance theorist Philip Auslander (2002) considers the meaning of *live* amid new advances in computer and recording technologies. He suggests that a "bot"—a piece of software that autonomously responds to various kinds of input and attempts to communicate, sometimes using techniques designed to disguise its non-human identity—challenges the concept of "live performance." In short, if the bot talks like a human, moves in real time like a human, and disappears at the end of the performance like a human, does the category of live actor still have weight in time-based performance?

Mixed reality theater practitioners have an equally vexing relationship with the notion of "live." In attempting to construct virtual characters programmatically, they ask what they should look like, how they should behave, how they should be structured internally, and how they should signify agency. In effect, they are trying to determine what "liveness" consists of, how it can be represented, and what aspects of "liveness" are sufficient and necessary for virtual characters to be useful and effective. In the virtual and mixed reality community, Mel Slater was the first to theorize the related concept of *presence*. His experiments strove to identify the elements that make a human participant treat a virtual environment and characters as if they are real or alive. He has linked his concept of presence to an actor's stage presence (Slater and Wilbur 1997). At a workshop on presence in the fall of 2006, researchers from many disciplines seemed to converge on the notion that presence is a default state; rather than suspending disbelief to experience the virtual, the human has to make an effort to treat the virtual differently from the real.

Auslander's argument suggests that there is a destabilization of the categories of live human and computer-generated actor. The work of the presence community suggests that participants routinely blur the distinction between real and virtual reality. Nevertheless, in a mixed reality context, practitioners have to be aware of potential differences in the power and impact of virtual and real actors. Contrariwise, there is dramatic capital to be made from smart, context-aware deployment of those differences. Part of mixed reality theater practice is to understand and handle the different ways in which real and virtual entities can grab the audience's attention and project authority.

Our experience with CAVE systems in the 1990s illustrates a context in which a live human outweighs the virtual. CAVEs are room-sized virtual reality systems: multiple real people stand close together in the same real space to view a virtual environment (VE), with one participant controlling navigation and interaction (Cruz-Neira et al. 1992). Although typically considered virtual reality systems, the co-presence of a group of real people gives these systems a mixed reality aspect. Very often the designer of a particular VE would stand in the CAVE to explain the VE and guide the participant. It was evident that it was hard for a virtual character or a smart virtual environment to command the same level of attention and authority as a real human being. If they were confused or hesitant, the participants would always turn to the human for help, even if the environment was offering advice.

This insight was crucial when we developed *The Thing Growing* (2000), an interactive VR drama that depended on the unfolding of a relationship between the participant and the virtual characters. The piece was exhibited without any human guide in the CAVE to usurp the authority of the virtual characters (Anstey, Pape and Sandin 2000). Between 2000 and 2005 we were part of a group of artists who exhibited networked VR projects worldwide on CAVE systems and low-cost CAVE-like VR systems. In this networked situation, the participant would be interacting with avatars of other real people who had joined the VE from remote locations. Even in this case, where the avatars were controlled by other real people, the person standing next to the participant tended to command more attention and authority than the "virtual" people.

The power and impact of real and virtual entities are related very importantly to questions of scale and proximity. In Coates's productions, when real actors are chased by a virtual eyeball or placed in a virtual birdcage, the huge size of the virtual images makes them diminish the live stage presence of the actor. The challenge in this kind of spectacular production is to give appropriately significant meaning to small human entities surrounded by large-scale projections. The audience of this type of mixed reality theater is watching from a distance, so the viewer's own size has no relevance. However, in more interactive productions such as in a CAVE, the participants are aware of their own bodies being inserted into the mixed reality world, thus giving them an embodied sense of scale. If the virtual actors, real actors and participants are close together and nearly equal in size, we argue that real people have more presence, more "liveness," more impact.

A powerful illustration of this comes in *Desert Rain*. In this production, one of the greatest moments of dramatic tension occurs when a live actor walks through the rain curtain that has until that moment served as a screen for the VE. Seconds before, the participant was fully immersed in that VE, chasing down a virtual target. When the actor steps through the curtain, it is a visceral shock—he shatters the notions of virtual and real as he appears to come out of virtual space. However, this action also serves to join the concepts of virtual and real, as if there is an underlying continuum: what you do virtually, technically, remotely has real, local, physical consequences. Blast Theory deliberately uses this contrast between the real and the virtual to communicate the conceptual message that this virtual game of chasing a target has a real-life analog in which real live targets are taken out by real live people.

In the *WoyUbu* production, the attention of the audience watching on the *Woyzeck* side had to shift regularly from the real actors onstage in *Woyzeck* to the virtual actors of *Ubu Roi* projected onto the walls. Typically the shift was accomplished by the live actors freezing, by the actor playing Woyzeck focusing all his attention on the projections while the second actor ignored them (see

Figure 5.2 "Woyzeck" observes a projection of the green-screened *Ubu Roi* performers.

Figure 5.2), and lighting and sound cues. To complicate matters of authority, the projected virtual characters had a variety of scales and degrees of photorealism. The projections included live video streams of real people or physical puppets (green-screened over still or moving backgrounds) that appeared roughly double the size of the real actors, and cat-sized "8-bit" video characters and slightly larger 3-D animations, both chasing around in video games. The live actor playing Woyzeck was typically placed farther from the projections when they were large and photorealistic, emphasizing his vulnerability and powerlessness in the face of these hallucinations. However, he would move closer to the wall to try to grab the smaller video-game characters, signaling how very lost he was inside his own mind. Shifting attention back to the real actors was accomplished by completely turning off or freezing the *Ubu Roi* projections, giving light and sound cues, and moving the actors—and the audience's gaze— in front of the projections belonging to the *Woyzeck* play (see Figure 5.2).

The audience on the *Ubu Roi* side had a very different experience. They were seated among the crew, watching or taking part in the live video feeds, operating the video games and shooting at robots (see Figure 5.3). They saw the live actors of *Woyzeck* through small security cameras, so they appeared insignificant compared to the actors and technicians right in front of them.

A culminating moment of shock for both audiences—which depends on the relative weight of the real and virtual actors—comes at the end of the performance. A maddened Woyzeck plunges into a projection of a lake, ripping the

Figure 5.3 The *Ubu Roi* side of *WoyUbu*, with the audience watching performers in front of the green screen.

paper screen and stumbling into the *Ubu Roi* space. The members of the *Ubu Roi* audience, used to his small, ineffectual presence on the security camera monitors, are suddenly confronted by a disheveled, sweating, mentally disintegrating, real live man in their midst. Moments later, the *Ubu Roi* actors rush through the same breached screen onto the *Woyzeck* stage. The audience on this side, which has just watched "Woyzeck" kill his wife in a fit of maddened, jealous rage, now has to endure the laughing *Ubu Roi* crew escaping the virtual space—the interior of Woyzeck's mind—physically invading their neat theater space and lasciviously commenting on the "loveliness" of the murder.

Questions of audience role

A second interesting set of issues for mixed reality theater is the audience's participation and role. There are at least three vectors to think about: audience numbers and level and kind of participation.

Productions such as *Placeholder* and *Desert Rain* have very small audiences, and each member of the audience is a fully immersed participant; there is no role for an observer and there is no production without the participants. But the participation in these two productions is very different in kind. *Placeholder* offers an open-ended play-space structure, while *Desert Rain* follows a narrative and time-driven model.

WoyUbu opted for a mixed audience model. About fifty audience members sat in tiered seats on the *Woyzeck* side and watched a live performance of the play's scenes intercut with multimedia *Ubu Roi* scenes projected on the walls. A smaller audience of about twenty went "behind the scenes" into the *Ubu Roi* space, which included a green screen, live cameras, computer game stations and a set for the robot battle. They were seated in an ad hoc manner among the actors, camera people and technicians, given snacks and beer, and invited to participate in production of the real-time media streams. The participants' actions were constrained by the dramatic context and pacing, and the flow and content of the production was not radically altered by their participation. On the *Woyzeck* side of the experience, the effect of audience participation was negligible, but degree of participation and choices made about how to participate were crucial to the experience on the *Ubu Roi* side.

Since mixed reality theater often includes audience participation, part of staging a production is managing and making clear the audience role. Creative teams need a very clear idea of what that role is, how they want the participants to feel, and how to handle participants' nervousness, unfamiliarity, confusion and self-consciousness. A crucial part of the design process is working out how instructions to audience members are embedded into the experience. For example, in *Placeholder* the creative team added the Goddess character when it became clear that the participants needed more guidance in order to take advantage of all the opportunities afforded by the environment. They decided to disguise the purely utilitarian role of guide as a goddess who could give inspirational suggestions as well as practical or technical advice in this sandbox environment. The Goddess was improvised live by one of the creative team, who could observe the participants on monitors and who could be heard but not seen by them.

In *Desert Rain*, the progress of the participants though the experience was very carefully stage-managed. The actors were guides but their guidance came in the context of the story's dramatic arc, and they stayed in character. The first actor the participants met gave them their mission and took them to and instructed them in the usage of the VE booths. The second actor walked dramatically through the rain curtain but then, in a much more utilitarian manner, gave participants the swipe card that indicated the next action; he then walked each of them through the sand tunnel to the hotel room where they could use the swipe card. Participants in this unfamiliar game-like experience might have been tempted to chat and comment on things, but the seriousness of the *Desert Rain* concept meant that the makers needed to thwart any such tendency and keep the mood intense and somber. The piece was about tracking and surveillance; the participants received the impression from the actors and from the set that they were also being observed … so don't muck about! The actors did not just direct the participants through the experience; their behavior was serious and intense so that the participants would take behavioral cues from them.

In *WoyUbu*, observers on the *Woyzeck* side had a traditional role as theater audience and needed no special guidance. However, on the *Ubu Roi* side, one of the actors explicitly acted as the stage manager, funneling audience members through the ongoing stream of media-making, handing out roles and props as appropriate, and using autocue boards to elicit sound effects from the crowd. As befitted the carnivalesque and licentious atmosphere of *Ubu Roi*, the stage manager was not played straight but in the character of a cabaret emcee. His job was to create an atmosphere that was both intimate and transgressive: to put the audience at ease so they would be able to participate in a variety of ridiculous antics without crippling self-consciousness. This job was made easier because the *Ubu Roi* audience was small, the seating was around the media staging area, the cast and crew were sitting casually among them when not onstage, and much of the participation was done by all. But the emcee also had to identify and guide those who were willing to take larger participatory roles, acting in front of the green screen and playing the video games.

Notions of virtual and physical space

The roles and relationship of virtual and physical space are vital components of mixed reality theater. In *Placeholder* this relationship was very simple: there was a dimly lit stone circle in which the participant stood wearing a VR helmet. The physical set worked on multiple levels. Semiotically, it connoted a natural landscape, but also the firepit around which one tells stories and makes shadow puppets. Technically, the stone circle was needed to control the participant, as the VR helmet was tethered by its necessary electronic wires. Without the circle to contain their movements, participants were in danger of moving too far away and disconnecting the helmet. Dramatically, the stone circle acted as a stage or the magic circle of a game. It is typical that both technical and conceptual ends are served in the relationship of real and virtual space, and perhaps also typical that technical ideas about the intersection of the two can drive a piece conceptually.

The technical innovation at the heart of *Desert Rain* was the rain projection screen for the virtual environment. Projecting on water meant that the creative team could radically destabilize the separation between real and virtual space by enabling a real person to emerge out of the virtual space. The transgressed interface between the real and virtual was the center of the piece conceptually, spatially and temporally. It catalyzed the team's conceptual process as they built a dramatic scenario that meditated on the way abstract technical networked space serves real-war ends. It worked spatially and temporally because the moment of transgression between real and virtual had a careful buildup and letdown. Participants began their dramatic arc in a physically built set with other real people and real actors. Next, the introduction of VE technology and their manipulation of it as they accomplished a story-based task served as a virtual contrast. Then came the collapse of real and virtual. Once the actor had walked through the rain curtain, the water was turned off and the participants were returned to mundane reality. This process served to jolt the participants— trudging through real sand to the last scene, they were invited to contrast this heavy, grounded physicality in real space with the dream of effortless virtual motion.

The key concept for *WoyUbu* was to mash together two plays conceptually and temporally but to give each its own real space and to play with virtual space in the mechanisms created for observing the other play. The two plays were performed simultaneously, one on each side of a wall. The *Woyzeck* space was clean, containing nothing more than a bench and a few props on hooks. Computer graphic projections on the two long side walls of the space took the place of scenery. While the scenes were being performed, the projections depicted slowly changing nineteenth-century themes of increasing urbanization, poverty and medical practices. The *Woyzeck* audience sat in neatly tiered matching seats. In contrast the *Ubu Roi* side was a messy raw space filled with technological equipment for live production of multimedia. The audience sat on kitchen chairs around the edges of the production space, squashed in to make room for an area set aside for the robot wars. As they were produced, the compiled *Ubu Roi* scenes were shown on the projection walls seen by the *Woyzeck* audience. Meanwhile, the *Ubu Roi* audience interacted with the pre-compiled scenes, for example, actors being filmed in front of green screens, with the backgrounds on monitors; they could also watch the *Woyzeck* scenes via small security cameras. The net result was a shifting reality that mixed the live worlds of the *Woyzeck* and *Ubu Roi* actors and the multiple virtual worlds augmenting each.

Movement and navigation of space must also be considered in mixed reality productions. Typically, the extent to which an audience member controls these elements relates to the level of participation. In *Placeholder* the participant has complete control of her navigation in the virtual environment but, as mentioned above, is constrained in the physical world. In *Desert Rain*, participants are required to move about in both real and virtual space. In the real space they are strictly controlled, led by actors along a fixed path. In the virtual space they control navigation via footpads and are free to roam anywhere they like. At an early stage in the planning of *WoyUbu*, we had imagined an audience free to move between the two sides. But logistical and conceptual factors meant that we finally determined on fixed seats for the folk on the *Woyzeck* side and some guided physical freedom for the *Ubu Roi* audience members. The only real moment of control of navigation in this production comes when participants play (sequentially) two video games that are part of the *Ubu Roi* scenes.

It is clear from these examples that mixed reality spatial arrangements and navigation practices can work powerfully to carry specific semiotic load in these performances. The fusion of real and virtual space can also provide a framework for very different metaphorical connections. In *Desert Rain* the mapping is between the real physical implications of virtual networked technological space; in *WoyUbu* the mapping is between the exterior and interior of a mind.

The Egyptian Oracle in this context

The Egyptian Oracle is a mixed reality production based on a scholarly reconstruction of a public ceremony set in an Egyptian temple. The physical setup includes a large projection screen for the virtual environment, a hidden station for a live puppeteer who operates the virtual characters in the VE, space for a live performer who engages with audience participants, and seating for the audience. To contextualize our discussion, we briefly summarize the action here; for more details on the performance, see "Narrative Structure and Key Moments" in Chapter 4, and on the puppeteering, see Chapter 7.

The experience starts in the pylon area outside the temple. The live performer takes the role of a temple musician, Atumirdis. She briefly explains that today is the New Year ceremony and that she will guide this group to meet the god Horus. They move inside the courtyard of the temple and she teaches the group members how to pound their chests and ululate instead of clapping when they are pleased (a reconstruction of traditional ancient Egyptian "applause"). The mood changes and becomes more respectful as the group enters the festival hall. In this hall full of columns, Atumirdis shows the group a small family shrine with gifts of food and water or wine. Suddenly she catches sight of the high priest approaching with the god riding in his richly decorated boat, the sacred barque, carried by eight priests. The spirit of the god is thought to inhabit a small statue, the divine image, which is unseen because it is inside a box-like structure on the boat.

From this point the live performer interacts with both the audience and the high priest, Petiese, a virtual character animated and voice-acted by the puppeteer. They lead the group through reenactments of a number of New Year ceremonies. First the old mayor retires and the god chooses a new one. Next the god decides whether to allow a group of priests and musicians to advance in their respective callings. Then everyone moves outside to watch the god judge a dispute between neighbors, and the guilt or innocence of a man accused of stealing water. Finally the whole group moves back out to the pylon, where the god bestows blessings. The audience members have been given colored cue cards that assign them roles in these proceedings. The god's decisions are made visible in two ways: the boat moves close to a person chosen and dips down at the front, or the boat moves backwards for no and forwards for yes. In all cases the priests carrying the boat scramble to keep up with its momentum—which is supplied by the god.

The Egyptian Oracle sits in a tradition of cultural heritage works (Addison 2000). These projects leverage virtual, mixed and augmented reality to create immersive experiences of historically and culturally rich places and events; they will be discussed at greater length in the following chapters. However, the Egyptian Oracle is also clearly related to works of mixed reality theater and, like them, has to work at a dramatic level.

Relationship to mixed reality theater

Like *Placeholder*, the Egyptian Oracle is based on research rather than fictional material. The research domain of *Placeholder* was Native American myths and stories, and the cultural research was undertaken specifically for development of the production. In contrast, the Egyptian Oracle comes as but one fruit of a much deeper research project into the history and culture of Upper Egypt, and specifically into the practices of divination and the processional oracle (see Chapters 1 and 2). The *Placeholder* team's invention of "smart critters" imaginatively represented the role of these animals in Native American mythology, but the Egyptian Oracle team had to base their ceremonies, their virtual priests and their god in the scholarly evidence. Having created a solid hypothesis of how the priests acted in the ceremonies surrounding the divination and how the boat of the god moved, it was a daring move to represent the hypothesis in a mixed reality reenactment.

The move from research and scholarship to a mixed reality experience means that a wider, non-specialist audience has the opportunity to become immersed in a totally different era. One dramatic goal of such experiences must be to take the audience as far as possible into a different state of mind, to destabilize norms of culture and identity. Visual, narrative, behavioral and sound cues all support the audience as they make this imaginative leap. What *was* it like to be an Egyptian at oracle ceremonies or a Native American living in the area around Banff? In the case of the Egyptian Oracle there is an interesting doubling, because it is a reenactment of an experience that was itself dramatic in character. Chapter 1 discusses the relationship of the ceremonial, the religious and the dramatic in this era, and we will not trespass further into this complex area. But we suggest that using a dramatic framework to represent the drama of the New Year ceremony gives the audience an accessible entry point to a culture and tradition that is profoundly alien. How the Oracle team handled this process is discussed in the sections below. (See Chapter 6 for audience feedback on the Egyptian Oracle performances.)

Like *Desert Rain* and *WoyUbu*, the Egyptian Oracle is time-based and has a narrative arc. Although participation and improvisation are part of the process, a script is also followed. Like many of our paradigmatic examples, it has to handle the dramatic implications of mixed reality theater, dealing with issues of real and virtual actors, audience role and participation, and real and virtual space.

Virtual beings

The virtual entities in the Egyptian Oracle include the high priest, Petiese, and an assemblage comprising the god's boat and the eight priests who are carrying it. The behind-the-scenes puppeteer is the voice-actor for the high priest. Using a standard video-game console, he controls all the virtual characters and is also the navigator through the virtual environment. Much of his puppeteering is high-level control: both the boat group and the high priest have automated animations and navigation pathways that the puppeteer triggers. For example, taking cues from the live performer, the puppeteer triggers the entry of the high priest and the sacred barque into the festival hall. They move along a preset navigation pathway, and the body animation of the eight priests carrying the boat and of the high priest, walking backwards in front of it, are also automated.

The role of virtual entities in the Egyptian Oracle is both to demonstrate the ceremonial activities and to draw the audience more fully into the virtual experience. This issue of "liveness" recurs—if these entities can appear to be present, command attention and have a lifelike aura, they are more likely to succeed. Visuals, movement and behavior all contribute to the liveness of the virtual characters. Although these overlap, we separate them in the paragraphs below to understand better the dramatic choices of the Egyptian Oracle creative team.

The priests and the boat are 3-D models; visually they are highly resolved and detailed. In two dimensions the equivalent would be lifelike drawings consistent with ancient Egyptian artwork, rather than photorealism (there is a similar abstraction in their movement, which aims at a smooth but simplified level of realism). These design decisions meant the team avoided the problems of the "uncanny valley"—ultra-realistic 3-D animations that make people uncomfortable because they just miss being human (Mori 2012). But because these virtual characters are located in the realistic rendering of the temple, they could not be abstracted much more or there would be a jarring mismatch of styles. We argue that photorealistic graphics are not a necessary precondition for virtual characters to appear live and present. A wide variety of visual styles, including very abstracted graphics, do not lessen the audience's response. It is more important that the visuals are compelling and that a coherent design is reflected in all aspects of the virtual environment and characters, as is the case here.

In our discussion of liveness and movement, we would like to focus on the main virtual character, the high priest Petiese. The Egyptian Oracle puppeteer has very interesting hybrid control over the animation of this character. He can trigger entire movement sequences (such as that described above) to move the priest from place to place; he has control over a small library of arm and torso animations—set gestures lasting a few seconds—and he can use an analogical stick to move the head around naturalistically. Taken together, these last two elements give the puppeteer tools to refine his performance and for live improvisation (see "Controlling the Digital Puppets" in Chapter 4 for details).

Using the library of animations, the puppeteer can rehearse effective sequences of gestures to accompany his more formal set speeches. The library gestures are large and sweeping and connote ritual. In dance and ceremony, gesture carries semiotic weight. The limited set of movements helps the actor to make each choice more marked and more significant. Once familiar with the controls, the puppeteer can also combine library gestures and head movements to respond to the live performer and the audience "on the fly." It is of the utmost importance that he does not have to wait for one gesture to complete before starting another. The animation engine interpolates smoothly between the actions and can combine gestures, giving him a large movement space in which to play. This flexible system for animating the high priest adds substantively to his liveness.

Obviously the look of virtual entities and their animation are components of their behavior. We believe that responsive behavior—appropriate awareness of and interaction with other people—carries the most weight in terms of conveying liveness and presence. Both the high priest and the sacred barque are responsive, but they have very different roles in this reenactment and must be discussed separately.

The puppeteer controls Petiese, who has two behavioral modes, official and casual. In his official mode he is doing his job as the interface between the

Egyptians who have come to the ceremony and the god Horus. He speaks in ritualized language and makes ritual gestures. In this mode he is giving information via demonstration and stressing the strangeness of this experience. He has ultimate authority (further discussed below) but he is more distanced from the audience, less accessible, less "live." In his casual mode he interfaces with the live performer and the audience. It is here that his liveness is established and reinforced. He may comment on or directly address an audience member, his head turns naturally and appropriately as Atumirdis organizes the interactive activities, and he comments on what is happening. He makes it clear that he can see and hear the audience, that he is right there with them.

The puppeteer also controls the god's boat, but the controls are simple. He can choose between four large compound movements: (1) move forward to dip in front of the left side of the screen; (2) dip in front of the right side of the screen; (3) tilt up and forward to indicate a yes answer or approval; and (4) tilt down and back to indicate a no answer or disapproval. The actress organizes the action, first by disambiguating the meaning of the boat's movements. For example, in the last scene the god is asked to choose among the willing (i.e. standing) members of the audience for a great honor. When the boat tilts vaguely to the left or right side of the screen, the actress singles out an audience member who could be the target of its intention. Similarly, when the god is asked to judge who is right in a dispute between two parties, the actress positions them in front of the screen at the two points to which the boat can point, so that the puppeteer can have it definitely choose one of them.

The priests carrying the boat all look the same and pretty much behave the same way, except for one in the back, who keeps picking up his leg as if he has an itch. They have some waiting behavior, which includes very slight movement, to maintain the liveness of the scene. The behavioral programming for the sacred barque assumes that the god shifts his weight to communicate his wishes. When the god shifts his weight forward, the priests stagger and dip forward. When the god shifts his weight backwards, they stagger backwards, struggling to maintain the boat upright. It is entirely appropriate, given their role in the ritual, that they should not evidence much autonomy or agency. They are effectively programmed to be live the way guardsmen are live: they mustn't move out of turn. However, what they effectively do is give evidence of the god's liveness. They communicate an eeriness, especially when the god causes them to canter forward and dip in front of an audience member. They add a sense of brooding presence to the event itself.

That idea that the god is the motive force in the processional oracle is explicitly described in the original Egyptian texts. It is not a theatrical device created by the creative team but was invented by the original authors of the ancient ceremony. To the Egyptians, religious drama and theater were very important, and a central goal of this performance is to make sure the audience knows that.

Questions of attention and authority

The Egyptian Oracle combines a live performer in front of the virtual environment and a virtual character in the VE, voice-acted and animated by the puppeteer. As we saw above, since they are peers in terms of size, we would expect the live performer to command more attention and exude more authority. The Egyptian Oracle team used multiple techniques to offset this problem, and the relationship between live performer and virtual character that develops also provides a pathway into the experience for the audience.

The live actor playing the part of the musician Atumirdis is introduced first, and she handles the pacing of the performance and the interactivity. She uses body language to direct attention into the virtual environment and back out to the audience. When the VE moves, she faces into it, like a guide taking a group around the temple. When it stops, she turns and talks to the group, gesturing back at the items of interest.

The god and the high priest make their entrance when Atumirdis and her group are in the festival hall. Multiple cues take attention away from the actress and turn it toward the virtual characters. There is a fanfare as Atumirdis interrupts her story and faces into the VE, babbling excitedly about the arrival of the sacred barque. The shift of attention to and the authority of the high priest are established by repositioning the VE so that Petiese is central, and by the priest's first line, in which he admonishes Atumirdis for talking so loudly in the sacred space. It is crucial to establish that the virtual character's awareness and influence extend to outside the virtual space. This small speech lets the audience know that Petiese can see and hear them, and that he is the one in command.

The Egyptian Oracle team maintains the relative authority of Atumirdis and Petiese in a variety of ways. Visually, he is further away than she is and therefore smaller, but he is higher and more central. At first all the communication between Petiese and the audience is directed through Atumirdis. He announces what they are going to do, and she passes on the information and works out the details with the audience. Only later does the priest speak directly to the participants. This makes clear that Petiese has a higher place in the temple hierarchy than Atumirdis. The audience, taking the role of ordinary Egyptians, are even lower down in the hierarchy, so it is not surprising that there is an intermediary between them and the high priest, which also disrupts people's tendency to defer to the real rather than the virtual person. As the audience becomes more familiar with the virtual character and is drawn more fully into the proceedings, more direct communication between Petiese and the participants works. Atumirdis always maintains an in-character attitude of deference toward the virtual Petiese: she bows to him, and if they talk at the same time during improvisation, she stops talking. And both Petiese and Atumirdis defer to the authority of the god. The priest never turns his back on the shrine of Horus, and both bow when the god's boat approaches.

Audience participation and roles

The Egyptian Oracle team leads the audience members very gently into their interactive roles, with clear directions at every step. The interface for the interaction is the live actor playing Atumirdis. Without the commanding presence of a real live person it is doubtful whether the audience would feel comfortable, secure and pressured enough to interact. Atumirdis switches between two modes, out of character and in character. She introduces herself as a temple musician and identifies her role within the drama, but she also steps out of character to act as guide and stage manager for the interactive components of the experience.

In the opening scene at the pylon of the temple, Atumirdis establishes a casual rapport with the audience, asking and eliciting questions and answers to establish a basic framework of information: she points out an image of the god Horus on the wall, she explains that they are to take part in a New Year's ceremony, and she informs the audience of their role—they are ordinary Egyptians. Once the group has traveled into the courtyard she teaches the men to pound their chests and the women to ululate to indicate pleasure. This exercise builds rapport among the group members so that individuals will be more comfortable when called upon to take part in the interactive episodes that follow. It is in some ways similar to the simple affirmations given during modern religious ceremonies, such as the chanting of "amen" when prompted.

On arrival in the performance space, some audience members were given color-coded cards that describe the roles they will be playing—retiring mayor, mayoral candidate, musician, priest, disputing neighbor or alleged water thief.

This in itself might cause nervousness or excitement, but the circumstances are relaxed and the first episode in which an individual is called on to participate is designedly low-key. The high priest Petiese announces that the mayor is retiring, the individual with the mayor card stands, and the audience members thank him or her by using the chest pounding and ululating as just taught. The next participatory step requires those with cards indicating that they are mayoral candidates to come forward and lay their résumés on the floor in front of the high priest. They stand to one side as the god determines which one to choose. The greatest degree of participation requires the two neighbors disputing about their mutual wall and the accused water thief to not only come forward but to state their case to the god. The interactive episode winds down with audience members being invited to ask personal questions or request blessings.

Use of space

In the Egyptian Oracle the real and virtual performers are deployed, as we have seen above, to bridge the gap between the real and virtual spaces. The in-character relationship of Atumirdis and Petiese establishes a continuity between the two, producing a seamless mixed reality temple into which the participants can imaginatively insert themselves. It is the work of the graphics to make the temple a compelling and immersive space. The audience first sees the temple walls with their magnificent paintings, they are then ushered into the vast courtyard open to the bluest of skies, and next they are plunged into the relative gloom of the festival hall with its closely placed columns. They are not permitted to wander freely, as navigation of the virtual environment is tied tightly to the unfolding of the narrative and controlled by the puppeteer. The benefit of this is that the group is always in the right place at the right time! Like a tour group in real space, they have an expert guide who shows them the highlights of the space, tells stories about it, is available to answer any questions and gets them front-row seats at show time.

The Egyptian Oracle has been shown in different real spaces, and it is clear that a variety of configurations between the real and virtual spaces is possible. Spatially the team has worked out a very effective way of positioning the real performer in relation to the virtual space, and her movements are carefully plotted to give a powerful sense of mixed space. It is a little harder to manage the spatial arrangements when real people step up to be judged by the god. They tend to occlude the virtual environment, and at times it is not clear whether they should face the VE and the god or face the audience.

Conclusion

The Egyptian Oracle effectively uses methods of mixed reality theater to communicate the experience of the New Year ceremony. The virtual setting quickly communicates a sense of place, history and ancient performance without long-winded explanations. The drama of the living god unfolds slowly. The audience members are drawn by slow steps into their own roles as common people attending the temple, both by the real actress and by the measured navigation of the virtual world. By the time they enter the festival hall they are curious, and their curiosity is nicely rewarded when the high priest appears, walking backwards in front of the sacred barque. The team allows the reenactment of the ancient ceremony to speak for itself. For the duration of the performance, audience members can take the role of mayor, neighbor or alleged thief and experience—as far as their own suspension of belief will allow them—the presence and judgments of Horus.

6

Educational Purpose and Results

Jeffrey Jacobson

The primary goal of the Egyptian Oracle performance is to show audiences how ceremony and drama were central to ancient Egyptian culture, something not well represented in most museum exhibitions and textbooks. More broadly, we want to sharpen their empathy for other cultures and connect ancient civic life with that of today. It is also an investigation of the educational power of mixed reality performance implemented through low-cost technologies developed by the game industry. The same approach could represent other times, places, scales and topics. The puppet could be a Roman emperor, a dinosaur or "Mr. Protein" guiding the audience through a human cell. By mixing physical and virtual reality, we gain many of the advantages of both, producing an immersive experience.

Even though the current performance is a first-run prototype, audiences received it well and felt that they had learned something. In our public performances we gathered preliminary data from audiences of children aged ten to twelve and from mixed family audiences of the general public. Generally most participants reported that they were fully engaged by the experience and learned something from it. Analysis of post-performance discussion indicates that they definitely absorbed new ideas and experienced a change in perspective about ancient Egypt, which was our primary goal. We now have enough data to form a basis for serious research with this form.

In this chapter we place the Egyptian Oracle within the world of serious games for education. It is also an educational example of mixed reality theater (Chapter 5), educational puppetry (Chapter 7), cultural heritage (Chapter 8) and Egyptology (Part 1). We also present our findings from data gathered at performances to date, and we set the performance in yet another context where it belongs—educational games.

Serious games for education

These are the key elements in an educational game: (1) the player works to achieve something; (2) there are rules; and (3) the activity is considered a form of play or competition (*OED* 2010). While this definition encompasses "skill and drill" types of games, most are much more complex, providing flexible and responsive narratives in which the player must test hypotheses, synthesize knowledge and respond to the unexpected (Dondlinger 2007). The fundamental goal is to motivate the student to learn something (Ang and Krishna 2008), but successful educational game design is not easy (Baker 2008). For a good survey of experimental evidence for the effectiveness of educational games, see Connolly et al. (2012) and also Girard, Ecalle and Magnan (2013).

The Egyptian Oracle is game-like primarily because the audience interacts with the narrative, an essential feature of educationally serious games (Ang and Krishna 2008). Also, a few audience volunteers play minor roles, embodying persona plausible for that historical era—a small but important example of role-playing (Barab et al. 2009; Dickey 2006; Squire 2008). Our interactive design is an example of a new class of mixed reality game interfaces that resemble virtual reality installations and arcade experiences (Laviola 2008).

According to Ang and Krishna (2008), the student can be motivated by ludology and by narrative. Ludology is iterative and creative competition or work toward goals, focusing on the game play. Narrative is the story itself, which the designer hopes will capture the students' attention because it is interesting. Within the narrative, the student can embody a character or persona (Barab et al. 2009; Dickey 2006; Slater, Spanlang and Corominas 2010; Squire 2008); as the character, he or she must understand the virtual context and ultimately transform it. In good game design, goals are structured flexibly so that the student can rise to a level that challenges his or her abilities (Dondlinger 2007). The goal is to keep the student in his or her "zone of proximal development," in Vygotsky's terms (1978).

However, an educational game must also motivate the student to learn what it was designed to teach, not just to play or "win" the game itself. Games can motivate through extrinsic or intrinsic rewards and goals (Dondlinger 2007). Extrinsic rewards, such as earning points or encountering something fun or pretty, are defined in the structure of the game but do not have any direct relationship with the material the student is expected to learn. Extrinsic rewards can engage the student, but they may also interfere with learning. According to Fisch (2005), when appealing elements are added to keep students interested, the students often remember those appealing elements and forget the content they were supposed to learn. Intrinsic rewards, on the other hand, are situated within the educational content. For example, in Dede's educational game *River City*, the goal of the game is to figure out what is making the townspeople sick—a perfect union of game and content (Dede et al. 2005).

Employing these terms, the Egyptian Oracle motivates students through narrative and not ludology. Participants are not seeking goals, but they are definitely playing, and the experience has rules. Of course we are employing game technology and interface techniques. Most importantly for a cultural heritage application, the rewards are intrinsic. The historical material, itself, is the star of the show and the reward for participation.

Performances and Testing Protocol

We devised a simple questionnaire, which we administered at the end of each performance (see Appendix B). The first half of the questionnaire asks two demographic questions (age and gender), two questions about the participant's role in the performance, two general assessment questions (Did you like it? Did you learn something?), and two knowledge questions. The back of the questionnaire asked for short answers, one testing knowledge and the rest asking for suggestions and opinions.

We administered no pre-test and we had no control groups. We also filmed each performance, and had an independent evaluator catalog and rate moments during the performance, such as when an audience member asks a good question. We developed this process on advice and eventual approval from the accredited Institutional Review Board at Carnegie Mellon University. It is appropriate for general audiences and K-12 venues under school supervision. In all our performances, we received a great deal of cooperation. Audiences were also eager to offer their suggestions for improvements to the show.

The overall purpose was to gather preliminary data to help us posit a more formal study later. Nevertheless, some interesting trends have emerged from the data, already. For full details, including the tests, the scoring rubric, raw data, IRB materials, and detailed protocol, see the project final report (Jacobson 2011a).

In each performance we had an independent evaluator tally the responses to the items on the first page of the post-performance questionnaire and enter the data in a summary form. Some of the answers were ambiguous and required judgment. The following descriptive statistics characterize the results; the full raw data are available in Jacobson (2011a: sect. 11.3). Our evaluators treated the short essay answers on the back of the questionnaire as anecdotal feedback. We combined that feedback informally with comments made during the after-show discussion.

Results are based on a total of 359 audience members responding: 181 self-reported males, 156 females and 22 not reporting their gender. Among the adults, there was a fairly even age distribution from teens to septuagenarians. The following performances were evaluated.

- Puppet Showplace Theater, Brookline, MA, May 20, 2011: general public audience of all ages, including three children.
- Immersive Education Initiative Summit, Boston, May 13, 2011: an audience of at least 150 K-12 educators and educational researchers, some graduate students and one child. Ages (not counting the child) ranged from the mid-twenties to the eighties. Thirty-six attendees completed the questionnaire.
- Carnegie Museum of Natural History, Pittsburgh, July 21, 2011: twelve teenaged volunteers at the museum (this is not the CMNH show depicted in the online video).
- William Diamond Middle School, Lexington, MA, September 19, 2011: nearly a hundred students, all around eleven years old. The show was part of their required studies on ancient civilizations but was presented as a special treat. Seventy-seven students had the necessary parental permission to fill out the questionnaire.
- William Diamond Middle School, March 16, 2011: more students from the same population. We were able to gather data from 154 students.
- AXIOM Gallery, Boston, February 16, 2012: a public audience of adults, mostly artists interested in new media. We gathered data from thirty-five, approximately 50 percent of the audience.
- Northeastern University, Boston, July 13, 2012: a public audience of adults, mostly from the technology community. Only twenty-one attended but we gathered data from all of them.

We also gave one performance at the Museum of Science, Boston, on May 11, 2013. Results from that population are not included in the totals above or the following analysis. See below for a summary of the results.

Affective measures and knowledge questions

On the questionnaire across all groups, responses to the question "Did you enjoy the show?" showed that most did. Self-reported enjoyment of the show was nearly identical for the middle-school children and the adults, averaging 4 on a scale of 1 to 5. The percentages were as follows:

It was bad!	1%
It was not good.	1%
It was okay.	22%
It was good.	46%
It was great!	30%

Responses to the question "Did you learn anything interesting?" were similar, with the average of all responses being a solid yes:

Nothing	1%
No	4%
A little	32%
Yes	51%
Yes, lots!	12%

Just as important, enjoyment and perceived learning were clearly correlated (Pearson's $R = 0.46$). This parallels one of the more frequent suggestions in the free-response section of the questionnaire: that we add more content and information to the presentation. In other words, audiences wanted more depth and detail.

There was also a small but statistically significant difference between the children and adults; the children reported that they learned from the show more often than the adults ($P < 0.010$, two-tailed uneven samples T-test). That difference may be a result of students' expectations in the school setting.

About three-quarters of respondents answered the question "Who is the High Priest?" correctly ("the man talking to us and to the actress"). About half of the audience members chose the correct answer for "What was MAAT?" ("harmony, peace and justice"). Although we did not have a control group to which we could compare this result, it is very unlikely that people in the general population would know the answers. It takes far more than two questions to really probe learning effectiveness, but the responses we did get showed that the audience was listening and absorbing information. We found no significant relationship between performance on these questions and age, gender or venue.

The adults scored better on the two knowledge questions, "What was MAAT?" ($P < 0.002$) and "Who was the High Priest?" ($P < 0.001$).

Results from open-ended questions

The 254 children at William Diamond Middle School filled out the comments section on the second page of the post-show questionnaire. We analyzed their comments to summarize their feedback into four categories, shown below. Under each category is a phrase that describes something from the show; the number following indicates how many statements mentioned that thing. The statements are arranged so that more specific answers follow more general but related statements. For example, thirty-two people stated generally that they liked the computer graphics, while thirteen people liked the computer-generated characters in particular. Each number refers only to the statement itself and is not in any way influenced by the answers to statements it is linked to. For example, thirty students wrote that they liked the audience roles generally but did not specify, while another six said they liked the role of the mayor, giving a total of thirty-six students who approved of the audience roles.

Students liked
Computer graphics	32
"Graphic characters"	13
Sacred boat	11
Junior priest scratching his leg	1
Details of the temple	10
Audience participation	96
Humor	12
Physical actors	17
Actress/narrator	19
Audience roles	30
The mayor	6
Interaction with animated characters	58
The high priest	47
Horus (the god spirit in the boat)	26

Students did not like
Revealing how the show worked	2
Junior priest scratching his leg	5
The real actors	4

Actress/narrator	19
Slow	3
Boring	2
Humor	2
Chanting	4

Students wanted more

Action and drama	7
Real actors	12
Actresses	8
Roles for audience	12
Graphic characters	20
Questions (querying the oracle)	35
Content and information	10
Temple details	6
Longer duration for the peformance	16

Students' suggestions for improving

Use real actors	5
Improve the actress/narrator	8
Computer graphics	33
Lighting	10
The boat	23
Graphic characters	3
Stop junior priest scratching his leg	3
Temple details	3
Information and content	9

We summarized the written comments from 130 adult audience members in a similar way. Filling out the forms was voluntary, and the adults wrote extended comments less often than the middle-school children.

Adults liked

Audience participation	13
Physical actors	2
Actress/narrator	1
Humor	7
Interaction with the graphics	22
Computer graphics	7
Sacred boat	3
High priest	3
Temple	2

Ritual	3
Horus (god spirit in the boat)	26

Adults did not like

Revealing how the show worked	3
Actress/narrator	1

Adults wanted more

Content and Information	9
Virtual locations	1
Real actors	3
Animated characters	4
Speed up the show	3
Audience participation	6
Allow more audience questions	4
Make show longer	3

Adults' suggestions for improvement

Actress's costume	3
Computer graphics	15
Temple detail	3
Graphic characters	6
The priests carrying the boat	4
High priest	3
Boat accuracy	6

From these charts it is apparent that the audiences liked what they saw, they wanted more information and more depth, and they wanted more to do—more interaction. They also wanted higher-quality computer graphics, likely because we were using an old projector capable of only 1024 × 768 resolution. Experiments with a very high-resolution video wall have shown that the graphics and the game engine work well in that environment, presenting a much better image. We leave the reader to draw further conclusions by examining the charts. It is interesting to compare them to analysis of audience behavior during the show and discussion afterwards, presented in the following section.

Results from the videos and discussions

For each performance we had two independent evaluators watch the results and fill out the video scoring rubric (Jacobson 2011a: 96–101). The purpose was to characterize how the audience members were interacting with the show while they were "in the moment." The following descriptive statistics characterize the results; the full raw data are available in Jacobson (2011a: 101–5). Note that the group in the video of the Carnegie Museum of Natural History (CMNH) performance was from an overnight camp for girl scouts from grades 4 through 7, who came with family members and younger siblings—about forty people in total (this was a different CMNH performance from the one that produced the completed questionnaires). At this point there are not enough data to justify statistical analysis, so the results are anecdotal, but some interesting trends emerge:

- Audiences definitely had no trouble following the action and participating.
- Our strategy of selecting people for specific parts (e.g., the disputing neighbors) ahead of time appears to have worked well. Most of the volunteer actors did a good job.
- The show worked better if there were at least some children in the audience. Even a few children engaging with the show seemed to have a strong positive effect on the adults.
- Children aged six and seven seemed to get something out of the show, but they did not engage fully. Those aged eight to twelve did very well.
- The adults tended to do well when acting out their parts but they were less enthusiastic in the general interactions, such as the Egyptian-style applause.
- The show depends on audience feedback; it usually did not work well with an adult crowd of fewer than twenty people.
- Many audience members liked how one of the priests carrying the boat keeps scratching his leg with the other foot.
- When the priest was addressing someone or pointing to something, the live actress often had to interpret for the audience. With monoscopic projection, the direction the priest is pointing in looks different to different members of the audience, depending on the location of the observer. Experimentation with the new 3-D projectors is warranted.
- The puppeteer's ability to engage with the audience through the avatar was remarkable, even though he could see them only through a single low-resolution webcam and a sliver of view past the edge of the curtain.
- In all the after-show discussions we asked the audience some version of this question: "When did you realize that the priest was not just a recording or a program following some particular script? When did that happen for you?" Every audience member who answered the question identified a point in the narrative when the priest interacted with a volunteer audience member

on stage. For some it was almost the first interaction, but for others it was not until later in the performance (see Figure 4.8).

Performance at the Boston Museum of Science

The Egyptian Oracle was performed on May 11, 2013 at the Museum of Science, Boston, in its Cahners Theater. The audience was drawn from their general public, visitors who were at the museum at the time. The audience (twelve people) had a good age range, with the youngest being four and the oldest sixty-four. Four were male and eight female. The following summary is excerpted from an internal evaluation report by Ryan Auster, and is presented here with the museum's permission:

> Exit surveys were collected from all audience members (N=12) following the performance to determine the effectiveness of the show's format and audience engagement in an avatar-based learning experience. Several visitors (N=4) were also interviewed at the Cahners Theater exit to ask follow-up questions about their experiences.
>
> The analyses to follow pertain to the single performance data collected from a small number of Museum visitors and should be interpreted as somewhat limited in their generalizability. These results suggest that those who attended the Egyptian Oracle show found it to be at least as entertaining as other things at the Museum (92%), and that a majority of the audience (75%) felt they learned a lot from the performance. Both the live presenter and the onscreen avatar held "a lot" of attention for visitors (67% and 82%, respectively), and almost all of those who saw the show would recommend it to others in the Museum (88%). Qualitative data indicate that the show could be improved by increased attention to the quality of the animation and features of the technology (e.g., sound system), and that finding strictly historical content in the Museum of Science was curious. Visitors seem interested in the extension of this type of show to other content areas but remained positive in their comments overall ...
>
> The exit survey completed by visitors also asked if those who saw the show would recommend it to other Museum patrons. Overwhelmingly, attendees to this show would "absolutely" recommend the show to other visitors [88%], with only one audience member responding "maybe," and none responding "no."

The museum used a post-show questionnaire nearly identical to ours, precisely to allow comparison with data from previous shows. The results were essentially the same, so we do not include them here. Anecdotally, answers to the interview

Table 6.1 Interview responses, Museum of Science, Boston (N=4)

Question	Response
Can you please tell me (more) about what you liked or disliked most about this show?	The script could have been more sophisticated. It has potential though. The kids were really with it, and I loved the interaction. Does the content always have to be about history? Could it be about problem-solving? Could the audience invent more of their own questions instead of using the script? [F, 64]
	I didn't figure out it was a live performance until about halfway through, so that was neat. At first I thought it was more like Ada and Grace, just speech recognition. It was exciting to find out it was in real time. I think there could be more advanced animations. It seemed old, like from the 90s. [F, 24]
	Neat to see it on the big screen. She (referring to his daughter) does not often get to see big screens, and didn't seem to like the unfamiliar clapping. [M, 43]
	I liked the boat. [M, 6] Being able to go inside. [F, 29] Totally cool: it was like a tour, but for something thousands of years old. It was surprisingly authentic. [M, 45]
What kept your interest or helped you to pay attention?	I liked when they stopped walking and actually interacted with the audience. Maybe they could speed up the walking parts. The kids all looked engaged, they seemed like bright kids. It was a neat idea, but could use some more development. [F, 64]
	The live guide was nice. She was like this host into a virtual world, so it was more like a tour. [F, 24]
	It helped that the guy on screen was moving and talking. The presenter and the guy on screen worked together to tell a story. [M, 43]
	It was really lifelike. It felt like I was standing there. [F, 11] It was like the real world. [M, 6]
Overall, how did you feel about the live presenter and the on-screen avatar?	I am an actress and I own an acting company, so the acting seemed a little stilted. The presenter didn't have much to work with. She had good energy, but the script was just predictable. They need a playwright. [F, 64]
	I liked them. They were very personable. [F, 24]
	(Father explains the question to his daughter and asks if she liked the presenters; she nods yes, she liked them).
	It was really great. I felt like they weren't in a video. [F, 11] It blurred the line between TV and reality. It kept my attention, the presenters were good. [M, 45] I was a bit distracted sometimes. It was hard to see the images on the screen. They were kind of blurry. [F, 29]

* **NOTE:** Gender and age of each respondent is indicated in brackets, and in cases of group interview are listed for each individual responding.

questions are broadly similar to comments made at other shows as well (see Table 6.1).

We are grateful to the Museum of Science for sponsoring the performance and providing their evaluation results. The experience was instructive for everyone.

Other lessons learned and conclusion

Making an early prototype of the Egyptian Oracle performance was a good experience for us, exposing a number of issues that we might not have anticipated had we attempted full implementation. In no particular order, these are some of the lessons learned:

- It is nearly impossible to describe the performance in words alone to anyone who has not seen something similar. Fortunately, our ninety-second introductory video works well and needs very little additional explanation. This video can be seen at http://publicvr.org/html/pro_oracle.html.
- We are quite pleased with Unity3D as a software platform for this work (see http://unity.com for further information).
- Projects like this would benefit from having a single art director, that is, someone to look after the artistic nature of the whole production. We will do that next time.
- We must spend more effort on music and sound effects, involving a sound person from the very beginning of the design.
- Our very best ideas came from the original historical sources, which makes sense—the Egyptian processional oracle was a highly developed genre of religious performance.

The educational potential of the Egyptian Oracle is very great, primarily through its ability to engage audiences and change their perceptions of ancient Egyptian culture. While most of our performances were for the general public, the three K-12 performances went well (in some ways best of all), and the Egyptian Oracle could easily be made part of a K-12 curriculum. Chapter 7 describes where the show connects with Common Core State Standards for education. Furthermore, it is part of the trend of experimentation in mixed reality theater described in Chapter 5, which should lead to more shows like it.

Part Three

The Technology

7

Puppetry and Virtual Theater

Lisa Sturz (with contributions from Tim Lawrence, Wendy Morton, Brad Shur and Kirk Thatcher)

Puppetry is an ancient art form that developed out of religious ritual, folklore and magic. It is defined as the process of giving life to an inanimate object, often anthropomorphic, through direct manipulation, strings or rods. As numinous objects, puppets have served as mediators between the spirit and the material world, echoing the miracle of creation (Ryu 2008). For at least four millennia puppets have captivated the imagination of various civilizations with their uncanny ability to connect with their viewers (Blumenthal 2005).

The Egyptian Oracle Project uses a puppet as a transformative vehicle for both the performer and the audience, echoing its ancient roots (Ryu et al. 2008). The goal is to capture some of the excitement and meaning of the original ritual by exploring the technical and psychological dimensions of the virtual reality. By bridging ascending layers of abstraction and sacredness in the oracle performance, we hope that our hyper-modern offspring of traditional puppetry can help to extend the meaning of ritual for the digital age.

Hieroglyphs reveal that the ancient Egyptians enacted religious rituals and celebrations of Isis and Osiris by using "walking statues." Four-thousand-year-old articulated puppets, made of clay and ivory and controlled by wire and string, have been found in Egyptian tombs. The Greek traveler Herodotus, writing in the fifth century BCE, described an Egyptian festival that used string-operated fertility figures in a procession for Osiris (Blumenthal 2005). It seems only fitting that the Egyptian Oracle Project include puppetry as a major player in the reenactment.

Educational puppetry

Puppetry is widely acknowledged as an educational tool for young audiences. Through colorful characters, broad movements, visual metaphor and animated storytelling, puppetry has won a place at the heart of American culture (Bernier and O'Hare 2005). For the past four decades, Sesame Workshop, formerly known as the Children's Television Workshop, has been on the leading edge of early childhood education with the creation of *Sesame Street* (Fisch 2004). The program's engaging characters are seen regularly in 150 countries, teaching vocabulary, math and science. To quote a *Newsweek* article, "No show has affected the way we think about education, parenting, childhood development and cultural diversity, both in the United States and abroad, more than Big Bird and friends. You might even say that *Sesame Street* changed the world, one letter at a time" (Fisch and Truglio 2001; Guernsey 2009).

Numerous national studies show that students who participate in hands-on interactive learning activities in the classroom do better statistically in reading, math and science (Michael 2006). Students are more engaged in what they are learning, spend more time on activities, use outside time to learn more about a specific topic, and earn better grades. These findings have informed artful curriculum-based puppet shows presented every year in school auditoriums and libraries (Fisler 2003).

Curriculum encompasses almost everything experienced in the classroom. Historically, individual states in the USA developed their own curriculum standards. Now most states have adopted national Common Core State Standards, which outline age-appropriate learning goals in academic subjects, including language arts, math, science and social studies (CCSS 2014). The standards, developed in collaboration with teachers, school administrators and childhood education specialists, also include character education and citizenship. The versatility of puppetry can address specific academic goals while exploring sensitive moral and emotional issues such as friendship, jealousy, bullying and even life and death in a warm and fuzzy way.

The Center for Puppetry Arts in Atlanta, Georgia, is an educational facility committed to "touching lives through puppetry." It houses a museum with both a permanent historical collection and special exhibits and offers live and filmed performances for children, teens and adults (CPA 2014). For thirty-five years the mainstay of the Center's season has been curriculum-based puppet shows and hands-on puppet-building activities. For the past ten years it has been using technology to offer nationwide distance-learning programs, using puppetry in virtual classrooms connected through video conferencing, webinars and recorded content tailored to specific classroom topics that complement national curriculum standards (Aretta Baumgartner, personal communication, 2014).

Arts-infused learning is vital to educators who are familiar with the cognitive research on multiple intelligences by Harvard professor Howard Gardner (1983). He found that students possess different kinds of minds and therefore learn, remember, perform, understand and retain information in different ways. He identified seven different types of intelligence that most people possess in different measures. Gardner argues that our educational system has been biased toward linguistic, mathematical and logical learning and often misses the mark for students whose learning styles depend more heavily on visual, kinetic or spatial aptitude. He advocates for a combination of learning experiences that address the multiple ways in which individuals learn.

Puppetry appeals to learners' visual, cognitive, auditory and kinetic intelligences simultaneously. As a practicing puppeteer and the artistic director of Red Herring Puppets (RHP 2014), I have created shows that explore history, astronomy, mythology, electricity and magnetism, fables and folklore. We bring together diverse subject areas into a compelling integral experience that

Figure 7.1 "Lewis Latimer" and "Thomas Edison" and their incandescent bulb.

enhances classroom learning. Through our unique breed of educational theater, we take a creative approach to difficult subjects and leave the audience with memories that resonate for years.

For example, in our puppet show *Electricity!*, which explores electricity and magnetism, we have a scene in which Thomas Edison and Lewis Latimer are testing different filaments to use in their light bulb (see Figure 7.1). We feel their fatigue as they work for months without positive results. We understand the perseverance needed to keep going as Edison remarks, "Don't give up; success is within our grasp. We now know over ten thousand ways in which a light bulb *won't* work." They review the 6,000 plant and mineral fibers they have tested until they are ready to pull their hair out—which they then test as a filament. The audience gasps when they finally test carbonized cotton fiber and the bulb turns on. Viewers have commented, "I will never forget that moment. I feel like I was there."

Students viewing the Egyptian Oracle performance are likewise absorbing information through multiple intelligences. They are able to interact with characters from a historical time period, thus creating visceral memories. They experience the performance with their bodies by participating in the drama, and they are able to ask questions of the performers in real time.

Connection to Common Core State Standards

The Egyptian Oracle Project is closely aligned with specific curriculum goals in several grades. Following are a few examples.

Literacy standards for grades K-5 specify integration of knowledge and ideas through illustration as well as words. They want students to comprehend different forms of literature, including stories, drama and poetry. Students are expected to recount stories such as fables, folktales and myths from diverse cultures; determine the central message, lesson or moral; and explain how it is conveyed through key details in the text (CCSS 2014: CCSS.ELA-Literacy.RL.3.2).

Sixth-grade English-language arts require students to integrate information presented in different media or formats as well as in words to develop a coherent understanding of a topic or issue (CCSS 2014: 6.RIT.7). Writing skills include the use of technology, including the Internet, and collaboration and interaction with others to produce writing samples (CCSS 2014: 6.W.6). New York State social studies standards expect sixth-grade students to know the social and economic characteristics—customs, traditions, child-rearing practices, ways of making a living, education, socialization practices, gender roles, foods, and religious and spiritual beliefs—that distinguish different cultures and civilizations (NYSED 2014).

Literacy standards in grades 11 and 12 require students to integrate and evaluate multiple sources of information presented in diverse formats and by diverse media (CCSS 2014: CCSS.ELA-Literacy.RH.11-12.7), including visual information from charts, graphs, photographs, videos or maps (CCSS 2014: CCSS.ELA-Literacy.RH.6-8.7). They are urged to make strategic use of digital media (textual, graphical, audio, visual and interactive elements) in presentations to enhance understanding of findings, reasoning and evidence and to add interest (CCSS 2014: CCSS.ELA-Literacy.SL.11-12.5).

Puppets meet technology

Background

Puppetry has gone through many transformations since ancient Egyptian times. Early puppets were made from wood, clay, bone, ivory, beads, feathers, leather and other natural materials. Today's puppet-builders often use foam, fabric, aluminum, latex, polyurethanes, lightweight carbon fibers and plastics (Blumenthal 2005: 12). As puppet performance became popular in the twentieth-century world of film, television and other recorded media, complex mechanical and electronic devices were added to the repertoire. With the advent of recent digital technology, puppeteers have the ability to manipulate space and time inside a new "silicon universe" of virtual reality. It is through this digital portal that the Egyptian Oracle Project finds its place in the digital age, by using a blend of gaming technologies and computer-generated images (CGI) that exist only in our virtual world. What hasn't changed, despite all the makeovers, is the role of the skilled puppeteer in bringing the figures to life (Sturz, Jacobson and Lawrence 2013).

Puppets in film

In the 1950s a few puppeteers were admitted to the Screen Actors Guild (SAG) in the category "special acts." Stunning examples of classic puppetry of the time include Bill Baird's marionettes in *The Sound of Music*, Burr Tilstrum's hand puppets in *Kukla, Fran, and Ollie* (Latshaw 2000), Margot and Rufus Rose's performance of Howdy Doody (Latshaw 2000), Topo Gigio on the *Ed*

Sullivan Show (Ilson 2009) and Shari Lewis's Lamb Chop (Harrington 1958). With the popularity of shows such as *Sesame Street* and *The Muppet Show*, beginning in the 1970s, on-camera puppeteers required specialized training to work with monitors to master precise eye focus, lip-syncing, body posture and arm motions. Within the Screen Actors Guild, puppeteers were upgraded to principal performers, with the same benefits and residuals as other SAG actors.

In pre-digital Hollywood, if your film required a fantastic character, you had few choices for how to achieve it: puppets, costumes or stop-motion animation (Johnson 1996). Each of these approaches had advantages and drawbacks, and the best effects were often a combination of all three. Often the choice involved how much of the character the camera needed to see. If using a puppet, it was necessary to disguise or hide the puppeteer and the puppeteer's controls. Puppeteers were stuffed into plants, hidden under floorboards or squeezed behind furniture while operating puppets over their heads and responding to a monitor behind them. These contortions were somewhat alleviated in the 1980s, when technicians learned to use the Quantel (later Harry) Paintbox television graphics system for rod removal (Thornton 1990). Another innovation of the time placed puppeteers clad in colored bodysuits

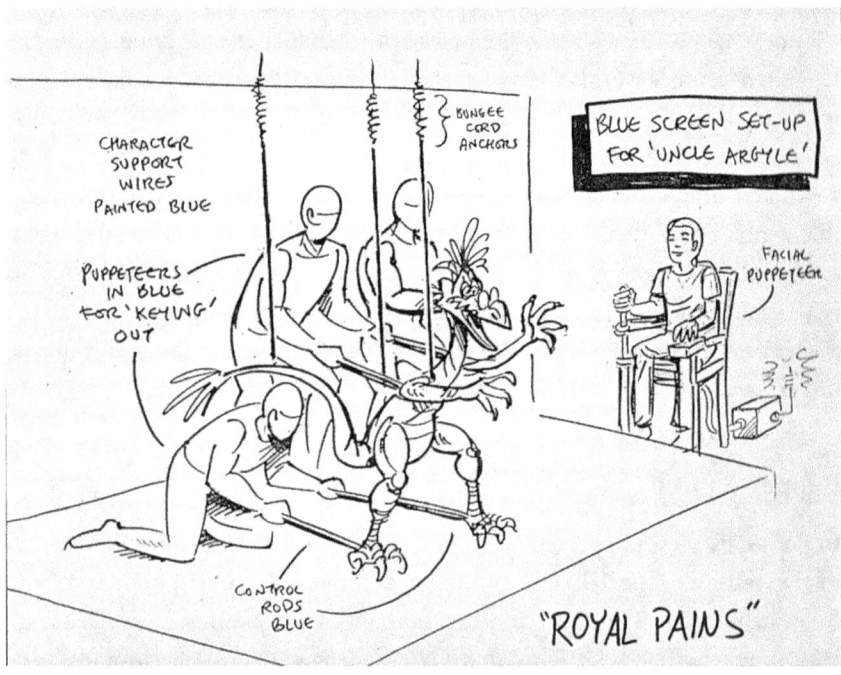

Figure 7.2 Blue-screen setup for "Uncle Argyle." Illustration by Pete Von Sholly.

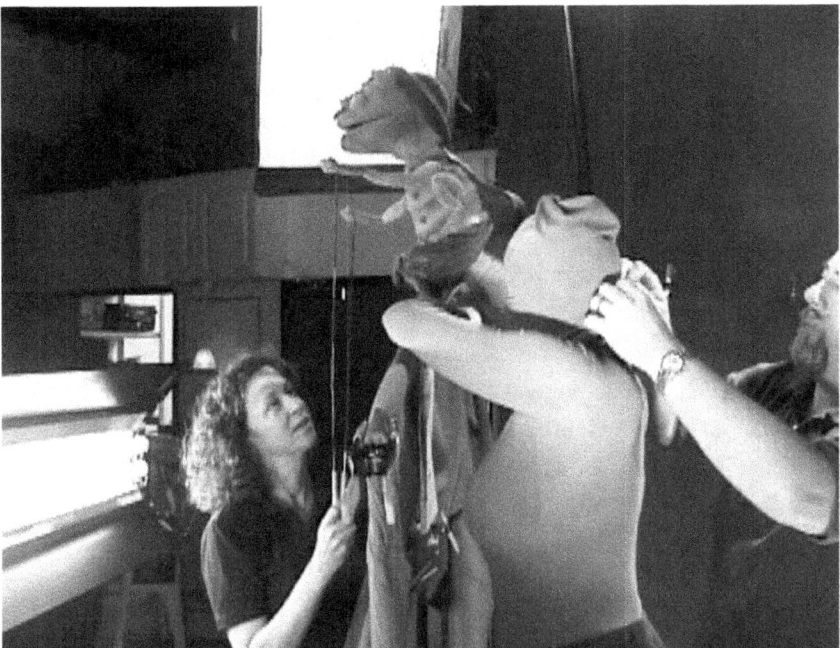

Figure 7.3 Lisa Sturz (in blue) controlling the puppet "Archie," with Wendy Morton (left) assisting.

in front of matching blue or green screens. They manipulated their characters while taking care not to move a rod or hand in front of the puppet (Figure 7.2). The puppeteers were keyed out in post-production and the performance was then layered into a previously filmed scene (Figure 7.3). This technique allowed full-body figures to inhabit more complex scenes but was touchy to light and restrictive to the performers.

By the 1980s and 1990s, technology was advancing quickly. Household computers were becoming the norm, and a rare breed of young geeks was learning to navigate, improve and create software. This new generation matured around the beginning of *Sesame Street* and *The Muppet Show*, and many were diehard fans. They grew up playing with mechanized gadgets and robots and they dissected radios, televisions and computers for fun. As they entered the workforce, many found a home in the motion picture industry just as the film elite were nurturing society's appetite for fantasy, horror and alien productions. The friendly hand-and-rod puppets of *The Muppet Show* were becoming latex figures with articulated expressions and mechanized controls.

The inside track

The following is a memoir of the author's experiences as a puppeteer during this pivotal time. Most of the assertions made here are from personal observation.

I was lucky to be among a group of puppeteers in Hollywood who were living the transformation first-hand. Many of us were also puppet-builders who freelanced at the various "creature shops" popping up all over southern California and Marin County. We often were hired because we had been practicing with and troubleshooting the figures as they were being created. We stumbled through each new development and became comfortable with change. Sometimes the puppets worked smoothly, supporting our performer's instincts. But often the interface was counterintuitive, for example, with a back-and-forth lever controlling up-and-down movements of the puppet. We had to adjust quickly under pressure as the time-is-money clock raced and producers checked their watches. Hand controls morphed from wooden toggles to pistol-grip triggers, and then to custom remote-controlled (RC) thumb contours and hardwired telemetrics that allowed one person to do what three or four had done previously. We breathed deeply and did our jobs.

In 1984 legendary makeup artist Rick Baker was nominated for an Oscar for his fantasy chimps in *Greystoke: The Legend of Tarzan, Lord of the Apes* (see http://www.imdb.com/name/nm0000711/awards). Rick had developed a facial control called the "lip loop," which helped produce a wonderful range of expressions in the apes' foam latex faces; the cable-and-lever mechanism required teams of puppeteers to operate. A few years later he received another award for *Harry and the Hendersons*, which used primarily remote controls that reduced the number of puppeteers needed: Rick worked the lower lip, Tim Lawrence was the upper lip and Tom Hester worked the brows, while Kevin Peter Hall acted inside the "Harry" suit. For the television version, the sole puppeteer, Brock Winkliss, rebuilt the controls into a special "quad box."

In *Captain EO* the 3D Disney short, Captain Eo and the Space Knights produced by George Lucas and directed by Francis Ford Coppola, I worked Hooter the elephant (Tony Cox acted inside a suit for wide shots) and the two-headed "geex," Idy and Ody, which I shared with Terri Hardin. The latter had a heavy, elaborate mechanism to open and close the mouth and move the head up and down. After rehearsing for several hours, I asked Bruce Schwartz, our lead puppeteer, for permission to remove the mechanism. He agreed, and I was able to get more expression just using my hand. The device was awkward and unnecessary, but it was a step in a new direction. In that same production I learned to master cable-controlled eye mechanisms that allowed the characters to look from side to side and blink. The film featured a small cable-controlled animatronic creature, "Fuzzball," designed by Rick Baker's makeup and effects shop. The main creator in the shop, Tom Hester, skillfully operated its complex cable controls.

Meanwhile in England, a Henson protégé of special effects designer Faz Fazakas, Tad Krzanowski, was revolutionizing remote-controlled performance. There had been much discussion about RC versus hardwiring the controls during the making of *The Dark Crystal* (1982), but it was on *Labyrinth* (1986) that the ideas, schedule and budget came together for the first time. Tad's engineering genius shone through in the character "Hoggle"—a marvel of technology. Any remote-control single-person performance podium you see today is still heavily indebted to Tad's original designs.

Later that year I started work on Lucasfilm's production of *Howard the Duck*. The puppets were built in the creature shop at Industrial Light & Magic (ILM). Tad fashioned remotely controlled eye-blinks and facial expressions to within a micro-millimeter of accuracy. Tim Rose held up the body of "Howard" and worked his head while Steve Sleap operated the eye-blinks and other facial moves remotely. I manipulated the hands and had a tube in my mouth to make him breathe. We worked carefully together like chamber musicians, planning our movements to attain a natural blend. I also had opportunities to work Tad's remote controls, animating the character's face during scenes in which a little person (either Ed Gale or Jordan Prentice) worked inside a full suit. We carefully controlled the character's eye-blinks before he changed focus or came up with a thought. This animation involved more mental and mechanical focus than performing directly with a live puppet, but Tad's interface helped the movements flow.

Eric Allard's All Effects Company (http://allfx.com) designed and built the famous "Energizer Bunny." The bunny had several servomechanisms built into the body and actually ran on Energizer batteries, stored inside the drum. I maneuvered the remote-controlled figure for several commercials. Eric's technology allowed me to change directions quickly and spin the character in circles. All Effects also built the telemetry suit that moved "Number 5" in 1986's *Short Circuit*. Gordon Robertson puppeteered the robot for the movie, but I wore the telemetry suit for some public appearances. With the suit on, my limb movements were translated electronically to the robot. I had to practice a bit to account for any slight delays or exaggerations, but I easily got the hang of it. Even though the suit could transfer my movements accurately to the puppet, it still required thought and seasoned performance skills to determine the scale, mood and intention of each action.

In 1988 the Henson organization was front and center with its creation of the first modern digital puppet, "Waldo C. Graphic." Before its use in puppetry, "waldo" (after a character in a Robert Heinlein story) referred to mechanical arms, telemetry and other anthropomorphic gadgetry used by the NASA space fleet. Designer Kirk Thatcher created a mitten-like motion-capture device called a waldo that was controlled in real time by a puppeteer wearing a skeletal framework and standing twenty to thirty feet from the actual set. The computer image of "Waldo" was mixed with a video feed so that it could interact directly with physical puppets. Puppeteer and engineer Rick Lazzarini took the idea a little further. When faced with the challenge of making a head of lettuce spring to life for a Kraft salad commercial, he attached sensors to a helmet and affixed additional sensor probes to his face. He routed the wires through a computer circuit board and attached servomotors. When he raised his left eyebrow, his on-camera doppelganger did the same.

In 1990 I was hired by Phil Tippett as a puppeteer for the robot monster "Nemesis" character in *RoboCop 2*. At the audition Phil explained that the puppet was a big, gawky machine that required performers with mechanical dexterity, precision and stamina. I showed him the forklift license I had acquired while working for Walt Disney Imagineering. That, combined with the fact that I had ridden my bicycle from Hollywood to Santa Monica, got me the job. Once on set, we were armed with adjustable wrenches so that we could loosen the appropriate joint just before "Action" was called. We did several all-night shoots in the warm Texas location, so I decided to dress for the occasion in an elegant black sleeveless top with long black evening gloves. A candid photo made it into *Premiere* magazine.

Later that year I helped with some background shots for *Gremlins 2: The New Batch*, with characters designed by Rick Baker, who was determined to improve the mechanical controls that Chris Walas had created for the first movie. Most of the characters were slick hand-and-rod puppets covered with latex foam or fur, with fluid-cabled eye mechanisms. I was working one of many characters in a crowded scene while the "Brain Gremlin" sang "New York, New York." Tim Lawrence was in the lead, operating the body and head, while Steve Sleap assisted on the arms. Mark Setrakian worked the Waldo-inspired mechanism built to create accurate lip-syncing and subtle expression as Tony Randall's voice rang through the playback. Mark Wilson and Tom Hester operated the eyes, lids, brows and ears by remote control. Everyone performed together in perfect harmony. It was epic.

Film puppetry changed so much in one decade that producers started questioning whether puppeteers should be paid as actors. They argued that the animatronic figures were special effects and should be under the jurisdiction of IATSE, the technical union. In 1991 the Screen Actors Guild set up a National Puppeteers Caucus to define what an on-camera puppeteer does, discuss changes in the industry, and set professional guidelines. That summer I co-authored an article, "On Camera: SAG Puppeteers—The Modern Practice of an Ancient Art" (with Mark Bryan Wilson) for the Screen Actors Guild magazine; it addressed the new technologies such as cables, radio-control devices, hydraulics, pneumatics, electronics and waldos that had replaced or augmented more traditional hand-operated puppets.

The final showdown was well attended. We puppeteers introduced our position with a simple hand-and-mouth puppet character performed by direct manipulation. The puppet loosened up the crowd with humor and style, and everyone agreed it was a worthy performance. Rick Lazzarrini had prepared several versions of the same puppet that were each controlled differently. We puppeteers worked out an identical routine that we performed consecutively using hand, cables and remote control. The caucus concluded that puppeteers should continue to be credited as principal performers because they take direction from the film director and create dramatic performances just as actors do.

In 1993 I was one of three puppeteers for "Master Splinter" in *Teenage Mutant Ninja Turtles III*, with characters built by All Effects. (Henson Productions had created the figures for the first two *Teenage Mutant Ninja Turtles* movies, in which "Splinter" was controlled by Kevin Clash.) Tim Lawrence moved the head and body. Since I was light, agile and strong, with long arms, I was once again cast to manipulate the hands. I had to reach around Tim's body, straining to see a monitor off to the side. James Murray voiced "Splinter" while working the mouth and facial expressions remotely. It took a lot of discussion and coordination to work and breathe as a team. Tim and I could talk to each other directly, but we had to communicate with James via headset. All three of us studied the video feed to modulate our performance as it was being recorded, and we often used playback to review and refine our movements. We worked closely with the four turtle characters and timed our gestures with theirs. Each turtle had a physical performer inside the suit and a puppeteer outside, watching the performance on monitors while manipulating the complex mechanics that gave expression to the faces (Figure 7.4).

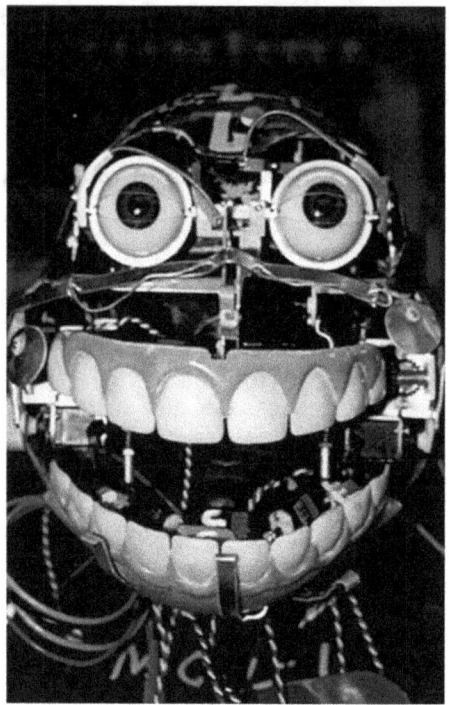

Figure 7.4a "Teenage Mutant Ninja Turtle," built by All Effects.

Figure 7.4b Puppeteers (from left to right) Jim Martin, Noah MacNeal, Gord Roberson and Rick Lyon.

Later that year I was on a team of puppeteers working on *The Flintstones*. Our first shot called for us to manipulate a fifty-foot-long brontosaurus. We had a dozen puppeteers carefully spaced inside the body according to size and strength, with ropes and cables to control the large neck. This time we worked more like dancers participating in a wave of choreography. I stayed on to become part of a smaller crew working the movements of the "Dictabird"; I was in charge of the remotely controlled eyes, part of my standard puppeteer vocabulary. I was also cast as one of the puppeteers for "Dino," the family pet. The day before rehearsals started, many of our cast and crew went to the opening of *Jurassic Park*, which was the first film to employ computer-generated imagery (CGI) on a large scale. We all knew it was a historic moment. The next day when we looked at the call sheet, we learned that the puppet had been replaced by CGI.

Phil Tippett Studios pioneered the prototypes for *Jurassic Park* back in 1988, by converting armatures built for stop-motion animation and transferring their movements to a computer. Joint movement was read and measured by rotary potentiometers that animated computer-generated dinosaurs. These digital input devices, or DIDs, revolutionized the industry once again (Figure 7.5). (For more on DIDs, see http://www.blep.com/rd/special-effects/dinosaur-input-device/).

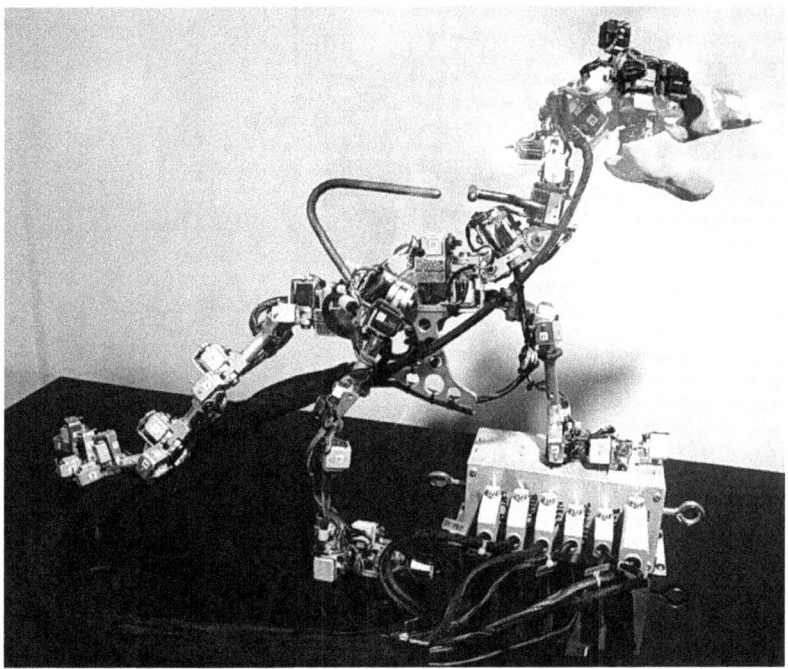

Figure 7.5 Digital input device (DID) used to control a large dinosaur puppet in *Jurassic Park*. Created by Craig Hayes, Rick Sayre, Brian Knep and Tom Williams.

In 1996 I was involved with another new technique, used in *Who Framed Roger Rabbit*. My job was to manipulate objects such as the dancing brooms in real time. The puppeteers worked with a choreographer and moved the brooms to music. The animation crew then painted out the puppeteers and used the footage as a road map for executing the two-dimensional cartoon brooms that appeared onscreen.

That same year I was on the cutting edge of another major transformation, as one of a few puppeteers hired by DreamWorks to experiment

Figure 7.6 Digital input device (DID) used to control a digital puppet, "Scooby Doo," © Hanna-Barbera. Illustration by Pete Von Sholly.

with motion-capture techniques for the first *Shrek* movie. The project literally began in Tim Lawrence's garage in North Hollywood. The idea was to combine motion capture, key-frame animation, puppetry and sculpted facial expressions digitized into the computer. Tim and Loren Soman fashioned uncovered articulated puppets based on the character illustrations DreamWorks provided. Each figure had several reflective spheres carefully embedded in the joints and extremities. Once in the studio, we were surrounded by cameras, each tracking the movements of the balls from its unique vantage point. The multiple feeds were sorted and analyzed by a master computer that used the information to animate two-dimensional figures on the computer screen. In this case our live performance was a digital input device that was read optically by the cameras.

Digital puppets and live reality theater

Brad Shur on the Egyptian Oracle Project

Brad Shur was the puppeteer for all of the Egyptian Oracle performances and played a central role in developing the show. The following is based on an interview with Brad in 2013.

When the Egyptian Oracle was first being envisioned, the main contributors thought they could easily find a puppeteer to plug into the project for the performances. They quickly realized that their committee of academics could do a great job with the historical content and accuracy of the model, but to create an engaging experience they needed a professional performer to influence the creative direction and development of the script.

The project greatly benefited from the participation of puppeteer Brad Shur. Brad has been a puppeteer for fourteen years and is currently a principal performer at the Puppet Showcase, outside Boston. Brad attended the Rhode Island School of Design, where he majored in film. There he had the opportunity to develop skills in traditional animation, video puppetry and digital animation. He studied hand puppetry for four years with Paul Vincent Davis, mastering the rigorous technique developed by Carol Fijan, which focuses on how to use the limited actions of a glove puppet in a thoughtful way to communicate emotional content. His prior training also included walking around inside a latex monster costume, creating improvised interactions with bystanders. And, like most men of his generation, Brad spent many boyhood hours with Game Boy and Nintendo technology that he has been able to translate into digital puppetry skills.

The puppeteer's concerns are the character that will be animated and what that character needs to do. In our story there is a live narrator, "Atumirdis" (played by Brenda Huggins), who serves as a facilitator between the modern audience and the ancient Egyptian setting. The priest puppet is the mouthpiece for the virtual Egyptian world. He guides the actions of the ritual and interacts with the audience. To resonate with the historical period and setting, his movements must be formal, decisive and clear. To prepare himself for answering audience questions, Brad had to study Egyptian culture and the role of the oracle; as well, the script contains much specific dialogue. Brad's job was to create a believable character and to express the text in a visually interesting and compelling way.

Many of Brad's ideas for the puppet had to be modified to fit the technical constraints of the controller. The biggest challenge was coming up with a movement vocabulary that could serve the demands of the script within the limits of the technology—in other words, to use cheap technology to make an expressive character. The control consists of six analog buttons, one arrow pad, one joystick and two buttons that work like volume controls but can be applied to actions for the movements; the software automatically blends the movements into a continuous phrase. It was not possible to have a full cycle of any one movement.

It took a lot of back-and-forth experimentation between Brad and Friedrich Kirchner, the programmer, to settle on the final configuration. Brad had to develop an understanding of what digital puppets can do effectively and what is difficult to program, and every gesture had to be preprogrammed. Together Brad and Frederick needed to create a specific map of the movements that could be accessed during the performance. For example, a repeated sequence consisted of the priest standing, tilting his head to look in a specific direction, and lifting his right arm to point.

An exciting part of the performance for Brad was the audience interaction. He was positioned backstage in such a way that he could partially see the audience. His station included a laptop monitor that showed what the audience could see, as well as a webcam that could scan the audience itself. Using these tools, Brad was able to bring the participants into his world; he could, for example, point directly at audience members and comment on what they were wearing. It would often be at least halfway through the presentation before the audience realized that the puppet had a live component, and that was when the magic really began to happen. Information started flowing both ways: the audience could talk to the priest puppet and Brad could respond appropriately and connect with them in a deeper way. Over the course of the twelve performances, Brad was able to get a sense of what worked and what didn't, and as with any performance, he was able to hone and refine it over time. The script was tightened and Brad figured out exactly where he could go off script to respond to the audience.

For future projects, Brad would like to experiment with non-human characters. His experience has given him a keen awareness of what digital puppets can do effectively—and what they cannot. Different puppets require different mapping. Given the limited control mechanism, there is only enough "juice" for one kind of interface at a time. Human characters use up much of the available technology in expounding and gesturing. One of the long-term goals of the Egyptian Oracle Project is to make better low-cost control schemes accessible to the public. Brad will be ready.

Kirk Thatcher on creating "Waldo C. Graphic"

Kirk Thatcher is a writer and director who has worked with the Muppets since 1989. He has also designed, built, painted and operated creatures in numerous films and music videos, for Industrial Light and Magic (ILM), Disney and his own production company.

I met and started working with Jim Henson in 1987 after working at ILM in the early eighties and watching the birth of Pixar and the dawn of computer-generated (CG) characters for film. Jim and I were both excited about how computer graphics were going to change and advance the way characters were done for films and television, and Jim had already spent a lot of money on the computer-generated owl for the opening of *Labyrinth*. We were both interested in seeing how CG characters could be performed and manipulated in real time by puppeteers, much like hand or rod puppets but without the constraints of physical materials or needing to hide the performers. That was the promise of computer-generated puppets—no restraints on the design because of physics!

On the other hand, computers were still fairly slow in terms of handling the tremendous amounts of data gathered during a live performance, so we decided a flying character without arms and legs would be a good start—a flying head, more or less. The performer could focus on the performance of the face and mouth and the computer wouldn't get bogged down by all the arm and leg motion data. So that's why "Waldo C. Graphic" looked the way he did: we couldn't overwhelm the computers with too much information.

It was tremendously expensive to develop Waldo for the *Jim Henson Hour* television series, but the little weirdo ended up being a perfect character to use in the Muppet 3-D attraction at Disney World, being computer-generated and easily converted to stereo-vision 3-D. He could fly right out over the audience and interact with them much more convincingly than a traditional Muppet could, and we didn't have to use an awkward green-screen setup to hide the performers—always a lot of work, and it still tended to look odd.

Sadly, Jim passed away soon afterward and the work we had done was put aside for a while. Ultimately, however, it became the basis for the Henson Digital Performance System (HDPS), which is now used to control both real-world rubber creatures and completely digital characters such as those in the PBS series produced by the Henson Company, *Sid the Science Kid*.

Conclusion

Today many of the puppets used in film are digital. These highly realistic, lifelike digital puppets, such as Gollum from *The Lord of the Rings* (Allison 2011), are driven by live motion capture of an entire human figure, similar to the puppet experiments we did for *Shrek*. For Gollum, the actor's movements were translated directly to the virtual body, which was digitally captured and merged with the live footage. This humanoid effect is perfect for detailed anthropomorphic figures; however, it is not the ultimate control interface for less human characters. The Henson Company and others use more abstract control mechanisms to amplify the power of caricature. They deliberately exaggerate the puppets' motions to achieve dramatic effect in a way that would be neither efficient nor possible with full-body motion capture.

For the Egyptian Oracle Project we use an Xbox 360 controller, which provides both precision and an acceptable range of expression (see Chapter 4). The control's contour is reminiscent of the mechanisms used to operate facial expression during the preceding decades. Thus the puppeteer and the controller form a bridge between analog and digital manipulation.

However a puppet is made to move—with a hand inside it; with strings, rods, cables, levers or electronic circuitry controlling its parts; or with a human being inside a motion-capture suit programming a computer—the common denominator is the puppeteer: a skilled human being who knows just how to move the figure to create the illusion of character, personality and emotion. The puppeteer understands who the character is, what the character needs to do physically and what emotions the character must convey—and, along the way, also becomes a master of the sometimes complex technology needed to accomplish those goals.

8

Introduction to Virtual Heritage

Erik Champion

Introduction and definition

The focus of this book—on archaeology and the classics reinvigorated by puppetry and performance, using digital environments—is an interesting and unusual contribution to the area of virtual heritage. In this chapter I wish to quickly cover some of the changes in the development and thinking behind virtual heritage, and to consider potential advantages of using performance and theatrical devices in the staging of virtual heritage.

Virtual heritage has generally been viewed as a hybrid marriage of virtual reality (VR) and cultural heritage, but there are few accessible examples of virtual heritage that incorporate live performance, let alone in a university. A definition closer to the potential contribution of performance was devised by Stone and Ojika (2000), who defined virtual heritage as "the use of computer-based interactive technologies to record, preserve, or recreate artifacts, sites and actors of historic, artistic, religious, and cultural significance and to deliver the results openly to a global audience in such a way as to provide formative educational experiences through electronic manipulations of time and space."

The Stone and Ojika definition is an interesting definition but I wish to modify it slightly, for it does not explicitly cover the preservation, communication and dissemination of beliefs, rituals and other cultural behaviors and activities. We also need to take into account authenticity of reproduction, scholastic rigor and sensitivity to the needs of the audience and to the needs of the audience while respecting the wishes of those who created and maintained the original cultural sites. Consider, for example, this definition: "Visualisation has been defined as 'to form a mental image of something incapable of being viewed or not at that moment visible'… (Collins Dictionary) … a tool or method for interpreting image data fed into a computer and for generating images from complex multi-dimensional data sets" (McCormick, DeFanti and Brown 1987). If we apply this definition, the more traditional aim of virtual heritage might be to visualize a culture through digital depiction of its artifacts; virtual heritage is often described as a "visualization" or "re-creation" of culture. In virtual heritage projects, the oft-cited aim is to recreate or "reconstruct" the past through three-dimensional modeling, animation and panoramic photographs. In more advanced examples, objects are laser-scanned so that accurate textures that used to be there can be applied to the resulting digital models.

Early examples of digital archaeology and virtual heritage

Although there have been earlier examples of digital archaeology (Forte 1997; Reilly 1990; Sylaiou and Patias 2004), Britain's Dudley Castle is one of the first examples of virtual heritage in a museum (Boland and Johnson 1996). The user could move one of two circular buttons to navigate the laser-disc-stored computer model "reconstruction" of the castle. The castle's website describes this project as a "virtual tour" or "virtual reality tour," but there was no head-mounted display, or even a wall projection that changed in viewpoint when users changed their position or gaze.

Tenochtitlán, one of the first web-based examples of virtual heritage, was both a model of a cultural heritage site and a showcase for new technology: Virtual Reality Modeling Language (VRML). With its offering of the second version (VRML 2.0) of this declared new 3-D standard for web models, Silicon Graphics provided a VRML model of the ancient Aztec city (Harman and Wernecke 1996). VRML was single user only, the browser software was often unreliable and not always maintained, and the models were large and very slow.

There were also several major computer-based virtual heritage projects in the early 1990s. Learning Sites (2011) has described its work on the Egyptian site of Buhen. Later in the decade the Federation of American Scientists released its educational "Discover Babylon," a free downloadable project but difficult to run on modern computers (http://www.discoverbabylon.org/). And there were many other projects, though often not labeled as virtual heritage; for example, one of the earliest books on the field was titled *Virtual Archaeology* (Forte 1997).

Missing cultural features in virtual heritage projects

Today we can view the above projects as ambitious challenges undertaken with an incredible amount of energy, but despite the resources and enthusiasm poured into these virtual sites, interaction was typically severely limited and depictions of inhabitants were scarce or unrealistic. Most important, differing cultural beliefs were not contestable and they were not learned through immersion in roles or rituals. No doubt this is because of the many issues involved in the presentation of culture. One is the definition of *culture* itself, the second issue is understanding how culture is transmitted, and the third is how to transmit locally situated cultural knowledge to people from another culture. In the case of virtual heritage, a fourth concern also arises: exactly how can this specific cultural knowledge be transmitted digitally?

It may seem that virtual heritage is simply re-creation of what used to be there. But what used to be *there* was more than just a collection of objects. Those objects had specific cultural meaning for the land's traditional inhabitants. So reproducing the artifacts is not enough; we must convey the importance of that cultural heritage to the public—and this is not easy. The culture may no longer exist and our understanding of it may be conflicted; conversely, it may be so ingrained that we do not normally notice or appreciate it, or the remains of the society or civilization may be currently inaccessible or scattered. For example, according to cultural geographer Yi-Fu Tuan (1998), culture is that which is not seen: "Seeing what is not there lies at the foundation of all human culture." He has further defined culture as a shared form of escapism. Such a definition raises an interesting paradox for the visualization of past cultures: how do we see what is not there?

So virtual heritage projects typically aim to provide three-dimensional interactive digital environments that aid the understanding of cultures and languages, rather than merely transferring learning terms and strategies from static, prescriptive media such as books. In a parallel but converging field of research, "serious games" typically use modified computer games as virtual learning environments. As an intersection between the two fields, game-based historical learning aims to provide ways in which the technology, interactivity and cultural conventions of computer gaming can help afford cultural understanding of the self, of the past, or of others with mindsets quite different from our own. The Egyptian Oracle is arguably such a project, but in an interesting twist, it also acts as a platform for classroom-based learning via plays, and social judgment is facilitated through real-time socially embedded narration and through avatar interaction as a form of puppetry.

Virtual environments are not virtual worlds

For Weckström (2003: 21), in order to achieve "worldliness," a virtual environment must allow for various ways of doing things: "The worldliness of 'the Roman world' is in the multitude of different characters involved in making it a world. For this Roman world to be rendered virtually, it should offer the user the possibility to choose from a multitude of things to do, and lives to lead." A world should be specific but it should allow you to do different things in different ways. First, the virtual environment offers at least one thematic cultural way of looking at things (for example, being a Roman). Second, there is more than one way of interacting with the world (you can invade countries, build roads or deliver speeches to the Senate). Third, the way of interacting with the virtual environment depends on your selection of a certain social role (although you can select different actions, this depends on whether you are a Roman centurion, engineer or senator).

Weckström's idea of worldliness may also mean that there should actually be at least two thematic cultural ways available in the world, for example, a Roman way and a "barbarian" way. In other words, the social and cultural framework is defined not just by how it allows people to communicate but also by the existence of a distinguishing framework. I believe that what he was searching for was *hermeneutic affordance*. Hermeneutics argues that we must grasp the world of the interpreter as well as the world of the interpreted in order to gain the meaning of the text or artwork. For example, the philosopher Hans-Georg Gadamer wrote that language is intersubjective, as exemplified by how children learn—by seeing how others respond to them. Learning is an interactive process; a language itself constitutes our life-world.

If we cannot experience the social presence of the original inhabitants, we need to feel their agency through their cultural presence. A feeling of strong cultural presence requires being physically embodied (we have a body that affects and is affected by other objects and forces), socially embedded (others are present to whom we feel socially bound) and culturally inscribed in the world (our actions and those of others leave a lasting and meaningful impression on it). The degree of complexity of such a virtual environment may range from causing us merely to believe that people with a different worldview existed in an environment to feeling that we are being rejected or assimilated by the other culture, to feeling that we are "home."

Currently I know of no virtual environment that can compare in emotional attachment to a real-world home. However, I would argue that online gaming environments such as *World of Warcraft* come closer to this feeling of home than traditional virtual environments, because communities (for lack of a better word) share content, meanings and some aspects of ritual-like behavior in these worlds, and the activities have some forms of social convention attached to them. There are games such as *Elder Scrolls: Skyrim* and a few virtual heritage projects that feature simulated rituals—such as the University of California at Berkeley's Virtual Samor Prei Kuk, Cambodia (http://www.ced.berkeley.edu/research/sambor/)—but without human actors they lack the feeling of intimacy, uniqueness and also social judgment that we experience in real-world rituals.

Public engagement

As Shackley has noted, public expectation and the journey may be as important as the visit itself (2001: 27). If content designers view virtual heritage environments as standalone re-creations of objects, visitors may be short-changed in terms of the learning experience. They will not have the background contextual knowledge of the archaeologist, nor can they be relied on to possess well-trained deductive logic or a scientifically honed ability to create and test hypotheses.

Research has indicated that the general public wants not realism but entertaining immersion. Various researchers have suggested that virtual environments (specifically heritage environments) often lack several features that would make them more engaging to the general public. "[T]he archaeological use of VR is at present all about the creation of pictures ... Only after they have been generated does attention turn to the uses to which such models can be put" (Gillings 2002: 17). Both Gillings and I suggest that it is not a lack of realism but a lack of meaningful content that impedes the enjoyment of virtual heritage. I have called it the "Indiana Jones dilemma" (Champion 2004). On the one hand, adventure films have popularized archaeology as an interactive and engaging pursuit; on the other hand, films and computer games typically destroy their very object of admiration.

For example, new media as interactive entertainment has often been advanced as a way of creating meaningful online worlds, but the reasons for the success of virtual environments as games often prevent their success as meaningful content-based environments. Digital media can recreate both objects and activities, but what sort of activity is both engaging and educational? How can we both significantly preserve and meaningfully communicate the past? Can we incorporate the procedural learning and intuitive conventions of interactive entertainment into the exploration of virtual worlds?

Game technology for cultural heritage

Computer games offer interesting opportunities to the audience, artist and critic. They are no longer shallow single-player interfaces; rather, they are turning into multivalent, multidimensional, user-directed collaborative virtual worlds. Commercial games are often bundled with world-creation technology and networking capability that are threatening to overtake the creation and presentation of displays of expensive, complex specialist VR systems. Facebook recently bought Oculus Rift, a virtual reality system startup company that did not even have a commercially ready product, for two billion dollars (Hern and Stuart 2014). This was revolutionary, as are the trading of virtual goods, fantasy and role-playing settings, user-based modification of virtual environments, and the creation of interesting hybrids through hijacking traditional media—for example, "machinima," the making of films from the virtual cameras in computer games.

A growing number of applications for cultural heritage have harnessed game technology and techniques (Anderson 2003; Champion 2012; Christiansen 2013; Dickey 2006; Leader-Elliott 2003; Mikovec, Slavik and Zara 2009; Wei and Li 2010). The heritage projects may use game engines (Bellotti et al. 2009) or be games in the fuller sense of the word (Chen et al. 2013; Jacobson, Handron and Holden 2009), and some may employ augmented reality (Papagiannakis et al. 2005). Surveys have recently been published on games appropriate to cultural heritage (E. F. Anderson et al. 2010; Girard, Ecalle and Magnan 2013; Mikovec, Slavik and Zara 2009; Mortara et al. 2011). To counter the burgeoning interest in games, there have also been papers warning about game ideas being applied to cultural heritage with disastrous results (Baker 2008; Leader-Elliott 2003).

Computer games are arguably the most successful form of virtual environment and the most interactive of all virtual environments, but they also pose problems for virtual heritage. The virtual environments that players explore are not typically "worlds" in any deep or profound sense. Despite their promise, I believe that both commercial computer games and conventional virtual environments lack a feeling of inhabitation, of animation (i.e. life), and do not afford full imaginative physical embodiment, social embeddedness or cultural presence. They are not inscripted through use.

In mainstream commercial games, content is "fragible"—intended to be destroyed rather than created—and the social positions of the participants are continually threatened rather than established. The player is physically embodied as a killing machine and learns to bend the rules rather than extend or create them. Typically players don't care where they are. They don't cultivate the world; they don't redecorate their surroundings to identify themselves or consider their surroundings in order to understand how people live there. They are not "dirt detectives," and in typical virtual environments they don't need to be.

One may argue that the audience members participating in a museum VR experience are not killing machines or zombies. Their minds are still active and questioning, they don't need instant reflexes, and their trip is singular, short and predicated on a need for some form of education. According to studies (Mosaker 2001; Tost and Champion 2011), when users wearing head-mounted displays visit virtual archaeology sites of high resolution and historical accuracy, projected using impressive specialist graphics technology, they are often disappointed because they cannot feel, live, breathe or thematically communicate with others. They expect real-time interaction of a high quality, not just in terms of interaction but also in terms of being able to talk to computer-generated people (social agency), to sit down (bodily movement) and to feel that the buildings are inhabited (sense of cultural presence).

Gamers, on the other hand, may display addictive behavior and conditioned reflexes, spending many hours transfixed by the screen, their darting eyes and beating fingers the only sign of life. Are they addicted to a meaningless, repetitive, socially immature digital environment? People have died from playing games to the exclusion of all else, and philosophers such as Dreyfus (2001) have warned us that internet usage leads to social exclusion, unhappiness and lack of physical intimacy and embodiment. There is also a growing concern among parents and teachers over the violence in games, and the dangerous link between sedentary behavior and obesity.

In treating extreme phobia cases with the use of virtual environments, photo-realistic detail is not needed; significant detail is. We may extrapolate these findings to capturing the cultural perspectives of a certain society: capturing what its members find evocative and important is arguably the most important aim. Philosophers of science have argued for many centuries that what we see is filtered reality, not actual reality. So virtual environments can be used to engage, distract or stimulate learning or particular phobias without being realistic. Photorealism is an admirable aim if we wish to test the extent of technology, but it may not be the most suitable aim for content.

For example, Clive Thompson wrote: "In 1978, the Japanese roboticist Masahiro Mori noticed something interesting: The more humanlike his robots became, the more people were attracted to them, but only up to a point. If an android become too realistic and lifelike, suddenly people were repelled and disgusted." Mori called this phenomenon the "uncanny valley," and it is further described and illustrated in Dave Bryant's online article "The Uncanny Valley: Why Are Monster-Movie Zombies So Horrifying and Talking Animals So Fascinating?" (2006). Not all game designers vie for photorealism (Schubert 2013; Walker 2013); however, they do attempt to evoke a sense of immersion.

Just as with virtual reality phobia studies, if a game correctly stimulates a user, the participant is too busy experiencing the sensation (horror, terror, etc.) to worry about nitpicking the quality of detail. My term for this—differing to some degree from philosophy (Hahn 2010; Lakoff 1987)—is *experiential realism*. On reflection, game participants feel that they experienced the same degree and nature of involvement as if they had been in a similar situation in the real world. Experiential realism is afforded when the experience is visceral, atmospheric and evocative rather than involving photorealistic capture of detail and rendering. Even films that feature the most advanced computer-generated imagery (CGI), such as *Lord of the Rings* and *King Kong*, often combine sophisticated digital technology such as motion capture with traditional acting and film techniques (Allison 2011).

Regardless of one's take on the actual impact of games, one has only to staff the multimedia stand at a university open house or teach game design to gauge the intense interest and enthusiasm that students have for courses, skills and opportunities to build electronic games. Thanks to the gamer communities, this has resulted in many commercial and shareware games becoming widely available, with level editors, applications for changing software formats, free 3-D models, maps and resources, and cheap and effective interface devices. As a result of the popularity of computer games and console games, we can now purchase affordable peripherals such as skateboards, exercise bicycles, 3-D joysticks, head-mounted displays, force-feedback devices, and "complete entertainment" electronic couches.

Increasingly powerful and more cost-effective cameras, sensors and trackers have now made the body itself an interface tool. We have seen the use of the body's shadow in new media; now we see the body silhouette as an interface mechanism with the Sony Move or the Xbox Kinect (Han et al. 2013), and breath and circulation as navigation controls via cheap biosensors in the meditation game *The Journey to Wild Divine* and in Neurosky and Emotiv peripherals. Hopefully, the next phase of virtual heritage will be able to use such elements of physicality to create ever richer, healthier and more satisfying forms of interaction. Today's players have more opportunities to become fitter, healthier, more expressive and more aware of other people and of their own physical states.

However, computer games lack one thing that traditional games often have—a game master, or moderator. Game masters can create rich outcomes based on player choices; they can help the story move along and develop its dramatic intensity; they can punish flagrant transgressions or offer enticing and changing rewards; they can retrigger shared memories that can lead to group identity; and they can determine which choices are contextually appropriate or historically accurate. In the next section I will suggest four scenarios in which their involvement could improve public engagement and understanding of virtual heritage.

Virtual reality and theatricality

The ability of the audience to share both passively and actively in the development of the performance is perhaps the most interesting and challenging aspect of new media. Aesthetic immersion can be by stealth, by infill. For example, in my teaching, students use commercial game engines to create interactive virtual archaeology projects, but not in terms of conventional realism. Instead they are asked to reanimate sacred places and other sites of beliefs of the past—to use new media to help dead places come alive.

Yet performance is seldom incorporated in virtual heritage projects. Why is that? Traditionally, virtual environments were for single participants; they were not powerful enough to display or record in real time advanced or nuanced interaction, and did not feature interactive narrative or realistic, believable characters. Academics may also have been worried about the audience members' interaction interfering with their understanding of historical scholarship. These constraints are now being overcome. As readers can see from publicVR's Egyptian Oracle Project site (http://publicvr.org/html/pro_oracle.html), combining performance and puppetry with virtual environments may enhance learning and understanding. In the following paragraphs I suggest four new opportunities that may maximize the potential synergy of performance and virtual heritage: (1) hybrid staging; (2) mimesis and social behavior; (3) interactive narrative and micro-stories; and (4) shifting degrees of agency.

As virtual heritage projects have also been shown as multi-wall and surround-space displays (Cruz-Neira, Sandin and DeFanti 1993), they lend themselves to theatricality—to *staging* events. Virtual environments are typically sterile; they appear staged, the virtual inhabitants (if there are any) may lack dramatic interest, events seem to lack spontaneity or dramatic danger, and personal motivation and individual character are seldom expressed. However, when we physically stage a virtual heritage environment, the audience may better grasp the unique physical and social features of the site and its inhabitants, from the places they dwell to the way in which rank and social roles are shown by the way they stand and behave near each other. It is important to remember that the staging of such a performance can be a hybrid affair. Props and backgrounds may be digitally simulated in real time and can form the backdrop to individual human actors. A trained director or game master could change the virtual props or environment, based on the performances of individual actors or on the engagement, understanding or performance of the audience.

Second, both virtual environments and games lack one important aspect of cultural learning that human performance can help redress. Roger Caillois (2001) has written that traditional games have one to four distinct elements: competition, chance, a sense of vertigo and/or play by imitation. Unlike games in society, digital games lack mimesis: we don't learn how to behave and perform through imitating others.

Camera tracking affords the ability to follow and incorporate the movements, orientation, gaze and even changing physiological states of not just one participant but several people simultaneously. Thanks to this technology, we are now able to track and incorporate both bodily movements and facial expressions. We can also incorporate participants' heartbeat, sweating and other physiological changes in their avatars, in the awareness of scripted characters, or in dynamic changes in the simulated environment. Actors have complained about missing the sensation of body heat when in virtual environments; new sensing technologies may resolve this issue for them.

Third, the instant interactive and reactive participatory audience is a new and foreign concept to many humanities academics. However, new ways of developing interactive narrative—through dramatic beats, through incorporating awareness of the human participants, through scientific discoveries about the brain and the way narrative is developed and understood—along with more powerful technology may one day allow for meaningful hybridization of personal stories and mainstream historical trajectories along with physiological responses.

By involving an audience and by incorporating actors, projects such as the one described in this book not only create social richness but may also afford us greater understanding of past events and practices as they affected people and reveal to us their differences and historical situatedness. And as Robyn Gillam mentions in her conclusion to Chapter 1, historical accounts often show us history only from the viewpoint of the elite. By allowing performers to role-play other characters, we can develop at least hypothetically more nuanced ideas of past societies.

Incorporating theatrical recitals into a virtual heritage project is also a powerful narrative device. There are human actors who immerse themselves in social role-playing; social judgment, thanks to the main narrator controlling the guide; and an audience that will give instant feedback on the liveliness of the content. Different archaeological perspectives could become different scenes of the same act, or human actors as narrators could reveal the same scene seen through the lens of different belief systems. Using camera tracking, audience reactions—for example, whether they think an element belongs or is a red herring—could affect the story or gameplay. Borrowing from improvised theater, their shouted cues might be incorporated by the human actors to try to uncover historical truths in the play. Or perhaps biofeedback from the audience could be aggregated into triggers that change the overall story or the presentation of micro-stories during the performance.

Fourth, the interactions and changes in agency among the audience, the human actors, the computer-scripted actors (non-playing characters, or NPCs) and the actors' or puppeteer's avatars could be more richly employed. The human actors could have varying degrees of control over their avatars that might be directly affected by the game master (the puppeteer or director) or the audience. The audience could control the interactive freedom or dramatic import of a human actor's avatar based on their judgment of the character's historical authenticity, believability or acting skills. Or the human actors could be like gods controlling the NPCs. There are many possible combinations of this interplay of interactive agency.

The above ideas may require highly skilled and trained actors, directors and puppeteers. There is no "one size fits all"; each situation will require contextually appropriate interaction, and the staging of the play itself may require specific spaces and conditions. Not every performance will "work," but that is part of the magic of theater.

Conclusion

Digital archaeology is not exactly virtual heritage. Virtual heritage, by definition, must convey the cultural significance of a site and explain why it needs to be preserved, but a digital archaeology model can ignore that aspect or take it for granted. Part of the reason for the slow progress in this field may be that few digitally simulated sites and models clearly explain their purpose. Are they meant to record archaeological data? Are they supposed to convey theories? Are they designed to educate and persuade the public? I doubt that many can fulfill all of those objectives.

As communicative media, virtual heritage environments must develop new metaphors and interface devices to better convey intangible sensations and cultural beliefs, and genres that are collaborative rather than just competitive. They need to become more holistically embodied and physiologically responsive and to foster enriched social interaction. Ideally they should have the ability to annotate and modify and to incorporate the sensations and opinions of the participants. Integrating aspects of performance and teaching with virtual heritage projects is thus, in my eyes at least, an exciting and important development.

Virtual heritage projects still need to more carefully distinguish among actual, conjectural, user-created and -related, and accidental events and objects. The tools must develop further beyond the mouse to accommodate different types of sensory input and multimodal approaches to object creation, for both the tangible and intangible heritage of past and remote places require many different types of sensory experiences. Hopefully more effective and appropriate but also unobtrusive evaluation and user testing will help achieve this goal, but it will not be easy.

With more responsive and more cost-effective technology, along with reintegration of aspects of performance, virtual heritage projects may be able to involve an audience more effectively, allow them to "inhabit" a digital space more imaginatively and richly, and afford them more intuitive and social means to develop ideas as to how past places were used and how social interactions between real and imagined historical characters may have taken place. I have suggested some ways in which theatricality and enhanced real human performance may further enhance the understanding and appreciation of virtual heritage, but far more remain to be discovered.

9

The Virtual Temple: Construction and Use

Jeffrey Jacobson

The reconstructed Egyptian Oracle ceremony takes place in our virtual Egyptian temple, the result of a separate and very long-running project documented at http://publicvr.org/html/pro_egypt.html. From the first version, built in 1993, to the present day, it was intended as an educational tool, a context for experiments in interactive media, and an exploration of the general characteristics of Egyptian formal temples. To date we have used the temple as a guide and teaching tool for understanding the Egyptian formal temple (Handron and Jacobson 2010), as a setting for live performances filmed with blue screen (Gillam, Innes and Jacobson 2010), as the basis for a study on immersive learning (Jacobson 2011a; 2013), and as the environment in which a live audience experiences the Egyptian processional oracle. The most recent version of the temple was funded by grants from the National Endowment for the Humanities (award HD-5120910) and the National Science Foundation (award 0916098). We also reconstructed the *Gates of Horus* game (see below) in this latest version.

The original virtual temple was constructed using a specific conceptual rationale and methodology. Since later versions of the temple still depend on this

Figure 9.1 The front of the virtual temple.

basic template, these will now be explained in some detail. The temple had to be historically authentic, but it also had to be complete. An accurate reconstruction of even the relatively well-preserved temple of Horus at Edfu would have to fill in many of the missing details from other sources and with scholarly judgment. An authentic simulation would also be quite large, have local idiosyncrasies, and be difficult for modern audiences to "read." As an introductory learning tool, the virtual temple must have all the essential elements of a real temple but must be expressed in a way that a modern audience can read.

To balance these priorities, we decided that the virtual temple of Horus would be an exemplar that embodies the most typical features of the formal Egyptian temple (Barsalou 1992). It does not represent any particular actual temple but instead visualizes a formal Egyptian temple that could have existed between 1500 BCE and 200 CE (Grajetzki 2003; Kemp 1989: 65–107). Within these parameters, we have felt free to select from materials that serve our educational goals. Most of the material comes from documentation of the funerary temple of Ramesses III at Medinet Habu, near Luxor in southern Egypt, and the temple of Horus at Edfu, located some ninety kilometers south of Luxor (see below). For cost and readability reasons, we also made the temple relatively small, containing just one pylon, one forward court, one festival hall and one inner sanctuary. Similarly, the decorations, while historically appropriate, are simple compared to those at many actual sites.

We developed the most recent version of the temple using the modern game platform Unity3D (2013), which is also the software platform for the Egyptian Oracle performance. Users can download the temple to their computers and run it as a standalone application. For the Egyptian Oracle Project, we use the simple desktop mode and copy the desktop image to a digital projector. By projecting the temple onto a wall at life size, we enable the audience and the actress playing Atumirdis to interact directly with the priest (see Figure 0.1). The temple application—available at PublicVR's website, http://publicvr.org—can be run on a Macintosh or PC computer or in a web browser.

Every version of the virtual temple was constructed from original Egyptian sources. By 2009, graphics technology had advanced to the point where we could put a great deal more accuracy and detail into the wall decorations and details of the virtual model. While we used the same basic floor plan, the technical and educational team led by Jeffrey Jacobson completely rebuilt the temple from fresh sources, which were selected and interpreted by Robyn Gillam. The materials involved were extensive and the design process complex enough to fill an entire book on its own. In this chapter we provide an overview of sources and describe how we created the virtual temple from the historical materials and made our design decisions, focusing on some key examples to illustrate the process. Then we discuss some of the ways in which the temple has been used and might be employed in the future.

Sources for the current virtual temple

The later versions of the temple that were used for the oracle performance were planned to include more material from the Ptolemaic period, from which the temple of Horus at Edfu, which supplied the basic ground plan, dates. Not only was this closer to the period that we had set the oracular performance in, but it was also when temples were decorated with materials that were particularly informative about the purpose and use of their space and surroundings (see above, Chapter 3), making them particularly suitable for educational purposes. Recent conservation work on later temples in Egypt (ARCE 2011) has rendered more feasible the use of their wall decoration in the virtual model and we began digital image capture at some of these sites for this purpose. It was also hoped many of the ancillary buildings and structures described above in Chapter 3 could also be added to the virtual temple surroundings. Unfortunately, lack of ongoing, stable funding has made the completion of these additions and alterations to the virtual temple impracticable at the present time. We hope that they may still be completed at some future date.

As a result of these funding problems we have had to continue to rely on earlier, New Kingdom sources for wall decoration. Much of the material used in the earlier versions of the temple was retained. It may be observed that basic decorative elements such as column and ceiling motifs remained relatively stable throughout the entire existence of the formal temple from the mid-second millennium BCE through the second century of the Common Era (Arnold 2003). Additions made to the decoration of the forecourt included a version of the frieze depicting the Festival of Sokar which is located on the south side of the inner courtyard of the Ramesses III temple at Medinet Habu (see Chapter 3 and Figure 3.3). Although this ensemble is over a thousand years earlier than the Edfu forecourt on which the virtual temple's forecourt is based, it may be pointed out that similar scenes depicting festival processions in honor of Horus and his consort Hathor are also in the forecourt of the later temple (Watterson 1998, 61–2). However, these reliefs are not well preserved or legible enough to be used in the digital model. Material must be able to be scanned and rendered into a readable form, as well as being easier to visually comprehend for the lay audience.

We chose to represent the shrine in the inner sanctuary as a later type, similar to the black granite example found in the sanctuary at Edfu. Shrines constructed during both the late and early Ptolemaic periods were massive objects carved from single blocks of hard stone. They had a large front door opening and, most commonly, a pyramidal top. Sometimes they were left undecorated, but many were covered with elaborate relief decorations consisting of an extremely complex arrangement of text and pictures. These could provide an encyclopedic record of the mythology and cults of the god, who was shown in many different forms. The reliefs also depicted protective deities that watched over the god as it rested during the night hours. Unfortunately, none of these shrines has been preserved in its original state, so we do not have exact details about the doors, contents or decoration (Roeder 1914; Spencer 2006).

The virtual shrine is undecorated, except for an inscription copied from an old image of Nectanebo's shrine in the Edfu temple (Rochemonteix 1892: 6–11). The inscription is in red to imitate the use of stone inlays popular during this period and to add to its numinous presence. The wooden doors stand open; they are hinged so they open outwards, because the god is thought of as coming into the temple from out of this world (Fischer 1996). The standing image of Horus is based on a large statue in the Walton Hall of Ancient Egypt at the Carnegie Museum of Natural History in Pittsburgh. It is not an artifact but a conceptual model built by Patrick Martin of the museum's Exhibits Division, under the direction of the Walton Hall designers (David Watters 2013, personal communication). At present only a transverse hall in front of the sanctuary and the beginnings of the corridors on either side have been constructed. Eventually we hope to surround the sanctuary with a "mysterious corridor" with radiating chambers (Sauneron and Stierlin 1975: 35).

Our choice of wall decorations was affected by the lack of high-quality open-source imaging. The reliefs of Ptolemaic temples such as those at Edfu and Esna were damaged by being buried in rubbish or fouled with bat guano (Kurth 1994: 38). Older publications used line drawings or black-and-white photographs to reproduce this material. To add some wall decoration to the columned hall, we made use of an old drawing from the *Description de l'Égypte*—a Napoleonic-era record of Egyptian monuments—of the astronomical ceiling of the temple at Esna (Jomard 1809–29: vol. 1, pl. 79), but our main source for wall decoration was the temple at Medinet Habu. For example, we used a watercolor reconstruction of the artwork on the pylon (Oriental Institute 1934: pl. 23) for the front of the virtual temple.

Most of the doorways have been augmented with decorative schemes from appropriate places in the temple at Medinet Habu. We added reliefs to the outer walls of the sanctuary entrance of the king admonishing visitors about purity, as is found at Medinet Habu and many other New Kingdom temples (Murnane 1980: 40). From Medinet Habu we have also used well-preserved reliefs of the festivals of Min and Sokar from the second court into the forecourt (Murnane 1980b: 26–39). While the forecourt at Edfu was also dedicated to the depiction and celebration of festivals, its images are on a small scale and in poor condition (Watterson 1998: 61–5). The images of the king presenting offerings to the god, from the screen wall at Medinet Habu (Oriental Institute 1957: pl. 322), were retained from an older version of the virtual temple after it was found that available images from corresponding walls at Edfu were not suitable for use. The images of the king making offerings to the god and of the divine barque in the shrine are from watercolor reproductions of images in the temple of Sethos I at Abydos (Oriental Institute 1930: pl. 7)—among the most beautiful such images in Egyptian art. The entrance to the temple's mud-brick enclosure has been improved with a reproduction of the gate of Ptolemy III Euergetes (145–116 BCE) at the temple of Khonsu at Karnak, also taken from the *Description de l'Égypte* (Jomard 1809–29: vol. 3, pl. 51).

In recent years the Ministry of Antiquities in Egypt has embarked on an extensive conservation program that includes cleaning and stabilization of painted relief decorations in many of the later temples, revealing their well-preserved and striking color schemes (ARCE 2011). It is hoped that digital images of some of these reliefs, captured by Robyn Gillam in 2011, will be added to the virtual temple when funding permits.

The virtual temple of Horus is a work in progress. Like a real Egyptian temple, it takes time and resources to construct. When these are not available, it remains unfinished, like the temple at Edfu during the Upper Egyptian rebellions of the second century BCE. It is also, like any scholarly project, subject to reappraisal and revision. Although it does not exist in a specific location, this temple is designed with an eye to the same social, economic and cultural factors that shaped the real buildings upon which it is based.

How we built the virtual temples

From 1993 to 2013 we reconstructed the temple five different times, with the help of many collaborators and contributors (see Acknowledgments for a full accounting). The first four rebuilds took advantage of new technologies and were carried out under the guidance of Lynn Holden as content expert. In 2009 Robyn Gillam took over as content expert and brought in new materials. We rebuilt the temple again to produce the current (2014) version. Despite the changes in software and hardware over the years, the general process of rebuilding the temple has always followed this pattern.

Phase 1

The Egyptologist (content expert) gathers evidence and explains it to Dr. Jacobson and whoever is doing the artwork. Jacobson and the Egyptologist work together to develop interpretation of the temple within the limits of the technology and to satisfy our educational goals.

Phase 2

Jacobson and the Egyptologist work with the artists to build the virtual temple's geometry, based on photos of existing temples. The artists use a 3-D modeling tool, usually Autodesk's 3ds Max (Autodesk 2014). The Egyptologist makes decisions about what features should or should not appear, based on the goals of the project and within the constraints of what is authentic. In the most recent temple we continue to have only one courtyard, one festival hall and one sanctuary so that we can concentrate our resources on quality rather than quantity.

Phase 3

Once the geometry is established, we have a three-dimensional space in which we can navigate. Then our artists use Photoshop (Adobe Systems 2014), relying on artwork from the original sources to produce images to put on the walls and other features of the temple. In industry parlance the images are called "textures"—while many contain complex artwork, many others are simply images of stone, sand, wood and so forth. In some cases we are able to take a photograph of artwork with surviving original colors, digitally

Figure 9.2 The artwork finished, textured and applied to the inner sanctuary gate of the virtual temple.

repair some of the damage and apply it directly to the model. Otherwise we start with monochrome tracings of hieroglyphics and fill in their colors with detailed guidance from the Egyptologist. Nearly all the artwork comes from the Oriental Institute's epigraphic study of Medinet Habu begun in the 1930s.

The exact content and placement of the artwork is done with great care and intention. Each of the elements must be authentic, must be correctly placed and must form a coherent whole consistent with Egyptian practice. For example, Figure 9.2 shows complementary images of Pharaoh on either side of the doorway into the inner sanctuary, warning that only the pure may enter. These images were scanned from the epigraphic study of the temple of Ramesses III at Karnak by the Oriental Institute of the University of Chicago (Chicago 1936, pl. 50). Figure 9.2 shows the final artwork applied to the virtual temple's gateway to the inner sanctuary. (This photograph has been modified from the original screenshot for illustrative purposes; it does not necessarily represent the current state of the virtual temple.)

To describe every decision of this type that we made throughout the temple would be beyond the scope of this book, but the example above illustrates the process. We did not "repair" all the damage to hieroglyphics, because of limitations of time and budget, but as the temple develops we will continue to fill in the details.

Phase 4

As the textured model takes shape, the process reveals contradictions and gaps in the original evidence. This problem is familiar to any archaeologist who creates 3-D reconstructions in any medium, physical or digital. It forces the author to make decisions and commit to a course of action. How these decisions are made and the tradeoffs involved are an important issue (discussed in Chapter 8).

Sometimes we have to make adjustments according to the intended purpose of the virtual model. In the latest version of the temple, for example, we had to eliminate the ramp between the open courtyard of the temple and its hypostyle hall, because it would have made some of the animations for the Egyptian Oracle Project considerably more difficult. Given the limited budget, we chose to delete the ramp so the animator could spend more time perfecting the ritual itself.

Phase 5

The 3-D model is then translated to a format appropriate for whichever 3-D viewing software we are using at the time. Preparing the simulated temple and its artwork for use by the game engine requires judgment and detailed knowledge of both the technology and the content. The engine has to produce a complete image of the virtual space thirty times per second to produce the illusion of moving through the space. Many techniques are needed to optimize performance, and many more to improve the visual quality. For example, we often place a layer of dirt and scratches over the artwork to give the temple a "lived-in" look.

Phase 6

At this point the temple is ready to use for new projects, all of which add some type of interactivity. For the *Gates of Horus* game we added an automated

Egyptian priest who explains features of the temple when the player clicks on them (Jacobson 2011). For the Egyptian Oracle we added the characters and the interactivity described in Chapter 4.

Throughout its history, a major problem in constructing the virtual temple has been the limited availability of materials that can be used to create wall decorations and objects in the temple that are freely available in the public domain. PublicVR provides the temple free to the public, primarily for noncommercial and educational uses (see http://publicvr.org/html/pro_egypt.html). Since funding is always an important issue, the option of creating such materials from scratch is not available. Because the meticulously accurate epigraphic copies of texts and images from the temple of Medinet Habu, with their well-preserved colors, are available for scholarly and educational purposes (Oriental Institute 1930), they were an obvious source of material and thus are what has been used in this project. From the beginning, images from this temple were used on the pylon, on the screen wall in the courtyard, and in the sanctuary. Given the varying conditions of preservation found in the Medinet Habu and Edfu temples, the virtual temple of Horus has made use of different aspects of both these ancient sites. Since the structure of the main building at the temple at Edfu is almost entirely preserved, it provided the basic structure and ground plan of the virtual temple.

Project history

The first version of the temple was developed under the auspices of the Interactive Egypt project at the Studio for Creative Inquiry, Carnegie Mellon University, in the summer of 1993. We used the first visual graphics card ever produced for a PC computer (an IBM 486) and the first commercial tool package for virtual reality applications on a desktop computer, World Toolkit (Blach et al. 1998). In the summer of 1994, the temple was exhibited at the Guggenheim Museum Soho to demonstrate this emerging artistic medium. Jeffrey Jacobson did the programming and the 3-D artwork under the direction of Egyptologist Lynn Holden.

In these early versions of the temple, there was only a short connecting passage to the sanctuary inside. Doors were omitted so that the viewer could see right into the sanctuary, making it easy for a guide to explain the basic parts of the layout. The model also included a couple of the large freestanding statues of falcons found by early excavators that were placed about the temple at

Edfu (Watterson 1998: 53). There was, however, one major difference from the Edfu temple. The transitions between spaces—the forecourt, the hall and the sanctuary—were provided with ramps like those found at Medinet Habu, which were common to most mortuary temples (Dodson 2010). Although ramps are not normally found in cult temples, their presence emphasized that the ground level rose up toward the sanctuary, which represented the primeval mound where the creator rested above the waters of chaos.

Later, in 1995, we rebuilt the temple in VRML format (Hartman and Wernecke 1996). This allowed a more advanced version of the temple to be viewed in a web browser (Jacobson and Holden 2005). Nicole Jackson was the artist.

In 2002 we worked with the artist Michael Darnell to rebuild the temple, using the game *Unreal Tournament* (UT, or UT2004) as the software platform (Jacobson and Holden 2005; 2007). UT came with a free 3-D editor that could take input from more advanced modeling packages; the publisher would accept virtual worlds designed by the game's players, which would then be distributed free through fan websites. Because UT was cheap and widely available, this also made it a useful platform for developing educational materials, and we were not the only educators to do so (Lewis and Jacobson 2002). This version of the temple owed more to temples of the New Kingdom than to those from later periods; at the time, more well-preserved colored temple reliefs and other visual material and artifacts were available from this earlier period. The shrine in the sanctuary resembled in shape the little golden shrine from the tomb of Tutankhamun (Reeves 1990: 140–1) but did not copy it, as images of this artifact are not freely available in the public domain. The latest version of the shrine is loosely based on the granite shrine found in the temple of Horus at Edfu (see Chapter 3).

Modern versions of the temple use Unity3D, a game production environment that allows us to produce a specialized computer program for each version of the temple with minimal programming work (Unity3D 2013). With the most recent versions of the temple, the user simply has to run the program for the temple to appear on the monitor screen. It can then be navigated by using the mouse and keyboard or other devices (see http://publicvr.org/html/pro_egypt.html).

Live museum tours of the temple

Beginning in 2002, we combined the virtual temple with another PublicVR project, CaveUT. The latter used the game *Unreal Tournament* to produce interactive environments for immersive displays (Jacobson 2002; Jacobson and Lewis 2005; Jacobson and Preussner 2010). Because the game gives its users the ability to modify the software, they can create additional artwork and new interactive content. CaveUT is one such modification that allows the user to create a large composite display of multiple monitors. Each monitor is plugged into a computer (usually a PC) and all the computers are connected through a standard local area network (LAN). Once CaveUT is configured, each monitor shows a particular view of the virtual world. Importantly, the composite display can surround the user so that she can look in many directions and see only the virtual world; in other words, each monitor acts as a window onto the virtual world. The monitors can be arrayed around the user in any orientation.

CaveUT provided a low-cost way of creating the illusion of "being there" in the virtual space. Today CaveUT is obsolete, but we are creating its successor, CaveUDK, which will be available through the PublicVR website. Many CaveUT installations use projectors instead of monitors, so that the projection screens can be much larger and the projections can join at the corners. See Jacobson (2002), Jacobson and Lewis (2005) and Jacobson and Preussner (2010), as well as http://publicvr.org/html/pro_caveut.html.

The best example of using the temple with CaveUT was in the all-digital Earth Theater at the Carnegie Museum of Natural History (CMNH) in Pittsburgh. The theater provided a 270-degree field of view for audiences of up to sixty people. It allowed presenters to give live tours of the virtual temple, during which they could reference the museum's Walton Hall of Ancient Egypt, just a few floors above the theater. On many occasions tour guides took visitors through the Walton Hall, then brought them downstairs and virtually toured them through the temple. This was especially popular with groups of K-12 schoolchildren on their overnight camps. In a similar way the museum thematically extended its dinosaur hall into virtual space (Handron and Jacobson 2010).

Beginning in 2005, Jacobson and Holden, and later Jacobson and Gillam, collaborated with computer art and animation modeling classes at the Art Institute of Pittsburgh. We directed the students to create simulations of objects found in the columned hall and the sanctuary. These included food offerings, private monuments, animal mummies and ritual equipment. Most of the objects were based on artifacts from the Walton Hall collection at the CMNH, while a few were based on photographic materials. Jacobson and Handron evaluated them for graphics quality and Holden and later Gillam evaluated them for authenticity. The most competently executed examples were placed in the virtual temple's festival hall and became part of the tour. All this activity employed the fourth version of the temple, which used *Unreal Tournament* as its software platform (Handron and Jacobson 2010).

Live reenactments (virtually) in the temple

Beginning in 2005, Robyn Gillam's students at York University, Toronto, used the virtual temple as a backdrop for their re-creations of Egyptian ritual performances. Under the direction of C. D. Innes, the students were filmed in front of a blue screen; then chroma-key technology was used to place their moving images over still images (computer screenshots) from the inside of the temple. The effect was that they appeared to be inside the temple acting out their parts, with each scene taking place in a historically appropriate context (Gillam, Innes and Jacobson 2010).

Accommodating these performances necessitated both temporary and permanent alterations to the temple. Performances of the daily cult ceremony (Gillam 2012) required temporarily removing the virtual shrine from the sanctuary because the students had constructed one to use as part of their performance. We also discovered that the ramp from the courtyard to the festival hall in earlier versions of the temple made it impossible for the blue-screen actors to move from one space to another. Therefore we removed the ramp and lowered the festival hall's floor down to the level of the courtyard floor. This also proved helpful for programming and animating the Egyptian Oracle.

Because there are a limited number of usable spaces in the virtual temple, existing ones had to be adapted. Purification of the person celebrating the daily cult could not take place in the *per duat*—a purification area annexed to the columned hall—as it had not been created as a usable space. The columned hall itself had to be used instead. Performances normally celebrated in closed areas were relocated to the sanctuary with the shrine removed, as it was the most usable small space. The virtual temple of Horus also currently lacks the peripheral buildings of an actual temple (Watterson 1998: 48–80). However, it does have a sacred lake, so the acting priest could perform his major purification next to it, as specified in the text being enacted in the performance. The consumption of a ritual meal by the priests in the offering hall had to take place in the space directly in front of the shrine, which combines that space with the central hall of the co-templar deities.

For some of the daily cult rituals in the sanctuary, the priests would often turn and face a new direction. Each time they did, we had to use a different background to indicate their location and which way there were facing in the temple. At times that was difficult to determine from textual and other sources, but the process was also illuminating (Gillam, Innes and Jacobson 2010).

Gates of Horus and our immersive learning study

In 2006 Jeffrey Jacobson and Lynn Holden devised the first version of the game *Gates of Horus*. During play, the user participates in a question-and-answer dialogue with a virtual Egyptian priest regarding the temple's major features and their meaning. Each time the player demonstrates sufficient knowledge of one area of the temple, a new gateway opens, allowing the player to move inside. The goal is to reach the inner sanctuary and unlock the shrine by answering all the questions there. The game is fully described in Jacobson (2011b), and the 2012 version is at http://publicvr.org/html/pro_gates.html.

Next Jacobson and Kerry Handron tested more than sixty students after they had played the game, and the results showed that the temple was an effective learning tool (Jacobson 2011a). In our study we had some of the students play the game on a standard desktop computer, while others saw the temple on a very large panoramic screen in the Earth Theater at the Carnegie Museum of Natural History. The screen is a partial cylinder that wraps 210 degrees around the user's viewpoint, filling her peripheral vision and allowing her to look in most directions. Otherwise, the game was exactly the same for both groups. Those who used the giant screen remembered more facts and were able to describe the temple in a more coherent manner. We surmise that this was because the panoramic theater allowed the viewer to see each interior space of the temple as a whole rather than with the tunnel vision that the standard monitor provides (Jacobson 2011a; 2013).

The purpose of the temple

The virtual Egyptian temple was always intended as a teaching tool—a way to introduce students and members of the public to the most important elements of Egyptian formal temple architecture. The traditional approach of providing descriptions and photographs of parts of old temples has the advantage of presenting only what is known and leaving out the rest. The downside is that the non-expert reader/viewer will develop a distorted and often contradictory mental model of what a temple looked like. The author thus loses control of the message, but can regain it by creating a 3-D model for the learner. The reconstruction shows all the elements of the temple in their proper places, helping the learner to see it as a whole. However, this approach has some risk of the viewer's not being able to distinguish between elements of the virtual temple that are well established and those that are more speculative.

Fortunately, the temple already has found good use as a virtual tour in museums and as the foundation for both the *Gates of Horus* learning game and the Egyptian Oracle. In the next chapter we discuss what has been accomplished and future possibilities.

Conclusion

Robyn Gillam and Jeffrey Jacobson

Throughout this work, with the assistance of our collaborators, we have attempted to define and explain both an ancient ceremony—the Egyptian processional oracle—and the augmented reality that we have chosen to re-present it in. This has not been an easy task. The processional oracle is not completely attested in the records of any part of the two millennia in which it was practiced, and both its form and content must be pieced together by using disparate materials from varying time periods, contexts and media. Although the oracle has been the object of intensive scholarly investigation from a number of differing perspectives, there has to our knowledge been little or no interest in its performative and dramatic character. While the study of ethnographic materials and cross-cultural analysis are certainly helpful in understanding the possible spatial and experiential permutations of a ceremony of this type, it must be noted that such materials must be understood as analogs only, not direct descendants or copies of the ancient Egyptian practice.

The concept and practice of augmented reality are difficult to grasp, let alone describe, without directly experiencing it. Augmented or mixed reality is a fast-evolving medium that stands at the intersection of a number of different fields and practices: virtual reality, immersive or interactive theater, and performance art on one hand, and active learning strategies and digital heritage interpretation on the other. Our project combines these elements, using scholarly research and archaeological theories about embodiment and space to create an interactive educational activity that incorporates experiential and spatial components of an ancient ceremony and its setting that are missing from more conventional treatments of the subject. With the help of our collaborators, who are experts in their various fields—the practices of mixed reality theater and digital puppetry and the theory and practice of virtual heritage—we have sought to explain and describe how our mixed reality presentation, the Egyptian Oracle, works. Let us briefly review the facts and arguments so far presented in this book.

Review

We began by introducing our work as a practice that stands at the intersection of a number of disciplines. It combines theories about performance and theater, education and archaeology with the theory and practice of constructing virtual worlds. The thread that connects all these is the human body and its conscious experience of an interactive event, in which it is called by both live and virtual performers to participate in witnessing and connecting with a spiritual presence that is virtually represented.

The content for our performance was selected by Robyn Gillam from an ancient Egyptian ceremony that interacts between the human and supernatural worlds, analogous in contemporary terms to the human and virtual worlds. This ceremony, the processional oracle, was carried out over a long period and is well documented. It consisted of a ritual in which questions were asked of a god whose spirit inhabited an image, which was carried in public procession by priests. The questioners were present, but the god could be hailed directly only by senior clerics. The god answered the questions through its statue, which was often housed in an elaborate shrine and compelled its bearers to move in specific ways that indicated affirmative, negative or preferential answers. The ceremony is attested and apparently developed over a long period, from the mid-second millennium BCE to the seventh century of the Common Era. The ceremony could vary considerably in presentation. Sometimes the god answered only through the movements of its bearers, while at other times it revealed its will by indicating written documents that could consist of anything from one-word answers to long and involved legal decisions. The ceremony could be conducted by important community figures who were not necessarily professional priests, and the etiquette of who could approach the god and speak directly to it was also subject to some variation.

Originally enacted in an elite setting, the ritual was later used by all social classes and was also adapted by neighboring cultures in Kush and Libya and the practitioners of a later religious faith, Christianity, indicating its transferability. Analogs can be found in nearby ancient cultures of the Near East as well as modern ones in West Africa and the African diaspora. Research on the divine oracle used by Maroon communities in Suriname allows for further understanding of the ancient ceremony through the analogy of a modern practice and its social and cultural context. In our study of the ancient ceremony we have included an imaginative reconstruction that emphasizes its performative and theatrical aspects. This is an essential step in understanding the process of how we developed the Egyptian Oracle in augmented reality.

Our performance aimed to recreate the Egyptian ceremony by using live and virtual actors, the latter in a virtual space projected on a wall, before a live audience whose interaction was integral to the whole. The virtual space was a temple constructed by Jeffery Jacobson and PublicVR as a setting for educational presentations at the Carnegie Museum of Natural History (CMNH) in Pittsburgh. The main actor was a virtual puppet or avatar comprising both the god's statue, in a boat-shaped shrine carried by junior priests, and the high priest of the temple, who mediates between the god and those who ask questions, who are played by members of the audience. The avatar was controlled by a live puppeteer who could see the audience and was able to react to and interact with them. The whole event was facilitated by a live actor playing a musician-priestess attached to temple; she explained to the audience the setting and parameters of the action so that they could successfully participate in it. Each performance was followed by a debriefing session during which audience members asked questions and filled out a participator survey.

Jacobson's detailed description of the construction and execution of our performances reveals it as an example of mixed reality theater, a form that has previously been utilized in high-concept art theater, as noted by Josephine Anstey and David Pape. Here we see the form adapted and developed in an educational setting that uses a virtual puppet operating both the god and the priest. Lisa Sturz notes that the use of the puppet has analogs in ancient practices, and that the evolution of virtual puppets still encompasses interaction with the human body. Puppets have also played an important role in the development of educational theater and the pedagogy of active learning.

In his discussion of virtual heritage, Erik Champion argues that it may be defined as what does not physically survive from the past. In a literal sense, the virtual is the hypothetical or the reconstructed in relation to the past. In an experiential sense, it is the connection between past and present bodies. The virtual reality temple described by Jacobson and the activities in this book that are performed in it exemplify these principles. Even the two best-preserved Egyptian temples, which provided the bulk of the source material for the virtual temple, cannot, as noted by Gillam, be understood without access to an extensive body of philological and archaeological evidence that is mostly accessible only in static, highly specialized, text-based media. On the other hand, the virtual temple, and our performance within it, shows what is no longer there by inhabiting the dead landscape of Egyptian ruins and creating life and interactivity.

Evaluation of the project

The debriefing surveys conducted by Jeffrey Jacobson point to a number of promising educational outcomes for the Egyptian Oracle activity. First, they indicated that both adults and children found the performance highly acceptable. They both liked the animated characters, and children particularly enjoyed its participatory character. The results of the educational game *Gates of Horus*, which was devised earlier for use with the temple, suggests that this form of presentation is a highly effective way for school-aged children to acquire, understand and retain information. Thus the Egyptian Oracle may be placed securely in a long tradition of educational theater and active learning.

The project is also an excellent example of collaborative teaching as well as learning. The enterprise would not have been possible without the invaluable contributions of Kerry Handron, a former educational programmer and interpreter at the CMNH, who wrote the original performance script, and Friedrich Kirchner, who wrote the programming for the virtual actors and was able to successfully combine technical exactitude with artistic effectiveness. There were many other contributors to this project, including Asa Gray, who provided the musical background, as well as numerous technicians who adjusted the programming and updated and modified the virtual temple.

Feedback from the audience surveys indicates a need for improvement of the animations, as well as a longer performance script and a more fully realized processional barque for the god. As noted in the body of this work, the movements of the animated figures and the construction of the barque were deliberately simplified, not only for legibility but also because additional funding is required to develop them further. The Egyptian Oracle is a pilot project; it must be seen as research and development for a more elaborate in-depth treatment of this subject, as well as a guide for the development of further educational mixed-media presentations. Put together on a very modest budget, in many ways it provides a roadmap for the direction of ongoing work in this developing field.

Significance and further implications of the project

The wider implications of the Egyptian Oracle Project are many. Its audience includes the general public, teachers and museum and other heritage educators, as well as academics such as archaeologists and anthropologists. Not only is the medium an immersive experience that intersects theater, virtual reality and education; it locates itself on the forefront of development of the fast-developing medium of mixed reality. The project is not just important for general educational purposes but can also add to the understanding of academic specialists and archaeologists who study this material, by casting light on the experiential and spatial dimensions of such ancient ceremonies. It does this by bringing together many different kinds of knowledge and perceptions, including the ethnographic, the spatial and the philological, and allows a number of widely different heuristic viewpoints to be considered together.

From an archaeological perspective, the opportunity for real and virtual actors to inhabit a reconstructed site in virtual reality could also prove invaluable in situations where visiting the actual location was, for various reasons, not possible. Where sufficient data exist, it should be possible to reconstruct entire buildings and built or natural environments that have been damaged or destroyed or are inaccessible, allowing researchers to model their spatial and lived aspects by moving around bodily within them. A highly sophisticated model could also include non-human environmental factors such as climate and seasonal variations of temperature, day and night, sun angles and so on. Such a capability could allow further insight into issues such as artifact spread, patterns of use and degradation within the site, and how it could have been affected by and have had an impact on various human and other interactions. Expanding in this way the understanding of how past spaces were inhabited should undoubtedly promote fresh insights into the economic, historical and cultural meanings of heritage sites that are able to be studied in virtual or mixed reality.

In an academic context, the advantage of mixed reality over more conventional VR formats that use helmets and screens is not only that it is genuinely immersive but also that it allows for more than one person, or even small groups, to enter the environment together and interact with each other as well, sharing insights and ideas. They are also able to interact directly with the digital actors and the persons controlling them. Although this may involve a degree of role-playing and theatricality not normally associated with academic activity, such routines may be modeled on the kind of active learning we have described in connection with the more general educational aims and uses of the Egyptian Oracle. Of course, the use of mixed reality to create immersive virtual environments for advanced academic research would entail much more elaborate programming than was created for our project, as well as extensive research and development and a very large budget, but it is certainly possible.

Final conclusion

What can be learned from this project and how can its methodology be further developed? We argue that the Egyptian Oracle is an important and innovative example of re-creating the performance of an ancient ceremony across time and through drama and the medium of mixed reality. It is an activity analogous to its ancient model and well illustrates the power and flexibility of the digital medium when it has good source material to work with. A compelling narrative allows the computer to demonstrate its particular suitability for this kind of activity. The medium also has the potential to be developed for more intensive academic applications, as argued above. The outcomes from the user surveys of the project show that a mixed reality educational format is also a powerful way to impart both factual information and experiential knowledge of complex and esoteric material. Although we have demonstrated its use in the area of heritage, it can also be adapted to other areas such as education and instruction in science and technology. We assert confidently that the Egyptian Oracle Project demonstrates not only the usefulness of mixed reality in a general educational sense, but also its suitability for any format that requires the combination of factual, spatial and experiential data.

Appendix A

A Funeral Procession in Modern Rural Egypt

Mary-Ann Pouls Wegner

Associate Professor of Egyptian Archaeology, Department of Near and Middle Eastern Civilizations, University of Toronto; Director, North Abydos Votive Zone Project, University of Toronto; Pennsylvania-Yale-Institute of Fine Arts, New York University Expedition to Abydos

In the winter of 1993 I was a doctoral student on my first archaeological fieldwork project in Egypt, working as a surveyor for the Ahmose-Tetisheri Project in Abydos under the field direction of fellow graduate student Stephen Harvey. Although I had traveled in Egypt previously, and it was my fascination with modern Egyptian culture that led me to pursue a career in the rarefied field of Egyptology at the University of Pennsylvania, I was still doing coursework and had a great deal yet to learn about ancient Egypt. My grandmother was born in Egypt, into a family that prized its Greek origins but had lived and worked in the cosmopolitan centers of Alexandria and Port Said for many generations. She looked Egyptian, with her bright dark eyes, luxuriant wavy hair and coffee-with-cream complexion. She exerted a powerful influence on me as a child. She was the keeper of esoteric knowledge derived from her distant homeland, and parables and pithy sayings colored her conversations. She also knew things that no one else in my limited purview knew, or even acknowledged: how to avoid the "evil eye" that arose from spite or envy; how to safeguard hair and blood and nail clippings so they would not fall into the wrong hands and be used to manipulate a person against his or her will; even, reputedly, how to instill illness or obsessive, overpowering love.

It was no doubt this contact with my resourceful *yia-yia* that instilled in me an early interest in popular religion and Middle Eastern cultures. When I found myself in a rural community in southern Egypt with Coptic Christians and Muslims living side by side, using strikingly similar practices to avert harm despite their different theological traditions, it was fertile ground for comparative cultural anthropology as well as archaeological research. I was often surprised to find villagers doing things my grandmother had done, humble, everyday practices that evoked a worldview with roots so deep that no patina of formalized religion could entirely obscure it. Shoes could not be left upside down lest a disagreement ensue. A baby was rolled over the bed of a nuptial couple to ensure fertility. Praise of a child, even if unspoken, was followed by spitting three times to avert the "evil eye." Some villagers went so far as to deliberately dress their children in filthy, tattered clothes to discourage the envious gaze. But most wonderful and unexpected were the points of intersection between modern and ancient practices. One striking example of the persistence of beliefs about the dead was illustrated in a funeral procession that we witnessed that season.

Our archaeological excavations were focused on the eastern edge of the Greater Abydos area, near a Coptic village called el-Ghabat. The site adjoined a Muslim cemetery featuring the domed mud-brick tomb of an important local holy man, Sheikh Mohammed, who had also given his name to the adjacent village. The tomb probably dates from the nineteenth century, and the cemetery had expanded into the desert around it; by 1993 it bisected the archaeological site.

In the rhythm of the excavation day we began work at sunrise, fueled by strong, sweet tea and biscuits, and then took a break for a more substantial meal—"second breakfast"—at about 10:00 a.m. We ate it inside a rough shelter made of bundled reeds that provided respite from the sun and the insistent north wind. One morning during second breakfast, we were sitting in the reed shelter when we heard voices outside. Looking out, we saw six men bearing a body wrapped in white cloth that had been laid on a simple litter. The bearers were positioned on either side of the body, supporting it at shoulder height with long poles that formed the edges of the palanquin. Behind them were numerous men from the neighboring villages, including members of the families of some of our workmen. Most of the men were wearing traditional southern-style *gallabeyas*, long robes with wide sleeves that flapped crazily in the wind.

We watched in amazement as the bearers crested a rise from the direction of the sheikh's tomb, came to a halt with their burden and paused for a few moments, then suddenly lurched forward again, setting off across the dig site along one of the baulks that separated the excavation units. The accompanying men jogged along in a procession that followed the palanquin's unsteady progress across the landscape. The procession stopped and a hush fell over them; as it suddenly began to move again, they raised their voices excitedly in acknowledgment of the new direction, saying, "*Aywa* [yes]," and "*Ala kiddeh* [like that]." When the bearers halted, it seemed as if the accompanying men were being held in suspense, uncertain of the direction the procession would take next until the bearers began to move again.

We watched the proceedings in amazement, sharing the feeling of suspense whenever the bearers paused. One of the workmen spoke with the men accompanying the procession; apparently the deceased had been a respected elder in the village of Sheikh Mohammed, and the bearers were accommodating his desire to see the work of the foreign archaeological expedition before his burial. He would urge them to carry him quickly or slowly and determined the direction they took; the bearers would stop when they were unsure of his wishes and wait until one of them discerned the dead man's will. Ultimately they would take him to the cemetery for burial, but first they ran with him to the top of the denuded pyramid of Ahmose and moved sure-footedly along the baulks through the site. Despite the consternation this provoked in the director, no damage to the excavation resulted from the procession's passage. Eventually they turned back toward the village and we lost sight of them in the narrow streets, but we could hear the unusually persistent honking of a car horn. Word reached us that the dead man had expressed a desire to have a final ride before his body was committed to the earth. This news conjured up an image of the palanquin tied on top of a local taxi and proceeding at breakneck speed down the main road through the neighboring villages, accompanied by men who had known and respected him in life.

The local workmen who were with us confirmed that sometimes especially holy men expressed their wishes regarding the path their funeral procession took to the site of their interment; women were not known to direct their processions to the grave that way. The ability to communicate with the bearers was understood to be a function of the strength of will and moral fortitude of the deceased. The highly charged experience of participating in the procession created a feeling of what Victor Turner (1995) called communitas, uniting the community through shared emotional experience but also highlighting relative social distinctions. It established a formal hierarchy—deceased, bearers, followers and finally those not present—through an essentially performative activity in which the dead individual directed the actions that caused his body to move through the landscape. Transmission of the deceased's desires to the men who bore his funeral bier also confirmed the exemplary character of the deceased, attesting to his holiness and distinguishing him as one deserving of reverence in his community. In the context of the Islamic proscription on showy funerary monuments, this successful communication of the deceased's final wishes functions as an expression of his individual identity that lives on in the collective memory of the villages of Abydos.

Appendix B

After-Show Questionnaire

How old are you? _____

Are you a boy or a girl?

Boy   Girl   Prefer not to say

Did you get a role card? (circle one)

Yes   No   I don't know.

Did you act out any of the parts? (circle one)

Yes   No   I don't know.

Did you enjoy the show? (circle one)

It was bad!   It was not good.   It was okay.   It was good.   It was great!

Did you learn anything interesting? (circle one)

Yes, lots!   Yes, a little   No, nothing

What was MAAT to the Egyptians? (circle one)

A floor mat   The power of god   Harmony, peace, and justice   Horus

Who was the high priest? (circle one)

The live, human actress   Horus   The lead priest carrying the boat   The man talking to us and the actress

What makes the boat move when it answers a question? (Please write)

We want to make our show better. What parts did you like and we should keep? (Please write)

Give us some advice on how to make the show better (Please write)

Is there anything else you would like to tell us?

Thank you for your help!

Bibliography

Abdallah, A. G. (1984), "An Unusual Private Stela of the 21st Dynasty from Coptos," *Journal of Egyptian Archaeology* 70: 65–72.

Abrams, R. D. and Szwed, J. F. (1983), *After Africa: Extracts from British Travel Accounts and Journals of the Seventeenth, Eighteenth, and Nineteenth Centuries concerning the Slaves, their Manners, and Customs in the British West Indies*, New Haven, CT: Yale University Press.

Addison, A. C. (2000), "Emerging Trends in Virtual Heritage," *IEEE MultiMedia* 7, 2: 22–5.

Adobe Systems Inc. (2014), Photoshop.com, http://www.photoshop.com (accessed February 20, 2015).

Agnew, V. (2007), "History's Affective Turn: Historical Reenactment and Its Work in the Present," *Rethinking History* 11, 3: 299–312, http://dx.doi.org/10.1080/13642520701353108 (accessed September 29, 2013).

Allison, T. (2011), "More than a Man in a Monkey Suit: Andy Serkis, Motion Capture, and Digital Realism," *Quarterly Review of Film and Video* 28, 4: 325–41, doi: 10.1080/10509208.2010.500947.

Anderson, E. F., McLoughlin, L., Liarokapis, F., Peters, C., Petridis, P. and Freitas, S. (2010), "Developing Serious Games for Cultural Heritage: A State-of-the-Art Review," *Virtual Reality* 14, 4: 255–75, doi: 10.1007/s10055-010-0177-3.

Anderson, M. (2003), "Computer Games and Archaeological Reconstruction: The Low Cost VR, Enter the Past," paper presented at "Enter the Past," 31st annual conference of Computer Applications and Quantitive Methods in Archaeology (CAA), Vienna.

Ang, C. S. and Krishna, R. G. S. V. (2008), "Computer Game Theories for Designing Motivating Educational Software: A Survey Study," *International Journal on E-Learning* 7, 2: 181–99.

Anstey, J., Pape, D. and Sandin, D. (2000), "The Thing Growing: Autonomous Characters in Virtual Reality Interactive Fiction," Proceedings of IEEE Virtual Reality 2000, New Brunswick, NJ, March 18–22.

Anstey, J., Seyed, A. P., Bay-Cheng, S., Pape, D., Shapiro, S. C., Bona, J. and Hibit, J. (2009), "The Agent Takes the Stage," *International Journal of Arts and Technology* 2, 4: 277–96.

ARCE [American Research Center in Egypt] (2011), *ARCE Conservation 2011*, Cairo: ARCE.

Aristotle (1996), *Poetics*, trans. M. Heath, London: Penguin.

Arnold, D. (2003), *The Encyclopedia of Ancient Egyptian Architecture*, trans. S. H. Gardiner and H. Strudwick, N. Strudwick and H. Strudwick (eds.), Princeton, NJ: Princeton University Press.

Artaud, A. (1958), *The Theater and Its Double*, trans. M. C. Richards, New York: Grove Press.

Assmann, J. (1992), "Der Tempel der ägyptischen Spätzeit als Kanonisierung kultuereller Identität," in *The Heritage of Ancient Egypt: Studies in Honour of Erik Iversen*, J. Ösing and E. K. Nielsen (eds.), 19–25, Copenhagen: Niebuhr Institute.

Assmann, J. (1995), *Egyptian Solar Religion in the New Kingdom: Re, Amun and the Crisis of Polytheism*, trans. A. Alcock, London: Kegan Paul International.

Assmann, J. (2002), *The Mind of Ancient Egypt*, trans. A. Jenkins, New York: Holt.

Aufrère, S., Golvin, J.-C. and Goyon, J.-C. (1991), *L'Égypte restituée*, 2 vols, Paris: Éditions Errance.

Augustine of Hippo (1991), *Confessions*, trans. H. Chadwick, Oxford: Oxford University Press.

Auslander, P. (2002), "Live from Cyberspace: or, I Was Sitting at My Computer This Guy Appeared He Thought I Was a Bot," *PAJ: A Journal of Performance and Art* 24: 16–21.

Autodesk (2014), 3ds Max, http://www.autodesk.com/products/autodesk-3ds-max/overview (accessed February 20, 2015).

Azim, M. (1980), "La fouille de la cour du Xe Pylône: Rapport préliminaire," *Karnak* 6: 153–65.

Azim, M. and Traunecker, C. (1982), "Un mât du IXe pylône au nom d'Horemheb," *Karnak* 7: 75–92.

Bagnall, R. and Rathbone, D. (2004), *Egypt from Alexander to the Early Christians: An Archaeological and Historical Guide*, Los Angeles, CA: Getty Museum.

Baines, J. (2006), "Public Ceremonial Performance in Ancient Egypt: Exclusion and Integration," in *Archaeology of Performance: Theaters of Power, Community, and Politics*, T. Inomata and L. S. Coben (eds.), 261–302, Lanham, MD: AltaMira Press.

Baines, J. (2007a), "On the Status and Purposes of Ancient Egyptian Art," *Cambridge Archaeological Journal* 4 (1994): 67–94, reprinted in *Visual and Written Culture in Ancient Egypt*, 298–337, Oxford: Oxford University Press.

Baines, J. (2007b), "Visual, Written Decorum," Prologue to *Visual and Written Culture in Egypt*, 3–30, Oxford: Oxford University Press.

Baines, J. and Eyre, C. J. (1983), "Four Notes on Literacy," *Göttinger Miszellen* 61: 65–96.

Baines, J., and Parkinson, R. B. (1997), "An Old Kingdom Record of an Oracle? Sinai Inscription 13," in *Essays on Ancient Egypt in Honour of Herman te Velde*, J. van Dijk (ed.), 9–26, Groningen: Styx.

Baker, C. (2008), "Trying to Design a Truly Entertaining Game Can Defeat Even a Certified Genius," *Wired* 16(4).

Barab, S. A., Scott, B., Sinyahhan, S., Goldstone, R., Ingram-Goble, A., Zuiker, S. J.

and Warren, S. (2009), "Transformational Play as a Curricular Scaffold: Using Videogames to Support Science Education," *Journal of Science Education Technology* 18: 305–20.

Barguet, P. (1962), *Le temple d'Amon-Re á Karnak: Essai d'exégese*, Cairo: Institut français d'archéologie orientale.

Barns, J. (1949), "The Nevill Papyrus: A Late Ramesside Letter to an Oracle," *Journal of Egyptian Archaeology* 35: 69–71.

Barsalou, L. W. (1992), *Cognitive Psychology*, Hillsdale, NJ: Lawrence Erlbaum Associates.

Barta, W. (1980), "Kult," in *Lexikon der Ägyptologie*, vol. 4, W. Helck and E. Otto (eds.), 839, Wiesbaden: Harrassowitz.

Baumgartner, Aretta, personal communication.

Behrens, P. (1986), "Widder," in *Lexikon der Ägyptologie*, vol. 6, W. Helck and W. Westndorf (ed.), 1243–5, Wiesbaden: Harrassowitz.

Beinlich, H. (1978), "Ein ägyptischer Räucherarm in Heidelberg," *Mitteilungen des Deutschen Archäologischen Instituts Kairo* 34: 15–31.

Bellotti, F., Berta, R., De Gloria, A., Panizza, G. and Primavera, L. (2009), "Designing Cultural Heritage Contents for Serious Virtual Worlds," paper presented at 15th International Conference on Virtual Systems and Multimedia, Vienna, September 9–12.

Benford, S. and Giannachi, G. (2011), *Performing Mixed Reality*, Cambridge, MA: MIT Press.

Berlin, A. and Brettler, M. Z. (2004), "Historical and Geographical Background to the Bible," in *The Jewish Study Bible*, A. Berlin and M. Z. Brettler (ed.), 2048–61, Oxford: Oxford University Press.

Berlinerblau, J. (2005), *The Secular Bible: Why Non-believers Must Take Religion Seriously*, Cambridge: Cambridge University Press.

Bernier, M. and O'Hare, J. (2005), *Puppetry in Education and Therapy: Unlocking Doors to the Mind and Heart*, Bloomington, IN: AuthorHouse.

Blach, R., Landauer, J., Rösch, A. and Simon, A. (1998), "A Highly Flexible Virtual Reality System," *Future Generation Computer Systems* 14, 3: 167–78.

Blackman, A. M. (1925), "Oracles in Ancient Egypt," *Journal of Egyptian Archaeology* 11: 249–55.

Blackman, A. M. and Fairman, H. W. (1941), "A Group of Texts Inscribed on the Facade of the Sanctuary in the Temple of Horus at Edfu," in *Miscellanea Gregoriana*, 397–420, Rome: Tipografia Poliglotta Vaticana.

Blake, E. (1998), "Sardinia's Nuraghi: Four Millennia of Becoming," *World Archaeology* 30, 1: 59–71.

Blasius, A. and Schipper B. V., eds. (2002), *Apokalyptic und Ägypten: Eine kritische Analyse der releventen Texte aus dem griechisch-romischen Ägypten*, Louvain: Peeters.

Blumenthal, E. (2005), *Puppetry and Puppets*, London: Thames & Hudson.

Boal, A. (1979), *Theater of the Oppressed*, trans. C. and M. O. L. McBride, London: Pluto.

Boardman, J. (1964), *The Greeks Overseas*, Harmondsworth: Penguin.

Boland, P. and Johnson, C. (1996), "Archaeology as Computer Visualization: 'Virtual Tours' of Dudley Castle, c. 1550," in *Imaging the Past: Electronic Imaging and Computer Graphics in Museums and Archaeology*, T. Higgins, P. Main and J. Lang, 227–34 (eds.), London: British Museum Press.

Boorn, G. van den (1988), *The Duties of the Vizier*, London: Kegan Paul.

Bourriau, J. (2000), "The Second Intermediate Period (ca. 1650–550 BC)," in *The Oxford History of Ancient Egypt*, 184–217, Oxford: Oxford University Press.

Brand, P. (2001), "Sacred Barks," in *The Oxford Encyclopedia of Ancient Egypt*, D. B. Redford (ed.), New York: Oxford University Press, http://www.oxfordreference.com.ezproxy.library.yorku.ca/views/ENTRY.html?subview=Main&entry=t176.e0627 (accessed May 14, 2012).

Brand, P. (2007), "Veils, Votives and Marginalia: The Use of Sacred Space at Karnak and Luxor," in *Sacred Space and Sacred Function in Ancient Thebes*, P. Dorman and B. Bryan (eds.), 51–83, Chicago, IL: Oriental Institute.

Bransford, W. (1998), "The Past Was No Illusion," in Clark Dodsworth Jr. (ed.), *Digital Illusion*, 49–57, New York: ACM Press.

Breasted, J. H. (1906), *Ancient Records of Egypt*, vol. 2, *The Eighteenth Dynasty*, Chicago, IL: University of Chicago, http://www.etana.org/coretexts/search?keyword=breasted (accessed February 20, 2015).

Brecht, B. (1964), *Brecht on Theatre: The Development of an Aesthetic*, trans. J. Willett, London: Methuen.

Brettler, M. Z. (2004), "The Canonization on the Bible," in *The Jewish Study Bible*, A. Berlin and M. Z. Brettler (eds.), 2072–6, Oxford: Oxford University Press.

Briant, P. (2002), *From Cyrus to Alexander: A History of the Persian Empire*, trans. P. Daniels, Winona Lake, IN: Eisenbrauns.

Browne, G. M. (1987), "The Sortes Astrampsychi and the Egyptian Oracle," *Texte und Untersuchungen* 133: 67–71.

Bryant, D. (2006), "The Uncanny Valley: Why Are Monster-Movie Zombies So Horrifying and Talking Animals So Fascinating?", http://www.arclight.net/~pdb/nonfiction/uncanny-valley.html (accessed February 20, 2015).

Bunbury, J. (2012), "The Mobile Nile," *Egyptian Archaeology* 41: 15–17.

Burke, A. A. (2012), Review of *Glorious Mud! Ancient and Contemporary Earthen Design and Construction in North Africa, Western Europe, the Near East, and Southwest Asia*, by O. W. Van Beek, *Near Eastern Archaeology* 75, 2: 126–8.

Butzer, K. W. (1976), *Early Hydraulic Civilization in Egypt*, Chicago, IL: University of Chicago Press.

Cabrol, A. (2001), *Les voies processionnelles de Thèbes*, Leuven: Peeters.

Caillois, R. (2001), *Man, Play and Games*, trans. M. Barash, Champaign, IL: University of Illinois Press.

Calabro, D. (2012), "The Hieratic Scribal Tradition in Preexilic Judah," in *Evolving Egypt: Innovation, Appropriation, and Reinterpretation in Ancient Egypt*, K. Muhlestein and J. Gee (eds.), 75–84, Oxford: Archaeo Press.

Callender, G. (2000), "The Middle Kingdom Renaissance (c. 2055–1650 B.C.)," in *The Oxford History of Ancient Egypt*, 148–83, Oxford: Oxford University Press.

Calverley, A. M. and Broome, M. (1933–58), *The Temple of Sethos I at Abydos*, A. H. Gardiner (ed.), London: Egypt Exploration Society.

Caminos, R. (1974), *Late Egyptian Miscellanies*, Oxford: Cumberledge.

Case, F. I. (2001), "The Intersemiotics of Obeah and Kali Mai in Guyana," in *Nation Dance: Religion, Identity and Cultural Difference in the Caribbean*, P. Taylor (ed.), 40–53, Bloomington, IN: Indiana University Press.

Cauville, S. and Devauchelle, D. (1984), "Les mesures réelles du temple d'Edfou," *Bulletin de l'Institut français d'archéologie orientale* 84: 23–34.

Cavazza, M., Lugrin, J. L., Pizzi, D. and Charles, F. (2007), "Madame Bovary on the Holodeck: Immersive Interactive Storytelling," in *Proceedings of ACM Multimedia 2007*, Augsburg, Germany: ACM Press.

CCSS (2014), Common Core State Standards Initiative, http://www.corestandards.org

Černý, J. (1935), "Questions adressées aux oracles," *BIFAO* 35: 41–58.

Černý, J. (1942), "Nouvelle série de questions adressées aux oracles," *BIFAO* 41: 13–24.

Černý, J. (1962), "Egyptian Oracles," in *A Saite Oracle Papyrus from Thebes in the Brooklyn Museum (Papyrus Brooklyn 47.218.3)*, R. A. Parker (ed.), 35–48, Providence, RI: Brown University Press.

Černý, J. (1965), "Egypt from the Death of Ramesses III to the End of the Twenty-First Dynasty," in *The Cambridge Ancient History*, vol. 2, part 2, ch. 25, "History of the Middle East and the Aegean Region, c. 1380–1000 B.C.," I. E. S. Edwards (ed.), Cambridge: Cambridge University Press.

Černý, J. (1972), "Troisième série de questions adressées aux oracles," *BIFAO* 72: 49–69.

Černý, J. (1976), *Coptic Etymological Dictionary*, Cambridge: Cambridge University Press.

Champion, E. (2004), "Indiana Jones and the Joystick of Doom: Understanding the Past via Computer Games," *Traffic* 5: 47–65.

Champion, E. (2012), "Teaching Mods with Class," in *Game Mods*, E. Champion (ed.), 113–48, Pittsburgh, PA: ETC Press.

Chen, S., Pan, Z., Zhang, M. and Shen, H. (2013), "A Case Study of User Immersion-Based Systematic Design for Serious Heritage Games," *Multimedia Tools and Applications* 62, 3: 633–58, doi: 10.1007/s11042-011-0864-4.

Christiansen, P. (2013), "Capricious Fate: Videogames as Tools for Moral Instruction," Play the Past, http://www.playthepast.org/?p=4221 (accessed February 20, 2015).

Cline, E., Silberman, N. A., Holtorf, C. and Killebrew, A. E. (2008), "Forum: Archaeologists and the Media," *Near Eastern Archaeology* 71, 3: 172–80.

Cogan, M. and Tadmor, H. (1988), *II Kings: A New Translation with Introduction and Commentary*, Garden City, NJ: Doubleday.

Colin, M.-È. (2003), "The Barque Sanctuary Project: Further Investigation of a Key Structure in the Egyptian Temple," in *Egyptology at the Dawn of the Twenty-First Century: Proceedings of the Eighth International Congress of Egyptologists, Cairo, 2000*, Z. Hawass and L. P. Brock (eds.), vol. 2, 181–6, Cairo: American University in Cairo Press.

Connolly, T. M., Boyle, E. A., MacArthur, E., Hainey, T. and Boyle, J. M. (2012), "A Systematic Literature Review of Empirical Evidence on Computer Games and Serious Games," *Computers and Education* 59, 2: 661–86.

Cooney, K. (2007), "Labour," in *The Egyptian World*, T. Wilkinson (ed.), 160–72, London: Routledge.

Chosson, Michaël (2002), *La Consultation des Oracles en Egypte du Nouvel Empire à l'Epoque Chrétienne*, Maîtrise d'Histoire, l'Université de Marne-la-Vallée, 2002, http:// michael.chosson.free.fr (accessed 5 December 2010).

Courtney, R. (1980), *The Dramatic Curriculum*, London, ON: University of Western Ontario, Faculty of Education.

CPA (2014), Center for Puppetry Arts, Atlanta, GA, http://www.puppet.org (accessed February 20, 2015).

Cruz-Neira, C., Sandin, D. J., DeFanti, T. A., Kenyon, R. V. and Hart, J. C. (1992), "The CAVE: Audio Visual Experience Automatic Virtual Environment," *Communications of the ACM* 35, 6: 64–72.

Cruz-Neira, C., Sandin, D. J. and DeFanti, T. A. (1993), "Surround-Screen Projection-Based Virtual Reality: The Design and Implementation of the CAVE," paper presented at 20th annual conference of Computer Graphics and Interactive Techniques, Anaheim, CA.

Cryer, F. H. (1994), *Divination in Ancient Israel and Its Near Eastern Environment*, Journal for the Study of the Old Testament suppl. ser. 142, Sheffield: JSOT Press.

David, A. R. (1981), *A Guide to Religious Ritual at Abydos*, Warminster: Aris and Phillips.

David, A. R. (2007), "The Temple Priesthood," in *The Egyptian World*, T. Wilkinson (ed.), 105–17, London: Routledge.

David, B. and Thomas, J. (2008), *Handbook of Landscape Archaeology*, Walnut Creek, CA: Left Coast Press.

Davies, P. V, trans. (1969), *Macrobius: The Saturnalia*, New York: Columbia University Press.

Dawkins, R. (2006), *The God Delusion*, Boston: Houghton Mifflin.

Dede, C., Clarke, J., Ketelhut, D. J., Nelson, B. and Bowman, C. (2005), "Students' Motivation and Learning of Science in a Multi-user Virtual Environment," paper presented at the annual meeting of the American Educational Research Association, Montreal, 2004.

Demarée, R. J. and Egberts, A. (eds.) (1991), *Village Voices: Proceedings of the Symposium "Texts from Deir el-Medîna and Their Interpretation," Leiden, May 31–June 1, 1991*, CNWS Publications 13, Leiden: Centre of Non-Western Studies, Leiden University.

Derchain, P. (1965), *Le papyrus Salt 825 (BM 10051): Rituel pour la conservation de la vie en Égypte*, Brussels: Académie Royale de Belgie.

Dickey, M. D. (2006), "Game Design Narrative for Learning: Appropriating Adventure Game Design Narrative Devices and Techniques for the Design of Interactive Learning Environments," *Educational Technology Research and Development* 54, 3: 245–63, doi: 10.1007/s11423-006-8806-y.

Dixon, S. (2007), *Digital Performance: A History of New Media in Theater, Dance, Performance Art, and Installation*, Cambridge, MA: MIT Press.

Dodson, A. (2010), "Mortuary Architecture and Decorative Systems," in *A Companion to Ancient Egypt*, vol. 2, A. B. Lloyd (ed.), 804–25, Oxford: Wiley Blackwell.

Dominicus, B. 1994. *Gesten und Gebärden in Darstellungen des Alten und Mittleren Reiches*, Studien zur Archäologie und Geschichte Altägyptens 10.

Dondlinger, M. J. (2007), "Educational Video Game Design: A Review of the Literature," *Journal of Applied Educational Technology* 4, 1: 21–31.

Dreyfus, H. L. (2001), *On the Internet (Thinking in Action)*, 2008 edn, New York: Routledge.

During, S. (2010), "Mimic Toil: Eighteenth-Century Preconditions for the Modern Historical Re-enactment," in *Historical Reenactment: From Realism to the Affective Turn*, A. McCalman and P. A. Pickering (eds.), 180–99, New York: Palgrave Macmillan.

Eaton-Krauß, M. and Murnane, W. J. (1991), "Tutankhamun, Ay, and the Avenue of Sphinxes between Pylon X and the Mut Precinct at Karnak," *Bulletin de la société d'égyptologie de Genève* 15: 31–8.

Edwards, I. E. S. (1960), *Hieratic Papyri in the British Museum*, ser. 4, *Oracular Amuletic Decrees of the Late New Kingdom*, London: Trustees of the British Museum.

Engler, L. and Fijan, C. (1973), *Making Puppets Come Alive: A Method of Learning and Teaching Hand Puppetry*, New York: Taplinger.

Esposito, J. L. (2003), "Funerary Rites," in *Oxford Dictionary of Islam*, J. L. Esposito (ed.), Oxford University Press, http://www.oxfordreference.com.ezproxy.library.yorku.ca/views/ENTRY.html?subview=Main&entry=t125.e681 (accessed May 23, 2012).

Fairman, H. W. (1954), "Worship and Festivals in an Egyptian Temple," *Bulletin of the John Rylands Library* 37: 165–203.

Fairman, H. W. (1973), *The Triumph of Horus*, London: Batsford.

Fakhry, A. (1950), *The Oasis of Siwa: Its Customs, History and Monuments*, Cairo: Wadi el-Nil Press.

Fakhry, A. (1973), *The Oases of Egypt*, vol. 1, *Siwa Oasis*, Cairo: American University Press.

Faulkner, R. O. (1962), *A Concise Dictionary of Middle Egyptian*, Oxford: Griffith Institute.

Favro, D. and Wendrich, W. (2014), Digital Karnak, http://dlib.etc.ucla.edu/projects/Karnak/feature/OtherProcessionalWays (accessed May 9, 2014).

Fejfer, J. (2013), "Cyrene and Cyrenaica," in *The Encyclopedia of Ancient History*, R. S. Bagnall, K, Brodersen, C. B. Champion, A. Erskine and S. R. Huebner (eds.), 1896–1900, Oxford: Blackwell.

Finnestad, R. B. (1985), *Image of the World and Symbol of the Creator: On the Cosmological and Iconographic Values of the Temple of Edfu*, Wiesbaden: Harrassowitz.

Fisch, S. M. (2004), *Children's Learning from Educational Television: Sesame Street and Beyond*, Mahwah, NJ: Lawrence Erlbaum.

Fisch, S. M. (2005), "Making Educational Computer Games 'Educational,'" paper presented at the 2005 Conference on Interaction Design and Children, Boulder, CO.

Fisch, S. M. and Truglio, R. T. (eds.) (2001), *"G" Is for Growing: Thirty Years of Research on Children and* Sesame Street, Mahwah, NJ: Lawrence Erlbaum.

Fischer, H. G. (1978), "Five Inscriptions of the Old Kingdom," *Zeitschrift fur agyptische Sprache und Altertumskunde* 105: 42–59.

Fischer, H. G. (1996), "Egyptian Doors Inside and Out," in *Varia Nova*, 91–102, New York: Metropolitan Museum of Art.

Fischer-Elfert, H.-W. (2001), "Instructions of Amenemope," in *The Oxford Encyclopedia of Ancient Egypt*, D. B. Redford (ed.), Oxford University Press, http://www.oxfordreference.com.ezproxy.library.yorku.ca/views/ENTRY.html?subview=Main&entry=t176.e0345 (accessed February 20, 2012).

Fisler, B. (2003), "Quantifiable Evidence, Reading Pedagogy, and Puppets," *Research in Drama Education* 8, 1: 25–38.

Forte, M. (1997), *Virtual Archaeology*, New York: Harry N. Abrams.

Foster, B. R. (2005), *Before the Muses: An Anthology of Akkadian Literature*, 3rd edn, Bethesda, MD: CDL Press.

Foster, J. F. (2001), *Ancient Egyptian Literature*, Austin, TX: University of Texas.

Foucart, G. (1935), *Le Tombeau de Amonmos*, Cairo: Institut française d'archéologie orientale.

Frankfurter, D. (1998), *Religion in Roman Egypt*, Princeton, NJ: Princeton University Press.

Gaballa, G. A. and Kitchen, K. A. (1969), "The Festival of Sokar," *Orientalia* 38: 1–76.

Galán, J. M. (2003), "Amenhotep Son of Hapu as Intermediary between the People and God," in *Egyptology at the Dawn of the Twenty-first Century: Proceedings of the Eighth International Congress of Egyptologists*, vol. 2, *History, Religion*, Z. Hawass and L. Pinch Brock (eds.), 221–9, Cairo: American University in Cairo Press.

Gardiner, A. H. (1935), *Hieratic Papyri in the British Museum*, ser. 3, *Chester Beatty Gift*, London: British Museum.

Gardiner, A. H. (1947), *Ancient Egyptian Onomastica*, 2 vols, Oxford: Oxford University Press.

Gardiner, A. H. (1953), "The Coronation of King aremab," *Journal of Egyptian Archaeology* 39: 13–31.

Gardiner, A. H. (1961), *Egypt of the Pharaohs*, Oxford: Oxford University Press.

Gardner, R. (1983), *Frames of Mind: The Theory of Multiple Intelligences*, New York: Basic Books.

Geller, S. A. (2004), 'The Religion of the Bible,' in *The Jewish Study Bible*, A. Berlin and M. Brettler (eds.), 2021–40, Oxford: Oxford University Press.

Geßler-Lohr, B. (1983), *Die heiligen Seen Ägyptisher Tempel*, Hildesheim: Gerstenberg.

Gillam, R. (2005), *Performance and Drama in Ancient Egypt*, London: Duckworth.

Gillam, R. (2012), "The Daily Cult: Space, Continuity and Change," *British Archaeological Reports*: Bar S 2397.

Gillam, R., Innes, C. and Jacobson, J. (2010), "Performance and Ritual in the Virtual Egyptian Temple," paper presented at Computer Applications in Archaeology (CAA), Granada, Spain, April, http://publicvr.org/publications/GillamCAA2010.pdf (accessed February 20, 2015).

Gillings, M. (2002), "Virtual Archaeologies and the Hyper-real," in *Virtual Reality in Geography*, P. Fisher and D. Unwin (eds.), 17–32, London: Taylor & Francis.

Girard, C., Ecalle, J. and Magnan, A. (2013), "Serious Games as New Educational Tools: How Effective Are They? A Meta-analysis of Recent Studies," *Journal of Computer Assisted Learning* 29, 3: 207–19, doi: 10.1111/j.1365-2729.2012.00489.x.

Górski, H. J. (1990), "La barque d'Amon dans la décoration du temple de Thoutmosis III à Deir el-Bahari," *Mitteilungen des Deutschen Archäologischen Instituts, Abteilung Kairo*, 99–112.

Goyon, J.-C. (1972), *Confirmation du pouvoir royal au nouvel an*, Cairo: Institut français d'archéologie orientale.

Goyon, J.-C. (1978–81), "Une dalle aux noms de Menkheperrê, fils de Pinedjem I, d'Isetemkheb et de Smendès (CS X 1305)," *Karnak* 7: 275–80.

Graefe, E. (1971), "Untersuchungen zur Wortfamilie bj3," Ph.D. diss., Köln University.

Graf, F. (2008), "Divination," in *Religion Past and Present: Encyclopedia of Theology and Religion*, H. D. Betz, D. S. Browning, B. Jonouslou and E. Jügel (eds.), vol. 1, 98–9, Leiden: Brill.

Graham, A. (2012), "Investigating the Theban West Bank Floodplain," *Egyptian Archaeology* 41: 21–4.

Graham, A. and Bunbury, J. M. (2005), "The Ancient Landscapes and Waterscapes of Karnak," *Egyptian Archaeology* 27: 17–19.

Graham, G. (2001), "Insignias," in *The Oxford Encyclopedia of Ancient Egypt*, D. B. Redford (ed.), New York: Oxford University Press, http://www.oxfordreference.com.ezproxy.library.yorku.ca/views/ENTRY.html?subview=Main&entry=t176.e0339 (accessed February 22, 2012).

Grajetzki, W. (2003), "Types of Temples," *Digital Egypt for Universities*, London: University College, http://www.digitalegypt.ucl.ac.uk (accessed November 2, 2012).

Grandet, P. (1994), *Le Papyrus Harris I, BM 9999*, Cairo: Institut français d'archéologie orientale du Caire.

Grau, O. (2003), *Virtual Art: From Illusion to Immersion*, Cambridge, MA: MIT Press.

Grimal, N. C. (1992), *A History of Ancient Egypt*, trans. I. Shaw, Oxford: Blackwell.

Groot, J. de (2011), "Affect and Empathy: Re-enactment and Performance as/in History," *Rethinking History* 15, 4: 587–99.

Guernsey, L. (2009), "How *Sesame Street* Changed the World," *Newsweek*, May 22.
Hahn, R. (2010), *Archaeology and the Origins of Philosophy*, Albany, NY: University of New York Press.
Hajjar, Y. (1977), *La triade d'Héliopolis-Baalbek*, vol. 2, Leiden. Brill.
Hajjar, Y. (1990), "Divinités oraculaires et rites divinatoires en Syrie et en Phénicie à l'époque gréco-romaine," in *Aufstieg und Niedergang der römischen Welt*, II.18.4, *Religion (Heidentum: Die Religiösen Verhältnisse in den Provinzen* [Forts. I]) 4, Teilband, W. Haase (ed.), 2236–320, Berlin: De Gruyter.
Hall, D. (1994), "Civil War Reenactors and the Postmodern Sense of History," *Journal of American Culture* 17, 3: 7–11.
Hamilakis, Y. (2001), "Experience and Corporality," in Y. Hamilakis, M. Pluciennik and S. Tarlow, *Thinking Through the Body: Archaeologies of Corporeality*, 99–103, New York: Kluwer, Plenum.
Han, J., Shao, L., Xu, D. and Shotton, J. (2013), "Enhanced Computer Vision with Microsoft Kinect Sensor: A Review," *IEEE Transactions on Cybernetics* 43, 5.
Handron, K. and Jacobson, J. (2010), "Extending Physical Collections into the Virtual Space of a Digital Dome," *11th International Symposium on Virtual Reality, Archaeology and Cultural Heritage (VAST), Paris, September*, A. Artusi, M. Joly-Parvex, G. Lucet, A. Ribes and D. Pitzalis (eds.), http://publicvr.org/publications/HandronVAST2010.pdf.
Haring, B. (1997), *Divine Households: Administrative and Economic Aspects of the New Kingdom Memorial Temples in Western Thebes*, Leiden: Nederlands Instituut voor het Navije Oosten.
Haring, B. (2001), "Deir El Medina," in *The Oxford Encyclopedia of Ancient Egypt*, D. B. Redford (ed.), New York: Oxford University Press, http://www.oxfordreference.com.ezproxy.library.yorku.ca/views/ENTRY.html?subview=Main&entry=t176.e0345 (accessed February 20, 2012).
Harman, J. and Wernecke, J. (1996), *The VRML 2.0 Handbook: Building Moving Worlds on the Web*, Reading, MA: Addison-Wesley Professional.
Harrington, P. (1958), "Shari Lewis & Lamb Chop," *Look*, December 9.
Hart, G. (1986), *A Dictionary of Egyptian Gods and Goddesses*, London: Routledge & Kegan Paul.
Hartman, J. and Wernecke, J. (1996), *The VRML 2.0 Handbook: Building Moving Worlds on the Web*, New York: Addison Wesley Longman.
Hayes, W. C. (1962), "Egypt: Internal Affairs from Tuthmosis I to the Death of Amenophis III," in *The Cambridge Ancient History*, vol. 2, part 2, ch. 25, "History of the Middle East and the Aegean region, c. 1380–1000 B.C.," I. E. S. Edwards (ed.), Cambridge: Cambridge University Press.
Heathcote, D. and Bolton, G. (1995), *Drama for Learning*, Portsmouth, NH: Heinemann.
The Hebrew Bible in English, According to the JPS 1917 Edition, http://www.mechon-mamre.org/e/et/et0.htm (accessed December 12, 2013).

Heckl, R. (2008), "Die Errettung des Königs durch seinen Gott: Die literarische Quelle der Gebete Hiskijas im Kontext von 2 Kön 19f. (par.) und ihre Rolle bei der Ausformulierung des Monotheismusbekenntnisses," in *Mensch und König. Studien zur Anthropologie des Alten Testaments: Rüdiger Lux zum 60. Geburtstag*, A. Berlejung and R. Heckl (eds.), 157–70, Freiburg im Breisgau: Herder.

Heidegger, M. (1962), *Being and Time*, trans. J. Macquarie and E. Robinson, Oxford: Blackwell.

Heimpel, W. (2003), *Letters to the King of Mari: A New Translation, with Historical Introduction, Notes, and Commentary*, Winona Lake, IN: Eisenbrauns.

Helck, W. (1987), *Untersuchungen zur Thinitenzeit*, Wiesbaden: Harrassowitz.

Hern, A. and Stuart, K. (2014), "Oculus Rift: Facebook Sees Virtual Reality Future in $2bn Deal," *The Guardian*, March 26, http://www.theguardian.com/technology/2014/mar/26/facebook-buys-oculus-virtual-reality (accessed February 20, 2015).

Hillers, R. B. and Kashani, R. (2007), "Burial," in *Encyclopaedia Judaica*, 2nd edn, M. Berenbaum and F. Skolnik (eds.), vol. 4, 291–4, Detroit: Macmillan Reference USA.

Hillier, B. and Hanson, J. (1984), *The Social Logic of Space*, Cambridge: Cambridge University Press.

Hirmer, M., Lange, H. O. and Otto, E. (1968), *Egypt: Architecture, Sculpture, Painting*, London: Phaidon.

Hitchens, C. (2007), *God Is Not Great: How Religion Poisons Everything*, New York: Twelve.

Hölscher, U. (1934), *The Excavation of Medinet Habu*, vol. 1, *General Plans and Views*, Chicago, IL: University of Chicago Press.

Hope, C. A. (2013), "Egypt and 'Libya' to the End of the Old Kingdom: The View from Dakhleh Oasis," in *The Archaeology and Art of Ancient Egypt: Essays in Honor of David B. O'Connor*, Z. Hawass and J. Richards (eds.), 399–416, Cairo: American University in Cairo Press.

Hornbrook, D. (1989), *Education and Dramatic Art*, 2nd edn, London: Routledge.

Hornung, E. (1982), *Conceptions of God in Ancient Egypt: The One and the Many*, trans. J. Baines, Ithaca, NY: Cornell University Press.

IEVR (Institute for the Exploration of Visual Realities), http://www2.ku.edu/~ievr/ (accessed November 26, 2013).

Ilson, B. (2009), "Topo Gigio and the Obratsov Puppets," in *Sundays with Sullivan: How The Ed Sullivan Show Brought Elvis, the Beatles, and Culture to America*, 83–8, Lanham, MD: Taylor Trade Publications.

Ingold, T. (2000), *The Perception of the Environment*, London: Routledge.

Jackson, A. (2007), *Theatre, Education and the Making of Meanings: Art or Instrument?* Manchester: University of Manchester.

Jacobson, J. (2002), "Configuring Multi-screen Immersive Displays with Existing Computer Equipment," *Proceedings of the Human Factors and Ergonomics Society*

46th Annual Meeting, Baltimore, Maryland, September, 760–5, http://publicvr.org/publications/hfes-2002.pdf (accessed February 20, 2015).

Jacobson, J. (2011a), "Digital Dome versus Desktop Display in an Educational Game: Gates of Horus," *International Journal of Gaming and Computer-Mediated Simulations* 3, 1.

Jacobson, J. (2011b), *Egyptian Ceremony in the Virtual Temple: Avatars for Virtual Heritage*, white paper and final performance report to the National Endowment for the Humanities, Digital Startup Grant #HD5120910, http://publicvr.org/egypt/oracle/whitepaper.pdf (accessed February 20, 2015).

Jacobson, J. (2012), "The Egyptian Oracle," Public VR, http://publicvr.org/html/pro_oracle.html (accessed February 20, 2015).

Jacobson, J. (2013), "Digital Dome versus Desktop Display: Learning Outcome Assessments by Domain Experts," *International Journal of Virtual and Personal Learning Environments* 4, 3.

Jacobson, J. and Holden, L. (2005), "The Virtual Egyptian Temple," paper presented at World Conference on Educational Media, Hypermedia and Telecommunications (ED-MEDIA), Montreal, Canada, June, http://publicvr.org/publications/Jacobson2005e.pdf (accessed February 20, 2015).

Jacobson, J. and Holden, L. (2007), "Virtual Heritage: Living in the Past," *Techné: Research in Philosophy and Technology* 10, 3, http://scholar.lib.vt.edu/ejournals/SPT/v10n3/jacobsen.html (accessed February 20, 2015).

Jacobson, J. and Lewis, L. (2005), "Game Engine Virtual Reality with CaveUT," *IEEE Computer* 38, 4: 79–82, http://publicvr.org/publications/Jacobson2005i.html (accessed February 20, 2015).

Jacobson, J. and Preussner, G. (2010), "Visually Immersive Theater with CaveUT," paper presented at World Conference on Educational Multimedia, Hypermedia and Telecommunications (ED-MEDIA), Toronto, Canada, June, http://publicvr.org/publications/JacobsonEDMedia-2010.pdf (accessed February 20, 2015).

Jacobson, J., Handron, K. and Holden, L. (2009), "Narrative and Content Combine in a Learning Game for Virtual Heritage," paper presented at 37th annual conference of Computer Applications and Quantitive Methods in Archaeology (CAA), Williamsburg, VA.

Jànosi, P. (1999), "The Tombs of Officials: Houses of Eternity," in *Egyptian Art in the Age of the Pyramids*, J. P. O'Neill et al. (eds.), 27–9, New York: Metropolitan Museum of Art.

Jansen-Winkeln, K. (1999), "Die Wahl des Königs durch Orakel in der 20. Dynastie," *Bulletin de la Société d'Égyptologie de Genève* 23: 51–61.

Janssen, J. J. (1991), "Literacy and Letters at Deir el-Medîna," in *Village Voices: Proceedings of the Symposium "Texts from Deir el-Medîna and Their Interpretation," Leiden, May 31–June 1, 1991*, 81–94, CNWS Publications 13, Leiden: Centre of Non-Western Studies, Leiden University.

Jasnow, R. (1997), "A Demotic Omen Text? (P. BM 10238)," in *Essays on Ancient Egypt in Honour of Herman te Velde*, J. van Dijk (ed.), 207–18, Groningen: Styx.

Jomard, E. F. (1809–29), *Description de l'Égypte, ou, Recueil des observations et des recherches qui ont été faites en Égypte pendant l'expédition de l'armée française*: Antiquités, vols. 1 and 3, Paris: Publiée par ordre de sa majesté l'empereur Napoléon le Grand.

Jones, H. L. (1982–97), *Strabo: Geography*, Cambridge, MA: Harvard University Press.

Kahl, J. (2007), *"Re Is My Lord": Searching for the Rise of the Sun God at the Dawn of Egyptian History*, Wiesbaden: Harrassowitz.

Kákosy, L. (1980), "Orakel," in *Lexikon der Ägyptologie*, vol. 4, W. Helck and E. Otto (eds.), 600–6, Wiesbaden: Harrassowitz.

Kaper, O. E. (2001), "Local Perceptions of the Fertility of the Dakhleh Oasis in the Roman Period," in *The Oasis Papers 1: Proceedings of the First Conference of the Dakhleh Oasis Project*, Dakhleh Oasis Project, monograph 6, C. A. Marlow and A. J. Mills (eds.), 70–9, Oxford: Oxbow Books.

Karlshausen, C. (1995), "L'évolution de la barque processionnelle d'Amon à la 18e Dynastie," *Revue d'égyptologie* 46: 119–37.

Karlshausen, C. (2009), *L'iconographie de la barque processionnelle divine en Égypte au Nouvel Empire*, Leuven: Peeters.

Kemp, B. J. (1989), *Ancient Egypt: Anatomy of a Civilization*, London: Routledge.

Kenny, P., Hartholt, A., Gratch, J., Swartout, W., Traum, D., Marsella, S. and Piepol, D. (2007), "Building Interactive Virtual Humans for Training Environment," paper presented at Interservice/Industry Training, Simulation and Education Conference (I/ITSEC) 2007, Orlando, Florida.

Kitamura, K. (2010), "Recreating Chaos: Jeremy Deller's 'The Battle of Orgreave,'" in A. McCalman and P. A. Pickering (eds.), *Historical Reenactment: From Realism to the Affective Turn*, 39–49, New York: Palgrave Macmillan.

Kitchen, K. A. (1996), *The Third Intermediate Period in Egypt (1100–650 BC)*, Warminster: Aris and Phillips.

Klasens, A. (1975), "An Amulet Papyrus of the 25th Dynasty," *Oudheidkundige Medelingen* 56: 20–8.

Klotz, D. (2006), *Adoration of the Ram*, New Haven, CT: Yale University Press.

Knapp, A. B. (1988), *The History and Culture of Western Asia and Egypt*, Belmont, CA: Wadsworth.

Kruchten, J.-M. (1987), *Le grand texte oraculaire de Djéhutimose, intendant du domaine d'Amon sous le pontificat de Pinedjem II*, Brussels: Fondation reine Elisabeth.

Kruchten, J.-M. (1989), *Les annales des prêtes de Karnak (XXI–XXIIIèmes dynasties) et autres textes contemporains relatifs à l'initiation des prêtes d'Amon*, Leuven: Peeters.

Kruchten, J.-M. (1995), "La terminologie de la consultation de l'oracle de l'Amon thébain à la IIIème Période Intermédiaire," in *Oracles et prophéties dans l'antiquité: Actes du colloque de Strasbourg, 15–17 juin 1995*, J.-G. Heintz (ed.), Paris: Diffusion de Boccard.

Kruchten, J.-M. (2001a), "Law," in *The Oxford Encyclopedia of Ancient Egypt*, D. B.

Redford (ed.), New York: Oxford University Press, http://www.oxfordreference. com.ezproxy.library.yorku.ca/views/ENTRY.html?subview=Main&entry=t176.e0402 (accessed May 21, 2012).

Kruchten, J.-M. (2001b), "Oracles," in *The Oxford Encyclopedia of Ancient Egypt*, D. B. Redford (ed.), New York: Oxford University Press, http://www.oxfordreference. com.ezproxy.library.yorku.ca/views/ENTRY.html?subview=Main&entry=t176.e0402 (accessed May 21, 2012).

Kuhlmann, K. P. (1988), *Das Ammoneion: Archäologie, Geschichte und Kultpraxis des Orakels von Siwa*, Archäologische Veröffentlichungen, Deutsches Archäologisches Institut, Abteilung Kairo 75, Mainz: Zabern.

Kuhrt, A. (1995), *The Ancient Near East: 3000–330 BC*, London: Routledge.

Kurth, D. (1994), *Treffpunkt der Götter: Inschriften aus dem Tempel des Horus von Edfu*, Munich: Artemis.

Kurth, D. (2004), *The Temple of Edfu: A Guide by an Ancient Egyptian Priest*, trans. A. Alcock, Cairo: American University in Cairo Press.

Lacau, P. and H. Chevrier (1977), *Une chapelle d'Hatshepsout à Karnak*, Cairo: Institut français d'archéologie orientale.

Lakoff, G. (1987), *Women, Fire, and Dangerous Things: What Categories Reveal about the Mind*, Chicago, IL: University of Chicago Press.

Landström, B. (1970), *Ships of the Pharaohs*, Garden City, NJ: Doubleday.

Lane, P. (1996), "Past Practices in the Ritual Present: Examples from the Welsh Bronze Age," *Archaeological Review from Cambridge* 5: 181–92.

Latshaw, G. (2000), *The Complete Book of Puppetry*, New York: Dover.

Lauffray, J. (1979), *Karnak d'Egypte: Domaine du divin*, Paris: Éditions du Centre national de la recherche scientifique.

Laurel, B. (1993), *Computers and Theatre*, Reading, MA: Addison-Wesley.

Laurel, B., Strickland, R. and Tow, R. (1998), "Placeholder: Landscape and Narrative in Virtual Environments," in Clark Dodsworth Jr. (ed.), *Digital Illusion*, 181–208, New York: ACM Press.

Laviola, J. J. (2008), "Bringing VR and Spatial 3D Interaction to the Masses through Video Games," *IEEE Computer Graphics and Applications* 28, 5: 10–15.

Leader-Elliott, L. (2003), "Community Heritage Interpretation Games: A Case Study from Angaston, South Australia," *International Journal of Heritage Studies* 11, 2: 161–71.

Leahy, A. (1984), "Death by Fire in Ancient Egypt," *Journal of the Economic and Social History of the Orient* 27, 2: 199–206.

Learning Sites (2011), "The Transition to VR: The Fortress of Buhen, Egypt," February 11, http://www.learningsites.com/EarlyWork/buhen-2.htm (accessed January 6, 2014).

Legrain, G. (1916), "Un miracle d'Ahmes Ier à Abydos sous le regne de Ramses II," *Annales du Service des antiquités de l'Egypte* 16: 161–70.

Legrain, G. (1917), "Le logement et transport des barques sacrées et des statues des dieux dans quelques temples égyptiens," *BIFAO* 13: 1–76.

Leisten, T. (2013), "Baalbek," in *Brill's New Pauly*, H. Cancik and H. Schneider (eds.), Brill Online, http://referenceworks.brillonline.com.ezproxy.library.yorku.ca/entries/brill-s-new-pauly/baalbek-e210940 (accessed December 12, 2013).

Levi, P. (1971), *Pausanias: Guide to Greece*, vol. 1, Harmondsworth: Penguin.

Lewis, M. and Jacobson, J. (2002), "Game Engines in Scientific Research," *Communications of the ACM* 45: 27–31, http://publicvr.org/publications/Lewis2002.pdf (accessed February 20, 2015).

Lichtheim, M. (1976), *Ancient Egyptian Literature*, vol. 2, *The New Kingdom*, Berkeley, CA: University of California.

Lightfoot, J. L. (2003), *Lucian: On the Syrian Goddess*, Oxford: Oxford University Press.

Lloyd, A. B. (2000), "The Late Period" and "The Ptolemaic Period," in *The Oxford History of Ancient Egypt*, I. Shaw (ed.), 369–421, Oxford: Oxford University Press.

Lloyd, A. B. (2001), "Herodotus," in *The Oxford Encyclopedia of Ancient Egypt*, D. B. Redford (ed.), New York: Oxford University Press, http://www.oxfordreference.com.ezproxy.library.yorku.ca/views/ENTRY.html?subview=Main&entry=t176.e0311 (accessed May 26, 2012).

Lorton, D. (1977), "Treatment of Criminals in Ancient Egypt: Through the New Kingdom," *Journal of the Economic and Social History of the Orient* 20, 1: 2–64.

Lynskey, D. (2013), "Austerity Addicts: Why Is 1940s Nostalgia All the Rage?" *The Guardian*, 13 August, http://www.theguardian.com/lifeandstyle/2013/aug/13/austerity-1940s-war-vintage-fashion (accessed October 13, 2013).

McCalman, I. and Pickering, P. A. (2010), "Introduction: From Realism to the Affective Turn: An Agenda," in *Historical Reenactment: From Realism to the Affective Turn*, 1–17, New York: Palgrave Macmillan.

McCormick, B., DeFanti, T. and Brown, M. (1987), "Visualization in Scientific Computing," *Computer Graphics* 21, 6.

McDowell, A. G. (1999), *Village Life in Ancient Egypt: Laundry Lists and Love Songs*, Oxford: Oxford University Press.

Magnessen, S. and Justice-Malloy, R., eds. (2011), *Enacting History*, Tuscaloosa, AL: University of Alabama Press.

Mahoney, D. P. (1995), "Live Theater Gets a Virtual Boost," Computer Graphics World 18, 7: 76.

Mapes, D. P., Tonner, P. and Hughes, C. E. (2011), "Geppetto: An Environment for the Efficient Control and Transmission of Digital Puppetry," *Lecture Notes in Computer Science* 6774: 270–8.

Maul, S. and Bremmer, J. (2012), "Divination," in *Brill's New Pauly: Antiquity*, vols. 14 and 15, H. Cancik and H. Schneider (eds.), Brill Online Reference, http://referenceworks.brillonline.com.ezproxy.library.yorku.ca/entries/brill-s-new-pauly/divination-e321630 (accessed May 24, 2012).

Mazalek, A., Chandrasekharan, S., Nitsche, M., Welsh, T., Clifton, P., Quitmeyer, A. and Athreya, D. (2011), "I'm in the Game: Embodied Puppet Interface Improves

Avatar Control," in *Proceedings of the Fifth International Conference on Tangible, Embedded, and Embodied Interaction*, 129–36), ACM (Association for Computing Machinery).

Meeks, D. (2003), "Locating Punt," in *Mysterious Lands: Encounters with Ancient Egypt*, D. O'Connor and S. Quirke (eds.), 53–80, London: UCL.

Meeks, D. and Favard-Meeks, C. (1997), *Daily Life of the Egyptian Gods*, trans. G. M. Goshgarian, London: John Murray.

Meister, K. (2013), "D. Siculus from Sicily, Greek Universal Historian, 1st Cent. BC," in *Brill's New Pauly*, H. Cancik and H. Schneider (ed.), Brill Online (accessed December 9, 2013).

Merleau-Ponty, M. (2002), *Phenomenology of Perception*, trans. C. Smith, London: Routledge.

Michael, J. (2006), "Where's the Evidence that Active Learning Works?" *Advances in Physiology Education* 30, 4: 159–67.

Mikovec, Z., Slavik, P. and Zara, J. (2009), "Cultural Heritage, User Interfaces and Serious Games at CTU Prague," paper presented at 15th International Conference on Virtual Systems and Multimedia, Vienna, September 9–12.

Milgram, P. and Kishino, F. (1994), "Taxonomy of Mixed Reality Visual Displays," *IEICE Transactions on Information and Systems* E77-D, 12: 1321–9.

Mintz, S. W. and Price, R. (1992), *The Birth of African American Culture: An Anthropological Perspective*, Boston, MA: Beacon Press.

Montet, P. (1964), "Le rituel de fondation des temples Égyptiens," *Kêmi* 17: 74–100.

Morenz, S. (1973), *Egyptian Religion*, trans. A. E. Keep, Ithaca, NY: Cornell University Press.

Moret, A. ([1902] 1988), *Le rituel du culte divine journalier en Égypte*, Genève: Slatkine.

Mori, M. (2012), "The Uncanny Valley," trans. K. F. MacDorman and N. Kageki, *IEEE Robotics and Automation Magazine* 19, 2: 98–100.

Morkot, R. G. (2000), *The Black Pharaohs: Egypt's Nubian Rulers*, London: Rubicon.

Mortara, M., Bellotti, F., Berta, R., Catalano, C. E., Fiucci, G., Houry-Panchetti, M. and Petridis, P. (2011), "Serious Games for Cultural Heritage: The GaLA Activities," paper presented at 12th International Symposium on Virtual Reality, Archaeology and Cultural Heritage (VAST), Prato, Italy.

Mosaker, L. (2001), "Visualising Historical Knowledge Using Virtual Reality Technology," *Digital Creativity* 12, 1: 15–25.

Müller, S. (2013), "Siwa Oasis," in *The Encyclopedia of Ancient History*, R. S. Bagnall, K. Brodersen, C. B. Champion, A. Erskine and S. R. Huebner (eds.), 6274–5, Oxford: Blackwell.

Murnane, W. (1980a), "Opetfest," *Lexikon der Ägyptologie*, vol. 4, W. Helck and E. Otto, (eds.), 574–9, Wiesbaden: Harrassowitz.

Murnane, W. (1980b), *United with Eternity: A Concise Guide to the Monuments of Medinet Habu*, Cairo: American University in Cairo Press and Oriental Institute.

Murnane, W. (1995), *Texts from the Amarna Period in Egypt*, Atlanta, GA: SBL.

Myśliwiec, C. (2000), *The Twilight of Ancient Egypt*, trans. D. Lorton, Ithaca, NY: Cornell University Press.

Nambiar, A. (2011), "Sound Spatialization for the Egyptian Oracle," Master's thesis, Department of Digital Media, Northeastern University.

Nambiar, A. and Jacobson, J. (2012), "Spatialized Audio for Mixed Reality Theater: The Egyptian Oracle," presentation to International Conference of Auditory Displays, Atlanta, GA, June. (accessed February 20, 2015).

Naville, E. (1892), *The Festival Hall of Osorkon II in the Great Temple of Bubastis*, London: Egypt Exploration Fund.

Nicholson, P. T. and Shaw, I. (eds.) (2000), *Ancient Egyptian Materials and Technology*, Cambridge: Cambridge University Press.

Nims, C. F. (1965), *Thebes of the Pharaohs: Pattern for Every City*, London: Elek Books.

Niwinski, A. (1992), "Bürgerkrieg, militärischer Staatsstreich und Ausnahmezustand in Ägypten unter Ramses XI: Ein Versuch neuer Interpretation der alten Quellen," in *Gegengabe: Festschrift für Emma Brunner-Traut*, I. Gamer-Wallert and W. Helck (eds.), 235–62, Tübingen: Attempto.

NYSED (2014), New York State Curriculum and Instruction: Social Studies, http://www.p12.nysed.gov/ciai/socst/pub/sscore1.pdf

O' Connor, D. (1991), "Mirror of the Cosmos: The Palace of Merenptah," in *Fragments of a Shattered Visage: The Proceedings of the International Symposium of Ramesses the Great*, E. Bleiberg and R. Freed (eds.), Memphis State University: 167–98.

O' Connor, D. (2012), "The Mortuary Temple of Ramesses III at Medinet Habu," in *Ramesses III: The Life and Times of Egypt's Last Hero*, E. Cline and D. O'Connor (eds.), 209–70, Ann Arbor: University of Michigan Press.

OED [Oxford English Dictionary] (2010), http://oxforddictionaries.com (accessed December 17, 2010).

Oldfather, C. H. (1933), *Diodorus of Sicily*, vol. 1, London: Heinemann, http://penelope.uchicago.edu/Thayer/E/Roman/Texts/Diodorus_Siculus/home.html (accessed December 15, 2013).

Onstine, S. (2001), "The Role of the Chantress (šm'yt) in Ancient Egypt," Ph.D. diss., University of Toronto.

Onstine, S. (2012), "A Brief Report: The University of Memphis mission to Theban Tomb 16 in Dra Abu el-Naga," *Newsletter of the Society for the Study of Egyptian Antiquities* 2: 4–5.

Oriental Institute (1930), *Epigraphic Survey of Medinet Habu*, vol. 1, *Earlier Historical Records of Ramses III* (OIP 8), Chicago, IL: University of Chicago Press.

Oriental Institute (1934), *Epigraphic Survey of Medinet Habu*, vol. 3, *The Calendar, the "Slaughter House" and Minor Records of Ramses III* (OIP 23), Chicago, IL: University of Chicago Press.

Oriental Institute (1936) *Ramses III's temple within the great inclosure of Amon*, Chicago, IL: University of Chicago Press.

Oriental Institute (1957), *Epigraphic Survey of Medinet Habu*, vol. 5, *The Temple Proper, Part 1* (OIP 83), Chicago, IL: University of Chicago Press.
Otto, E. (1960), *Das Ägyptische Mundöffnungsritual*, Wiesbaden: Harrassowitz.
Otto, E. (1966), *Osiris und Amun: Kult und heilige Stätten*, Munich: Hirmer.
Otto, E. (1972), "Amun," in *Lexikon der Ägyptologie* I, W. Helck and E. Otto (eds.), Wiesbaden: Harrossowitiz.
Papagiannakis, G., Schertenleib, S., O'Kennedy, B., Arevalo-Poizat, M., Magnenat-Thalmann, N., Stoddart, A. and Thalmann, D. (2005), "Mixing Virtual and Real Scenes in the Site of Ancient Pompeii," *Computer Animation and Virtual Worlds* 16, 1: 11–24.
Parker, R. A. (1962), *A Saite Oracle Papyrus from Thebes in the Brooklyn Museum (Papyrus Brooklyn 47.218.3)*, Providence, RI: Brown University.
Parker-Starbuck, J. (2011), *Cyborg Theatre: Corporeal/Technological Intersections in Multimedia Performance*, New York: Palgrave Macmillan.
Parkinson, R. B. (2002), *Poetry and Culture in Middle Kingdom Egypt: A Dark Side to Perfection*, London: Continuum.
Parpola, S. (1997), *Assyrian Prophecies*, Helsinki: University of Helsinki.
Pavis, P. (1998), *Dictionary of the Theatre: Terms, Concepts, and Analysis*, trans. C. Shantz, Toronto, ON: University of Toronto Press.
Pearce, R. (2003), "University History," *History Today* 53, 8: 54–7.
Perrin, B. (1914–26), *Plutarch's Lives*, London: W. Heinemann, http://penelope.uchicago.edu/Thayer/E/Roman/Texts/Plutarch/Lives/home.html (accessed December 15, 2013).
Pfoh, E. (2009), *The Emergence of Israel in Ancient Palestine*, London: Equinox.
Pinch, G. (1993), *Foundation Deposits to Hatho*, Oxford: Griffiths Institute.
Pongratz-Leisten, B. (1999), *Herrschaftwissen in Mesopotamien*, Helsinki: University of Helsinki.
Porter, B. and Moss, R. (1972), *Topographical Bibliography of Ancient Egyptian Hieroglyphic Texts, Reliefs, and Paintings*, vol. 2, *Theban Temples*, 2nd edn, Oxford: Clarendon Press.
Posener, G. (1971), "Amon juge du pauvre," *Ägyptische Bauforschung und Altertumskunde* 12: 59–63.
Posener-Kriéger, P. (1976), *Les archives du temple funéraire de Néfererkare-Kakai, les papyrus d'Abousir: Traduction et commentaire*, Cairo: Institut français d'archéologie orientale.
Price, R. (1975), *Saramaka Social Structure: Analysis of a Maroon Society in Surinam*, Rio Piedras: University of Puerto Rico.
Quirke, S. (1992), *Ancient Egyptian Religion*, London: British Museum Press.
Radt, S. (2013), "Strabo," in *Brill's New Pauly*, H. Cancik and H. Schneider (eds.), Brill Online, http://referenceworks.brillonline.com.ezproxy.library.yorku.ca/entries/brill-s-new-pauly/strabo-brill130030 (accessed December 9, 2013).
Rattray, R. S. (1927), *Religion and Art in Ashanti*, Oxford: Clarendon Press.

Ray, J. D. (1976), *The Archive of Hor*, London: Egypt Exploration Society.
Reaney, M., Unruh, D. and Hudson-Mairet, S. (2004), "The Edge of the Illusion: A Virtual Reality Production of the Magic Flute," *Theatre Design and Technology* 40, 5: 10–19.
Redford, D. B. (1992), *Egypt, Canaan and Israel in Ancient Times*, Princeton, NJ: Princeton University Press.
Redford, D. B. (2000), "Egypt and Western Asia in the Late New Kingdom: An Overview," in *The Sea Peoples and Their World: A Reassessment*, E. D. Oren (ed.), 1–20, Philadelphia, PA: University Museum, University of Pennsylvania.
Redford, D. B. (2013), "Akhenaten: New Theories and Old Facts," *Bulletin of the Oriental Schools of Research* 369: 9–34.
Redman, C. L. (1978), *The Rise of Civilization from Early Farmers to Urban Society in the Ancient Near East*, San Francisco, CA: Freeman.
Reeves, N. and Wilkinson, R. H. (1996), *The Complete Valley of the Kings*, London: Thames and Hudson.
Refai, H. (1998), "Die Bestätigung im Fest: Zur Rolle der thebanishchen Feste bei der Erneuerung der Königsmacht," *Memnonia* 9: 181–8.
Reilly, P. (1990), "Towards a Virtual Archaeology," in *Computer Applications in Archaeology*, K. Lockyea and S. Rahtz (eds.), 133–9, Oxford: British Archaeological Reports.
RHP (2014), Red Herring Puppets, http://www.redherringpuppets.com/ (accessed February 20, 2015).
Richards, C. (1993), "Monumental Choreography: Architecture and Spatial Representation in Late Neolithic Orkney," in *Interpretive Archaeology*, C. Tilley (ed.), 143–78, London: Berg.
Rickitt, R. (2006), *Designing Movie Creatures and Characters: Behind the Scenes with the Movie Masters*, Abingdon: Taylor & Francis.
Ripat, P. (2006), "The Language of Oracular Inquiry in Roman Egypt," *Phoenix* 60, 3–4: 304–28.
Ritner, R. (2003a), "The Famine Stela," in *The Literature of Ancient Egypt*, 3rd edn, W. K. Simpson (ed.), 386–91, New Haven, CT: Yale University Press.
Ritner, R. (2003b), "The Romance of Setna Khaemuas and the Mummies (Setna I)," in *The Literature of Ancient Egypt*, 3rd edn, W. K. Simpson (ed.), 453–69, New Haven, CT: Yale University Press.
Ritner, R. (2009), *The Libyan Anarchy: Inscriptions from Egypt's Third Intermediate Period*, Atlanta, GA: SBL.
Roberts, A. (1995), *Hathor Rising: The Serpent Power of Ancient Egypt*, Totnes: Northgate.
Robins, G. (2005), "Cult Statues in Ancient Egypt," in *Cult Image and Divine Representation in the Ancient Near East*, N. Walls (ed.), Boston, MA: American Schools of Oriental Research.
Rochemonteix, M. de (1892), *Le Temple d'Edfou*, vol. 1, Cairo: Institut français d'archéologie orientale.

Roeder, G. (1914), *Naos*, Leipzig: Breitkopf and Härtel.
Rollicke, H.-J. (2009), "I Ching: Divination," in *Religion Past and Present: Encyclopedia of Theology and Religion*, H. D. Betz, D. S. Browning, B. Jonouslou and E. Jügel (eds.), vol. 6, 372–3, Leiden: Brill.
Roman Military Research Society, http://www.romanarmy.net/ (accessed October 13, 2013).
Romano, J. and Bothmer, B. (1979), *The Luxor Museum of Egyptian Art: Catalogue*, Cairo: ARCE.
Roth, A. M. (1991), *Egyptian Phyles in the Old Kingdom: The Evolution of a System of Social Organization*, Chicago, IL: Oriental Institute.
Roth, A. M. (1993), "Social Change in the Fourth Dynasty: The Spatial Organization of Pyramids, Tombs and Cemeteries," *Journal of the American Research Center in Egypt* 30: 35–55.
Ryholt, K. (1993), "A Pair of Oracle Petitions Addressed to Horus-of-the-Camp," *Journal of Egyptian Archaeology* 79: 189–98.
Ryu, S. (2008), "Redefining Puppet: Paradoxical Relationship Between Human and Object," in *New Realities: Being Syncretic*, R. Ascott, G. Bast and W. Fiel (eds.), New York: Springer.
Ryu, S., Faralli, S., Bottoni, P. and Labella, A. (2008), "From Traditional to Virtual Interactive Puppetry: A Comprehensive Approach," in *Proceedings of ISEA 2008: The 14th International Symposium on Electronic Art, 25 July–3 August 2008, Singapore*, 396–8, ISEA2008.
Sadek, A. I. (1987), *Popular Religion in Egypt during the New Kingdom*, Hildesheim: Gerstenberg.
Sagrillo, T. L. (2013), "Libya and Libyans," in *The Encyclopedia of Ancient History*, R. S. Bagnall, K. Brodersen, C. B. Champion, A. Erskine and S. R. Huebner (eds.), 4071–5, Oxford: Blackwell.
Salter, C. (2010), *Entangled: Technology and the Transformation of Performance*, Cambridge, MA: MIT Press.
Sauneron, S. (1954), "La justice à la porte des temples (à propos du nom égyptien des propylées)," *BIFAO* 54: 117–27.
Sauneron, S. (1959), "Les songes et leur interprétation en l'Égypte ancienne," in *Les songes et leur interprétation*, Paris: Éditions du Seuil.
Sauneron, S. (1962), *Les fêtes religieuses d'Esna aux derniers siècles du Paganisme*, Cairo: Institut française d'archéologie orientale.
Sauneron, S. (2000), *The Priests of Ancient Egypt*, trans. D. Lorton, Ithaca, NY: Cornell University Press.
Sauneron, S. and Stierlin, H. (1975), *Edfou et Philae: Derniers temples d'Égypte*, Paris: du Chêne.
Schäfer, H. (1986), *Principles of Egyptian Art*, trans. and ed. J. Baines, Oxford: Griffith Institute.
Schechner, R. (1988), *Performance Theory*, New York: Routledge.

Schechner, R. (2011), *Performing Remains and War in Times of Theatrical Reenactment*, London: Routledge.

Schott, S. (1952), *Das schöne Fest von Wűstentale*, Wiesbaden: Akademie der Wissenschaften der Literatur.

Schubert, D. (2013), "Do We Always Have to Strive for 'Realism'?" Gamsutra, http://www.gamasutra.com/view/news/196663/Do_we_always_have_to_strive_for_realism.php (accessed February 20, 2015).

Schwarz, A. (2010), "Just as It Would Have Been in 1861: Stuttering Colonial Beginnings in ABCs Outback House," in *Historical Reenactment: From Realism to the Affective Turn*, I. McCalman and P. A. Pickering (eds.), 18–38, New York: Palgrave Macmillan.

Seibert, J. (2006), "Introduction," in *Space and Spatial Analysis in Archaeology*, E. C. Robertson, J. D. Seibert, D. C. Fernandez and M. U. Zender (eds.), Calgary, AB: University of Calgary Press.

Shackley, M. (2001), *Managing Sacred Sites: Service Provision and Visitor Experience*, New York: Continuum.

Shaw, I. (2004), *Ancient Egypt: A Very Short Introduction*, Oxford: Oxford University Press.

Simpson, W. K., ed. (2003), *The Literature of Ancient Egypt*, 3rd edn, New Haven, CT: Yale University Press.

Skeat, T. C. and Turner, E. G. (1968), "An Oracle of Hermes Trismegistos at Saqqâra," *Journal of Egyptian Archaeology* 54: 199–208.

Slater, M. and Wilbur, S. (1997), "A Framework for Immersive Virtual Environments (FIVE): Speculations on the Role of Presence in Virtual Environments," *Presence: Teleoperators and Virtual Environments* 6: 603–16.

Slater, M., Spanlang, B. and Corominas, D. (2010), "Simulating Virtual Environments within Virtual Environments as the Basis for a Psychophysics of Presence," *ACM Transactions on Graphics (TOG)* 29, 4: 92.

Spalinger, A. J. (1998), "The Limitations of Formal Ancient Egyptian Religion," *Journal of Near Eastern Studies* 57: 241–60.

Spalinger, A. J. (2001), "Festivals," in *The Oxford Encyclopedia of Ancient Egypt*, D. B. Redford (ed.), New York: Oxford University Press, http://www.oxfordreference.com.ezproxy.library.yorku.ca/views/ENTRY.html?subview=Main&entry=t176.e0242 (accessed May 19, 2012).

Spencer A. J. (1982), *Death in Ancient Egypt*, Harmondsworth: Penguin.

Spencer, N. (2006), *A Naos of Nekhthorheb from Bubastis: Religious Iconography and Temple Building in the 30th Dynasty*, London: British Museum.

Spencer, N. (2010), "Priests and Temples: Pharaonic," in *A Companion to Ancient Egypt*, A. B. Lloyd (ed.), vol. 1, 256–73, Oxford: Wiley Blackwell.

Spencer, P. (1984), *The Egyptian Temple: A Lexicographical Study*, London: Kegan Paul.

Squire, K. (2008), "Video Games and Education: Designing Learning Systems for an Interactive Age," *Educational Technology* 47, 2: 17–25.

Stadlemann, R. (1996), "Origins and Development of the Funerary Complex of Djoser," in *Studies in Honor of William Kelly Simpson*, P. Der Manuelian and R. Freed (eds.), 787–800, Boston, MA: Museum of Fine Arts.

Stone, M. C. (1998), "The *hnw* Gesture: Reinterpreting Early Variants and Inferring Patterns of Movement," paper presented at Annual Meeting of the American Research Center in Egypt, Los Angeles.

Stone, R. J. and Ojika, T. (2000), "Virtual Heritage: What Next?" *IEEE Multimedia* 7, 2: 73–4.

Strong, H. A., trans. (1913), *Lucian: The Syrian Goddess*, London: Constable, http://www.sacred-texts.com/cla/luc/tsg/tsg07.htm (accessed December 3, 2013).

Sturz, L., Jacobson, J. and Lawrence, T. (2013), "Puppet Evolution: Film and Technology," *Puppetry Journal* 65: 12–17.

Sylaiou, S. and Patias, P. (2004), "Virtual Reconstructions in Archaeology and Some Issues for Consideration," *IMEROS: An Annual Journal for Culture and Technology* 4, 1, http://www.ime.gr/publications/print/imeros/en/04/article01.html (accessed February 20, 2015).

Szpakowska, K. (2003), *Behind Closed Eyes: Dreams and Nightmares in Ancient Egypt*, Swansea: Classical Press of Wales.

Szpakowska, K. (2010), "Religion in Society: Pharaonic," in *A Companion to Ancient Egypt*, A. B. Lloyd (ed.), vol. 1, Oxford: Wiley Blackwell.

Teeter, E. (2007), "Temple Cults," in *The Egyptian World*, T. Wilkinson (ed.), 310–24, London: Routledge.

Thoden van Velzen, H. U. E. and Van Wetering, W. (2004), *In the Shadow of the Oracle: Religion as Politics in a Suriname Maroon Society*, D. van der Elst (ed.), Long Grove, IL: Waveland Press.

Thomas, J. (2000), 'The Polarities of Post-Processual Archaeology," in *Interpretive Archaeology: A Reader*, 1–18, London: Leicester University Press.

Thompson, C. (2004), *The Undead Zone: Why Realistic Graphics Make Humans Look Creepy*, posted June 9, 2004 [electronic version]; retrieved http://www.slate.com/articles/technology/gaming/2004/06/the_undead_zone.html (accessed date January 15, 2015),

Thornton, R. (1990), "Painting a Brighter Picture (Computerised Picture Processing)," *IEE Review* 36, 10: 379–82.

Tilley, C. (1994), *A Phenomenology of Landscape*, Oxford: Berg.

Török, L. (1997), *The Kingdom of Kush*, Leiden: Brill.

Tosi, M. (1987), "Popular Cults at Deir el Medina," in *Egyptian Civilization*, Donadoni Roveri and Anna Maria (eds.), 162–77, Turin: Electa Spa.

Tost, L. P. and Champion, E. (2011), "Evaluating Presence in Cultural Heritage Projects," *International Journal of Heritage Studies* 18, 1: 83–102, doi: 10.1080/13527258.2011.577796.

Traunecker, C. (1997), "L'appel au divin: la crainte des dieux et les serments de temple," in *Oracles et prophéties dans l'antiquité: actes du colloque de Strasbourg, 15–17 juin 1995*, J.-G. Heintz (ed.), 34–54, Paris: Boccard.

Traunecker, C., Le Saout, F. and Masson, O. (1981), *La chapelle d'Achôris à Karnak*, vol. 2, *Texte [et] Documents*, Paris: Éditions A. D. P. F.

Tritton, A. S. (2012), "Djanaza," in *Encyclopaedia of Islam*, 2nd edn, Brill Online Reference, http://referenceworks.brillonline.com.ezproxy.library.yorku.ca/entries/encyclopaedia-of-islam-2/djanaza-SIM_1985 (accessed May 23, 2012).

Trowbridge, S. and Stapleton, C. (2009), "Melting the Boundaries between Fantasy and Reality," *Computer* 42, 7 (July): 57–62, doi:10.1109/MC.2009.228.

Tuan, Y.-F. (1998), *Escapism*, Baltimore, MD: Johns Hopkins University Press.

Turner, V. W. (1995) *The Ritual Process: Structure and Anti-structure*, New York : Aldine de Gruyter.

Tyldesley, J. (2000), *Judgement of the Pharaoh: Crime and Punishment in Ancient Egypt*, London: Weidenfeld & Nicolson.

Ullmann, M. (2007), "Thebes: The Origin of a Ritual Landscape," in *Sacred Space and Sacred Function in Ancient Thebes*, P. Dorman and B. Bryan (ed.), Chicago, IL: Oriental Institute.

Unity3D (2013), http://unity3d.com (accessed February 20, 2015).

Valbelle, D. (1985), *Les ouvriers de la tombe: Deir-el-Médineh à l'époque Ramesside*, Cairo: Institut français d'archéologie orientale du Caire.

Van Dijk, J. (2000), "The Amarna Period and the Later New Kingdom (c. 1352–1069 BC)," in *The Oxford History of Ancient Egypt*, 272–313, Oxford: Oxford University Press.

Vandier, J. (1952), *Manuel d'archéologie Égyptienne*, vol. 1, *Les époques de formation: Les trois premières dynasties*, Paris: Éditions Picard.

Vandier, J. (1955), *Manuel d'archéologie Égyptienne*, vol. 2, *Les grandes époques: L'architecture religieuse et civile*, Paris: Éditions Picard.

Vannoy, J. R. (1974), "The Use of the Word hāʾĕlōhîm in Exodus 21:6 and 22:7, 8," in *The Law and the Prophets: Old Testament Studies in Honor of Oswald Thompson Allis*, J. H. Skilton (ed.), 225–41, Nutley, NJ: Presbyterian and Reformed.

Veldmeijer, A. J. (2010), *Amarna's Leatherware*, Norg: DrukWare.

Vercoutter, J. (1972), "Apis," in *Lexikon der Ägyptologie*, vol. 1, W. Helck and E. Otto (eds.), 338–50, Wiesbaden: Harrassowitz.

Verner, M. (2001), *The Pyramids*, trans. S. Rendall, New York: Grove Press.

Vernus, P. (2003), *Affairs and Scandals in Ancient Egypt*, trans. D. Lorton, Ithaca, NY: Cornell University Press.

Von Beckerath, J. (1968), "Die 'Stela der Verbannten' im Museum de Louvre," *Revue d'égyptologie* 20: 7–36.

Vygotsky, L. S. (1978), *Mind in Society: The Development of Higher Psychological Processes*, Cambridge, MA: Cambridge University Press.

Walker, J. (2013), "Editorial: An Appeal for Unrealism," Rock, Paper, Shotgun, September 24, http://www.rockpapershotgun.com/2013/09/24/editorial-an-appeal-for-unrealism/ (accessed February 20, 2015).

Waterfield, R., trans. and ed. (1998), *Herodotus: The Histories*, Oxford: Oxford University Press.

Watson, I. (2002), "Staging Theatre Anthropology," in *Negotiating Cultures: Eugenio Barbo and the Intercultural Debate*, I. Watson (ed.), 20–35, Manchester: University of Manchester Press.

Watterson, B. (1998), *The House of Horus at Edfu*, Stroud: Tempus.

Weckström, N. (2003), *Finding "Reality" in Virtual Environments*, Helsingfors/Esbo: Arcada Polytechnic.

Wei, T. and Li, Y. (2010), "Design of Educational Game: A Literature Review," in *Transactions on Edutainment IV*, Z. Pan, A. Cheok, W. Müller, X. Zhang and K. Wong (eds.), 266–76, Berlin: Springer.

Weiss, L. (2012), "Individuum und Gemeinschaft: Methodologische Überlegungen zur Persönlichen Frömmigkeit," in *Sozialisationen: Individuum – Gruppe – Gesellschaft: Beiträge des ersten Münchner Arbeitskreises Junge Aegyptologie (MAJA 1)*, 3 (bis 5.12.2010), G. Neunert, K. Gabler and A. Verbovsek (eds.), 187–205, Wiesbaden: Harrassowitz.

Wettengel, W. (2003), *Die Erzählung von den beiden Brüdern: Der Papyrus Orbiney und die Königsideologie der Ramessiden*, Freiberg/Schweiz: Universitätsverlag.

Wildung, D. (1977a), *Egyptian Saints*, New York: New York University.

Wildung, D. (1977b), *Imhotep und Amenhotep: Gottwerdung im alten Ägypten*, Munich: Deutscher Kunstverlag.

Wilkinson, T. A. H. (1999), *Early Dynastic Egypt*, London: Routledge.

Wilson, P. (2010), "Temple Architecture and Decorative Systems," in *A Companion to Ancient Egypt*, A. B. Lloyd (ed.), vol. 2, 781–803, Oxford: Wiley Blackwell.

xbox.com (2013), "Controls and Remotes," http://xbox.com

Young, F. (2000), "Christianity," in *The Cambridge History of Greek and Roman Political Thought*, C. Rowe and M. Schofield (ed.), 635–60, Cambridge: Cambridge University Press.

Yurco, F. J. (1999), "The End of the Late Bronze Age and Other Crisis Periods: A Volcanic Cause?" in *The Gold of Praise: Studies on Ancient Egypt in Honor of Edward F. Wente*, E. Teeter and J. A. Larson (ed.), 455–63, Chicago, IL: Oriental Institute of the University of Chicago.

Zinn, K. (2011), "Temples, Palaces and Libraries: A Search for an Alliance Between Archaeological and Textual Evidence," in *Palace and Temple: Architecture – Decoration – Ritual. Symposium zur ägyptischen Königsideologie/5th Symposium on Egyptian Royal Ideology, Cambridge, July 16–17, 2007*, R. Gundlach and K. Spence (eds.), 181–202, Wiesbaden: Harrassowitz.

Index

The Adding Machine (Rice) 133
afaaka ("carry oracles") 75–7, 78
Africa 74–5, 78
Ahmose II (Amasis) 61
Ahmose-Tetisheri Project (Abydos) 217, 218
Akhenaten (Amenhotep IV) 23, 69
Alexander ("the Great") 61–2
Allard, Eric 175
All Effects Company 175, 177
Amenemope 19
Amenhotep I 46
Amenhotep III 22, 23, 49
Amenhotep IV (Akhenaten) 23, 69
Amenhotep, son of Hapu 22–3, 24
Ammân (god) 63
Ammon, oracle of (Siwa oasis) 60–3, 78
amuletic decrees 38–9, 126
Amun, 19, 25 *see also* Ammon; temple of Amun (Karnak)
    as Amun-Re 20, 25, 85
    boats of 20, 31
    estate (per) 19, 20–5, 34, 47, 90
    festivals 20, 37, 38–44, 54, 84–5
    as hidden god 19, 28
    and ordinary people 26, 41–2
    priesthood 26–7
    roles 20, 48, 85
    as ruler 25–6, 34, 48
    ruler chosen by 47, 52
    temples 20, 59
    worship of, 35–6, 41, 53–4, 59
Anstey, Josephine 137
Apis bull 50
Apollo 67
Apy (god) 101
archaeology 9–10 *see also* virtual heritage
    of Egyptian temples 81–2
    and reenactment 13
    virtual 186, 196, 215
Are/Are (Coates) 132
Aristotle 6

Ark of the Covenant 71
Artaud, Antonin 7–8
artifacts 187
    digital 185–6, 207
Art Institute of Pittsburgh 207
Ashanti 74–5, 78
Ashur (god) 65
Aspelta (Kushite king) 58–9
Assyria 65, 68–9
Atargatis (Hera) 66–7
audiences
    of Egyptian Oracle Project 114–15, 121–6, 150–1, 153, 154
    managing 140–1, 151
    in mixed reality theater 133, 134–5, 136–7, 139, 140–2
    as participants 9, 11, 140–1, 143, 161, 195
    role-playing by 154, 161
    in virtual environments 137, 191, 194–5
    of virtual heritage 189–90, 191, 193–5, 196
Augustine, Saint 12
Auslander, Philip 136
Auster, Ryan 162
avatars 133, 137, 195

Baal (god) 68
Baalbek (Heliopolis) 68–9
Babylonians 70
Baird, Bill 171
Baker, Rick 174, 176
barque of the god *see* sacred barque
bia 47–8
Bible (Hebrew) 70, 71–3, 74
Blast Theory 134, 138
Boal, Augusto 8
Book of the Temple 92
Boston Museum of Science 162–4
bots 136
Brecht, Bertolt 7, 8

Buechner, Georg 134
Buhen (Egypt) 186

Caillois, Roger 194
Captain EO (film) 174–5
Caribbean region 75–7
Carnegie Mellon University Studio for Creative Inquiry 205
Carnegie Museum of Natural History (Pittsburgh) 200, 207
  Egyptian Oracle Project at 4, 156, 161, 209
CAVE systems 137
CaveUT/UDK (PublicVR) 206–7
cemeteries 84, 85, 218
Center for Puppetry Arts (Atlanta) 168–9
Černý, Jaroslav 44–5
CGI (computer-generated imagery) 179, 192
Clash, Kevin 177
Coates, George 132–3, 137
Common Core State Standards 168, 170–1
Cox, Tony 174
Cutha myth 64
Cyrene (Greek colony) 61, 78

Dagan (god) 65
daily cult ritual 26, 27, 97–8
  offerings 26, 33–4, 83, 87, 96, 208
  significance 100, 101
  student re-creations 208–9
Dark Crystal, The (film) 175
Darnell, Michael 206
David (Hebrew king) 71
Davis, Paul Vincent 181
Deir el-Medina *see* Sut Maat
Description de l'Égypte 200, 201
Desert Rain (Blast Theory) 134, 138, 140, 141, 142, 143–4
DIDs (digital input devices) 179
Diodorus Siculus 62, 78
"Discover Babylon" (Federation of American Scientists) 186
distancing 7–8, 10, 148
divination 51, 64–5, 67–8, 70–4
Djhutymose, 54, 55
  inscription of, 40, 42–3
dreams, 50, 58, 64–5

DreamWorks 180–1
Dudley Castle (UK) 186

Edfu, 81, 92 *see also* temple of Horus (Edfu)
educational practice
  archaeology and 9–10
  arts and 169
  curriculum standards 168, 170–1
  Egyptian Oracle Project as 6, 10, 109, 153, 164, 170–1, 216
  hands-on 168
  learning styles in 169–70
  performance as tool 8, 14, 19
  puppetry as tool 168–71, 193
  technology and 9, 133
Egypt, 17–19, 103, 218–19 *see also* Nile River; *individual kings*
  agricultural foundation 101, 102
  bureaucracy 41–2, 48–9
  house design in 97–8
  influence of 59–60, 69–70, 71, 73–4
  justice system 48–9
  kings of 79–80, 82–4, 85, 102–3
  Ministry (Supreme Council) of Antiquities 201
  Ptolemaic period 50–1, 104
Egyptian Oracle Project xiii–xv, 1–3, 10–12, 211–15 *see also* Egyptian Oracle Project: evaluations; Egyptian Oracle Project: roles; virtual temple of Horus
  attention and authority in 149–50
  audience participation 114–15, 121–6, 150–1, 153, 154
  breaking the fourth wall 118–20
  educational goals 109, 153, 170–1
  as educational practice 6, 10, 109, 153, 164, 170–1, 216
  "Egyptian-style applause" 118, 150, 151
  funding for 197, 199
  gestures in 118, 128–9, 147–8
  as heritage experience 145–6, 187
  historical sources 3–4, 212
  improvisation in 121, 123, 125, 128, 146, 150, 183
  as mixed reality 145–6, 149–50, 213
  narrative structure 117–26
  personnel 4–6, 213, 214

puppetry in 167, 181–3
as serious game 154, 155, 187
significance 214–15, 216
technology use 116, 198, 202–4, 205, 206–7
as theater 10, 144–6, 152
videos of 3, 164
virtual beings in 146–50
Egyptian Oracle Project: evaluations 117, 153, 155–64, 213, 214
affective measures 157
after-show discussions 161–2
after-show questionnaire 155–6, 162–4, 221–2
lessons learned 164
questions asked 157–60
videos as 155, 160–1
Egyptian Oracle Project: roles
accused thief 114, 123–5
actress ("Atumirdis") 113, 115–17, 120, 122, 126, 128, 148, 150
ascending priest 114, 122
disputing neighbors 114, 123
high priest ("Petiese") 112, 117–20, 128–9, 147–8, 182
mayor 114, 120, 121–2, 151
puppeteer 115–19, 121, 122, 126, 146, 161, 182–3
Elder Scrolls: Skyrim (game) 189
Electricity! (puppet show) 170
Enumeration of the Mounds of the First Time 101
Esna (Egypt) 200

Federation of American Scientists 186
festivals
of Amun 20, 37, 38–44, 54, 84–5
Feast of the Valley 84–5, 87
of Min 88, 201
Opet 20, 37, 54
of Sokar 88, 199, 201
spaces for 95–6
at temple of Horus (Edfu) 95, 104–5
at temple of Ramesses III (Medinet Habu) 88
Festival of the Oracle of Amun *see also* oracles, processional
reconstruction 30–8, 212
sources 38–44

Fijan, Carol 181
First Prophet (high priest) 19–20, 32–7, 42, 43–4
The Flintstones (film) 177–9
Frankfurter, David 78
French Archaeological Institute (Cairo) 81
funeral practices
in Africa 74–5, 78
in Caribbean 75–7
Islamic 52, 218–19
pallbearers 74–5, 218–19
processions 52–3, 74–7, 218–19

Gaan Tata oracle 76–7, 78
Gadamer, Hans-Georg 188
Gale, Ed 175
Galli 67, 68
games (computer) 9, 154, 188–94 *see also individual games*
game master role 193
as motivating 154–5, 192
player interaction with 191, 192
serious 154–5, 187
tools for making 192–3, 206–7
in virtual heritage 190–3
as virtual worlds 188–9, 190
Gardner, Howard 169
Gates of Horus (game) 204–5, 209, 210, 214
George Coates Performance Works 132–3, 137
Gillam, Robyn 111, 202, 207, 208, 212
gods *see also* daily cult ritual; temples; *individual gods*
as advisors 20, 64–6
images of 26, 27, 103
kings and 34, 43, 83, 102–3
Gray, Asa 214
green screen technology 143, 172–3, 184
Gremlins 2: The New Batch (film) 176
Greystoke: The Legend of Tarzan, Lord of the Apes (film) 174

Haddad (god) 68
Hall, Kevin Peter 174
Handron, Kerry 6, 209, 214
Hapi (god) 97
Hardin, Terri 174

Harry and the Hendersons (film/television show) 174
Harsomtus *see* Horus
Hathor 84, 85, 100
Hatshepsut 47, 52
head-mounted displays (HMDs) 131–2, 133, 134, 142, 191
Heliopolis (Baalbek) 68–9, 78
Henson, Jim 183, 184
Henson Productions 176, 177, 184
henu gesture 118
Hera (Atargatis) 66–7
Herihor 19, 38
heritage *see* archaeology; virtual heritage
hermeneutic affordance 188
Herodotus 49, 61, 167
Hester, Tom 174, 175, 176
Hezekiah 74
Hieropolis 67–9, 78
high priest (First Prophet) 19–20, 32–7, 42, 43–4
Holden, Lynn 202, 205, 207, 209
hōn 45
Hopkins, David 111
Horemheb 23–4, 52
Hor of Sebennytos 50
Horus 11, 85, 96, 100, 103–4 *see also* temple of Horus (Edfu)
of Edfu (Djeba) 92
king as incarnation of 83, 85
Howard the Duck (film) 175
Howdy Doody 171
hut-netcher 97

improvisation 141, 195
in Egyptian Oracle Project 121, 123, 125, 128, 146, 150, 183
Industrial Light & Magic (ILM) 175
Innes, C. D. 208
Institute for the Exploration of Virtual Realities (IEVR) 133–4
Intermedia Performance Studio 134–5
Invisible Site (Coates) 132, 133
Isaiah 72
Ishtar 65
Isis 97, 104
Israel (ancient) 70–4

Jackson, Nicole 206

Jacobson, Jeffrey 205, 207, 209 *see also* PublicVR
Jarry, Alfred 134
Jim Henson Hour 184
Journey to Wild Divine, The (game) 192
Judah (kingdom) 70, 71, 72–3, 74
Jupiter of Heliopolis (Baal of Beqa) 68
Jurassic Park (film) 179

Khonsu
barque of 30, 31, 42, 111
temple of (Karnak) 25, 201
Kirchner, Friedrich 182, 214
Kruchten, Jean-Marie 40
Krzanowski, Tad 175
Kukla, Fran, and Ollie (television show) 171
Kush (Nubia) 58–60, 78

Labyrinth (film) 175, 183
Laurel, Brenda 133
Lawrence, Tim 174, 176, 177, 181
Lazzarini, Rick 176, 177
Learning Sites 186
letter prayers 64–6, 69, 73
Levant 66–70
Lewis, Shari 172
Libyan Desert 60–3
"liveness" 137–8, 146, 190–1
Lord of the Rings, The (film) 184, 192
Lucian 66–7, 78
ludology 154

maat 100, 103
as cosmic order 27, 83, 90, 99, 104
Macrobius 68–9, 78
Mari (kingdom) 64–5
Mariette, August 81
Maroons (Suriname) 75–7, 78
Martin, Patrick 200
Masaharta 39
Medinet Habu *see* temple of Ramesses III
mediums 75
Menkheperre 38, 42
stela of 41, 43
Meroitic culture 60
Mesopotamia 63–6, 71, 73
mimesis 194

mixed reality 211 *see also* theater, mixed reality
　Egyptian Oracle Project as 145–6, 149–50, 213
Mori, Masahiro 192
motion capture technology 130, 176, 180–1, 184, 192
multiculturalism 5–6
Muppet Show, The (television show) 172, 173
Murray, James 177
Mut (goddess) 20, 30, 31, 42

narratives
　Bible as 70, 73
　interactive 194–5
　of kings 66, 73
　in mixed reality theater 134, 140, 145, 146
　in serious games 154, 155
Ndyuka (people) 75–7, 78
Nectanebo II 92
nedjet-ro 47
Nekhen (Hierakonpolis) 92
Nephthys (goddess) 104
Nesikhons 39
Nile River 20, 22, 101
　temple access to 96–7
Nubia (Kush) 17, 58–60, 78
numinous objects 75–6, 167

oases 60, 63
Oculus Rift (game system) 190
Ojika, T. 185
Opet Festival 20, 37, 54
oracles 45, 57 *see also* oracles, processional
　of Ammon (Siwa oasis) 60–3
　amuletic decrees of 38–9, 126
　analogs and variants 49, 58–79, 212, 218–19
　"carry" (afaaka) 75–7, 78
　divinatory 50–2
　documents used 33, 35, 45–6, 48–9, 57, 64–6, 70, 72–3
　Egyptian influence on 59–60, 69–70
　elite perspective of 77, 78
　Gaan Tata 76–7, 78
　human intermediaries 50, 54–5
　interpretation of 51–5
　in Kush (Nubia) 58–60
　and legal issues 34, 38, 40, 48–9, 72, 73
　legitimation of king by 47, 52, 58–9, 65–6
　in Mesopotamia 63–6
　modern parallels 74–8
　petitions to 51, 53–4
　and political issues 38, 39, 50–1
　popularity of 48, 49–50
　private (royal) 58, 59, 62, 69, 72–3
　public nature of 48, 49, 55
　records of decisions 36–7, 39–40, 59
　statues as 67
　in Sut Maat 46, 53–4, 78
　"ticket" 50
　uses 3–4, 38–9, 47, 50–2, 72
oracles, processional 46, 62, 70, 71 *see also* sacred barque
　acquittal procedure 35, 36–7
　applicants to 33, 34, 43–4
　blessings from 38–9
　god's actions 34–5, 37–8, 39–40, 50, 54, 55
　historical/cultural context 17–20, 46–51
　hymns and prayers 35–6, 41
　incense use 31, 43
　priests' roles 43, 76
　sources for 42–6
Oriental Institute (University of Chicago) 81, 203
Osiris 85, 100
Osorkon 38
ostraca 44, 45–6

Paintbox (graphics system) 172
Pape, David 137
Papyrus Harris I 90
Paramesse 24
Pausanius 62
peh netcher 48, 49
performance, 6–8 *see also* theater
　audience as participants 9, 11, 140–1, 143, 161, 195
　as learning tool 8, 14, 19
　in virtual heritage projects 193, 194, 195
Persians 70

Pethauemdiamun 53–4
Philistines 71
Phil Tippett Studios 179
Piankh 19
Pinudjem I 20
Placeholder (Laurel) 133, 140, 141, 142, 145
prayers 35–6, 41
   letter 64–6, 69, 73
Prentice, Jordan 175
presence 136, 137–8
priests 26–7, 34, 54–5 *see also* daily cult ritual
   astronomer 30–1, 32
   First Prophet (high priest) 19–20, 32–7, 42, 43–4
   God's Fathers 34
   hem netcher 26–7
   in processional oracle ceremony 43, 76
   purification of 26, 32, 68, 98, 208
   sem (setne) 26, 32
   wab 26, 31, 33, 34, 37, 55
processional oracle *see* oracles, processional
projections 115–16, 131, 132–4
prophecy 50–1, 64–5, 67
prophets 26–7, 64–5, 67, 72–3 *see also* First Prophet
Ptolemy III Euergetes 79–80, 92, 97, 201
PublicVR, 3, 198, 205, 206–7 *see also* virtual temple of Horus
   Gates of Horus (game) 204–5, 209, 210, 214
puppetry, 167, 172–81, 184 *see also* puppets
   in Egyptian Oracle Project 115–19, 121, 122, 126, 146, 161, 167, 181–3
   as learning tool 168–71, 193
   technology and 173–7, 179
puppets 167
   computer-generated 176, 183, 184
   controls for 174–5, 176
   in film and television 171–81
   motion capture of 176, 180–1
   with multiple operators 174–5, 177–9
   operators 11, 172–3, 176–7, 184

Qadesh 69

Ramesses II 26, 46–7, 69
Ramesses III 17, 90 *see also* temple of Ramesses III
Ramesses IV 47
Re *see also* Amun; Horus
   Amun-Re 20, 25, 85
   Re-Horakhty 87
Real Dream Cabaret 134–5
reenactment 12–14
religion 53, 55
Rice, Elmer 133
Robertson, Gordon 175
RoboCop 2 (film) 176
role-playing 8, 154, 161, 195, 215 *see also* reenactment
Rose, Margot and Rufus 171
Rose, Tim 175

sacred barque 27–32, 100 *see also* oracles, processional
   bearers 29–30, 37, 52–3, 55, 67–8, 218–19
   design 27–30, 32, 42, 52
   god as motive force 52–5, 148–9
   of Khonsu 30, 31, 42, 111
   movements 32–3, 34–5, 37–8, 45, 46, 52
   of Mut 30, 31, 42
   in Nubia (Kush) 59
   shrines for 84, 87, 100
   stopping gesture 37, 45, 47
Saite Oracle papyrus 39–40, 43
Saramaka (people) 77
Saturnalia (Macrobius) 68–9
Schwartz, Bruce 174
Science Meets the Arts Society 132
Screen Actors Guild 171, 173, 177
"Sea Peoples" 60–1
Senemur 69
Sennacherib 71, 72–3
Sesame Street (television show) 168, 172
Seshat (goddess) 103
Set (god) 97, 103–5
Setrakian, Mark 176
shamans 75
Short Circuit (film) 175
Shrek (film) 180–1
Shur, Brad 181–3
Sid the Science Kid (television show) 184

Silicon Graphics 186
Siwa oasis 60-3
Slater, Mel 136
Sleap, Steve 175, 176
Soman, Loren 181
Sound of Music, The (film) 171
Stone, R. J. 185
Strabo 62, 78
Sturz, Lisa 174-81
Suriname 75-7, 78
Sutherkhedis 61
Sut Maat (Deir el-Medina) 42, 44-6
   oracles in 46, 53-4, 78
"The Syrian Goddess" (Lucian) 66-7

technology (computer) 8-9 *see also* virtual environments
   and education 9, 133
   in Egyptian Oracle Project 116, 198, 202-4, 205, 206-7
   projections 115-16, 131, 132-4
   in theater 132
   in virtual heritage 190-3
Teenage Mutant Ninja Turtles III (film) 177
television 12, 13, 172-3, 184 *see also individual programs*
temple of Amenhotep II (Karnak) 37
temple of Amun (Karnak) 19, 20, 89 *see also* temples
   courtyards 24-5, 30, 40
   history 20, 84
   layout and design 20, 22-5, 30-4
   processional way 20, 84
   pylons 22-4, 31
   reliefs and inscriptions 24, 40
   sacred lake 25, 32
   sanctuary 87-8
temple of Horus (Edfu), 79-81 *see also* virtual temple of Horus
   colonnades 93, 95, 102
   falcon as symbol in 93, 103, 104-5
   festivals at 95, 104-5
   flagstaffs 80, 104
   history 80-1, 92, 96
   layout and design 80, 92-6, 102
   as library/teaching tool 91-8, 99, 102-3
   light in 101-2
   outer wall 95, 103
   public access 95, 98
   Pure Walkway 95, 103-4
   reliefs and inscriptions 91-2, 95, 99, 101-4
   research on 81-2
temple of Isis (Philae Island) 97
temple of Khonsu (Karnak) 25, 201
temple of Mut (Karnak) 20
temple of Ptah (Memphis) 50
temple of Ramesses III (Medinet Habu) 79-82, 85, 87-91, 203 *see also* virtual temple of Horus
   daily cult ritual 97-8
   importance 82, 89-90
   layout and design 80-1, 87-91, 96-7, 100
   pylon gates 90-1, 104
   reliefs and inscriptions 87, 88-9, 90, 103, 111
   sanctuary 87-8, 97-8
temple of Sethos I (Abydos) 201
temples, 19 *see also* daily cult ritual; oracles; priests; *individual temples*
   archaeological research on 81-2
   conservation of 199, 201
   as cosmos/creation 90, 99-105
   cult 82, 83
   economic basis of 26, 34
   evolution of 80-1, 83-4
   as house of god 83-4, 97-8
   as information source 10, 99, 199
   layout and design 80, 82-3, 95-9
   meaning levels 98-100
   mortuary 82, 83-7
   music in 31, 71, 113
   orientation 20, 22, 96-7
   river access 96-7
   sanctuaries 26, 27, 101
   women's roles 31, 113
Tenochtitlán 186
Teudjoi (el-Hibeh) 19
Thatcher, Kirk 176, 183-4
theater 6-8, 9, 132 *see also* performance; theater, mixed reality
   as deceitful 11-12
   distancing in 7-8, 10
   Egyptian Oracle Project as 10, 144-6, 152

virtual environments as 9, 193–5
virtual environments in 132–3
theater, mixed reality 131–5 *see also* virtual environments
   audience participation 133, 134–5, 136–7, 139, 140–2
   avatars 133, 137
   Egyptian Oracle Project as 145–6, 149–50, 213
   guide figure 133, 137, 138, 141–2, 150
   impact 145–6
   implications 135–44
   live actors 133–4, 136–40
   "liveness" 137–8, 146, 147
   narratives 134, 140, 145, 146
   and physical space 142–4
   shock moments 138, 139–40
   technology use 131, 132–4, 143
   virtual actors 136, 137, 138–9
Thebes 19
Theodosius 81
The Thing Growing (Anstey and Pape) 137
Thoden van Velzen, H. U. E. 76–7
Thoth (god) 103
Thutmose III 47, 121
Thutmose IV 47
Tilstrum, Burr 171
Tippett, Phil 176, 179
Togo 78
Topo Gigio 171–2
Trajan 69
Tuan, Yi-Fu 187
20/20 Blake (Coates) 132–3

Ubu Roi (Jarry) 134 *see also WoyUbu*
"uncanny valley" effect 112, 146–7, 192
Unity 3D (software) 164, 198, 206
University of Nottingham (UK) Mixed Reality Lab 134
Unreal Tournament (game) 206–7
Uzzah 71

Van Wetering, W., 76–7
virtual environments 10, 137–8, 190–5 *see also* theater, mixed reality; virtual heritage; virtual reality helmets
   audience reactions 137, 191, 194–5
   body as interface 192–3, 194, 212
   interaction with 143, 188–9
   lighting in 132
   "liveness" in 137–8, 146, 190–1
   in phobia studies 191, 192
   and physical space 115, 116, 120, 142–4
   realism in 146–7, 189, 191–2
   as theater 9, 193–5
   in theater 132–3
virtual heritage 185–96, 213, 215
   audience interactions 189–90, 191, 193–5, 196
   content 185–6, 187, 189–90, 196
   guide figure 193–5
   human actors 189, 194, 195
   limitations 187, 190
   performance in 193, 194, 195
   and physical space 194
   technology 186, 190–3
   uses 186, 189 196
   "worldliness" in 188
virtual reality helmets 131–2, 133, 134, 142, 191
Virtual Samor Prei Kuk, Cambodia 189
virtual temple of Horus 4, 197–210 *see also* Egyptian Oracle Project
   artwork/graphics 160, 164, 200–4
   construction 202–5
   equipment 116, 127–30, 184
   evolution xi–xii, 197–8, 205–6
   as interactive 204–5
   layout and design 109, 198–200, 204
   as learning tool 209–10
   "liveness" in 146, 147–8
   physical setup 115–17
   projections 115–16, 161
   prototypes 79–82
   puppet controls 126–30, 147, 148, 182
   ramp issues 204, 206, 208
   "restoration" in, 202–3, 204
   sacred barque 110–12, 118, 121, 127–8, 146–7, 148
   scene transitions 117–18, 129–30
   shrine 200, 201, 206
   sound effects/music 116, 117, 164
   source materials 199–201, 205, 213
   space use 115, 116, 120, 151
   stylization in 111–12, 126–7, 146–7, 214

technology 116, 198, 202–4, 205, 206–7
    uses 207, 208–9
VRML (Virtual Reality Modeling
    Language) 186, 206

Walas, Chris 176
Waldo C. Graphic 183–4
waldos 176
Weckström, N. 188
Who Framed Roger Rabbit (film) 180
William Diamond Middle School
    (Lexington, MA) 156, 158–9
Wilson, Mark 176, 177
Wings (IEVR) 133–4
Winkliss, Brock 174

"Wisdom of Ani" 119
World of Warcraft (game) 188–9
World Toolkit 205
WoyUbu 134–5, 138–40, 141, 143, 144
Woyzeck (Buechner) 134 *see also WoyUbu*

Xbox 360 (game controller) 116, 127–9, 184

Yebu (Elephantine) Island 97
York University (Toronto) 208

Zeus 61
Zimri-lin (god) 65

www.ingramcontent.com/pod-product-compliance
Lightning Source LLC
Chambersburg PA
CBHW061438300426
44114CB00014B/1737